The Lean Entrepreneur

The Lean Entrepreneur

HOW VISIONARIES CREATE PRODUCTS, INNOVATE with NEW VENTURES, and DISRUPT MARKETS

**BRANT COOPER
and PATRICK VLASKOVITS**

WILEY

Published by John Wiley & Sons, Inc., Hoboken, New Jersey.
Published simultaneously in Canada.

For general information on our other products and services or for technical support, please contact our Customer Care Department within the United States at (800) 762-2974, outside the United States at (317) 572-3993 or fax (317) 572-4002.

Wiley publishes in a variety of print and electronic formats and by print-on-demand. Some material included with standard print versions of this book may not be included in e-books or in print-on-demand. If this book refers to media such as a CD or DVD that is not included in the version you purchased, you may download this material at http://booksupport.wiley.com. For more information about Wiley products, visit www.wiley.com.

Library of Congress Cataloging-in-Publication Data:

Cooper, Brant.
 The lean entrepreneur : how visionaries create products, innovate with new ventures, and disrupt markets / Brant Cooper, Patrick Vlaskovits. — 1
  p. cm.
 Includes index.
 ISBN 978-1-118-29534-2 (cloth); ISBN 978-1-118-33408-9 (ebk); ISBN 978-1-118-33523-9 (ebk); ISBN 978-1-118-33186-6 (ebk)
  1. Entrepreneurship. 2. Success in business. I. Vlaskovits, Patrick. II. Title.
 HB615.C6495 2013
 658.4'21—dc23
                                                          2012035450

Printed in the United States of America
10 9 8 7 6 5 4 3 2 1

For Riva and Eliza

—BC

For Kati, Shane, and the twinkle in my eye

—PV

Contents

Special Thanks

Without our early adopters, who believed enough in *The Lean Entrepreneur* to pre-order a book when it was merely a landing page with a silly video, we might not have survived the process of writing and publishing this book.

Their early feedback on content and exercises forced us to simplify, focus, and home in on how to move the needle for them.

Thank you,
Brant & Patrick

The Lean Entrepreneur Early Adopters*:

@$H0K
@WojKwasi
Aalap Parikh
Abraham Williams
Adalsteinn Ottarsson
Adam Gibson
Adam Jong
Advanced VA
Akili King
Al Bsharah
Al Shaw
Alan David Rojas Yacolca
Alan Lattimore
Alan Turner

Alberto Jr
Alex Wolfe
Alexander Bastien
Alexander Ginsberg
Alexander Konowka
Alexander Osterwalder
Alexandre Marcondes
Alexandre Zamarion Cepeda
Alfred Lo
Alfredo Osorio
Alison Anthoine
Alison Gibbins
Alline Watkins
Alon Goren

Amiel Zwier
Andersen Andre
Andrea Amedeo
Andreas Cem Vogt
Andreas Klinger
Andres Arias
Andres Buritica
Andres Riggioni
Andrew Hemsley
Andrew Korf
Andrew Mohebbi
Andrew Payne
Andrew White
Andrey Gridnev

*to view this list of names online, please visit http://leanentrepreneur.co/earlyadopters.

Anita Leffel

Antonio Lucena de Faria

Arden Grady

Armando Maldonado

Arthur Dodge

Arturo Garrido

Basil Elway

Beat Goetschi

Becky Smith

Beihua Yu

Benjamin Biddel

Benjamin Patock

Bergson Fogaca de Oliveira

Bernard Lebelle

Bernardo Mazzini

Bill Carver

Bill Kenney

Brendan Baker

Brenton O'Brien

Brittany Lynch

Brunno Cruz

Bryan Hall

C Crouch

Camilo Zamora

Carol Gunby

Casey Armstrong

Cassiano Porreca

Catherine Colgan

Chan Keung

Chandan Kanodia

Chantal Botana

Chin Eugene

Chonchayong Trairatkeyoon

Chris Elam

Chris Gallo

Chris Healy

Christian Fahlke

Christian Kramer

Christopher Conrey

Claudio Perrone

Clayton Levering

Colin Tuggle

Craig Aron

Cristian Valbuena

Cv Harquail

D Elley

Dale Larson

Damien Saunders

Damon D'Amore

Dan Kaplan

Dan Mattrazzo

Daniel Donado

Daniel Fulep

Daniel Haran

Daniel Horowitz

Daniel James Scott

Daniel Politzer

Danny Beckett Jr.

Danny Currie

Darren Fehrmann

Dave Blackman

David Andujo

David Drake

David Fishman

David Hooton

David Stevens

Davorin Gabrovec

Daylin Breen

Deane Sloan

Dennis Cabarroguis

Desiderio Gutierrez

Dmitri Leonov

Donna Klym

Dr. Ernie

Drew Sanocki

Eduardo Burgel

Elio Maggini

Emily Cotter

Emmanuel Devries

Eneko Bilbao

Eric Fader

Eric Galen

Eric Pantera

Erich Buri

Erick Herring

Erik Saltwell

Erika Callahan

Erin Mcclarty

Esteban Quijano

Farez Rahman

Ferenc Fekete
Fernando Labastida
Fernando Saenz-Marrero
Ferran Giones
Francesc Mutge
Francesco Fullone
Frank Dale
Fuat Koro
Gabriele Lana
Garth Humbert
Gary Chiu
Gary Hellen
Gary Marcos
Gary Percy
Gavin Heer
Geert Bollen
George Komoto
Gerard Charlot
Gibran Abarca
Gideon Walker
Gijsbert Koren
Gil Doukhan
Gilbert Bagaoisan
Giles Farrow
Giorgio Casoni
Glenn Marcus
Gonzalo Santos
Graham Kehily
Guilhem Bertholet
Hampus Jakobsson

Hao Chen
Helge Hannisdal
Hendrik Bohn
Hiroshi Menjo
Howard Iii
Ira Herman
Iren Elisabeth Ovstebo
Ivan Rapin-Smith
Iyas Alqasem
Jacob Taylor
Jake Waxenberg
Jakub Musialek
James Gagel
James Katzenberger
James Levine
James Manias
James McGilvray
James Sutherland
Jan Belke
Jane Garrity
Jared Hardy
Jason Bowser
Jason Fitts
Jason Fraser
Jason HJH
Jason Yip
Jay Beecham
Jay Cranman
Jay Grieves
Jeanne Pi

Jeff Chen
Jeffrey Howell
Jeffrey Mohr
Jeffrey Poole
Jeffrey Tingle
Jennie Enholm
Jeremy George
Jesse Nowlin
Jim Chesebro
JM Bonthous
Joanna Piotrowska
Joe Bailey
Joe Gerber
Joe Waltman
Joel Abraham
Joel Gascoigne
Joel Jenkins
John Asalone
John Beadle
John Carter
John Halpern
John Holcroft
John Hornbaker
John Morrow
John T. Chapman
John Wark
John Wolpert
Jon Gold
Jon Lawrence
Jonatan Alava

Jonathan Buccella

Jonathan Drillings

Jonathan Gray

Jonathan Tarud

Jonathan York

Jonathon Schuster

Jonny Lennon

Jordana Adler

Joseph Draschil

Joseph Morgan

Joseph Vandervest

Joshua Kerievsky

Joshua Lewis

Joshua Steimle

jozi9

Juergen Anke

Justin Coetsee

Justin Homkow

Justine Lam

Kahlil Corazo

Kangtao Chuang

Karin Lehner

Karl Shaikh

Kathleen Meairs

Keenahn Jung

Keiron Mccammon

Kelvin Tham

Ken Hejmanowski

Kent Mcdonald

Kim Silva

Kirk Lashley

Kutlu Kazanci

Lars Kristian Aasbrenn

Lars Teigen

Lawrence Schoonover, DDS

Lee Heathfield

Lee Munroe

Leslie Hunter

Lindsey Nagy

Lord Fernandez

Louis Galipeau

Lowell Lindstrom

Lowell Winer

Luigi Matrone

Luigi Montanez

Luis Luengo

Lukas Fittl

Luke Scoates

Lynn Pearce

Lynn Rasmussen

M Keeffe

Maciej Czarnik

Makoto Miyagawa

Marc Havener

Marcelo Pimenta

Mark Horoszowski

Mark Morris

Marko Vasiljevic

Martin Alcala Rubi

Martin Giorgetti

Martin Hrdlicka

Matias Waes

Matthew A

Matthew Bellows

Matthew Dally

Matthew Ownby

Mauricio Montilla

Melissa Foster

Melissa Navarro

Meng Wong

Michael Grassotti

Michael Hawkins

Michael Lira

Michael Maretzke

Michael Petronaci

Michael Porcelli

Michael Thompson

Michael Yevdokimov

Michel Gelobter

Michele Battelli

Michelle Hoang

Mikhail Nikolaev

Mila Vukojevic

Mitchell Villani

Morgan Linton

Mr O'Flynn

Mrs Oliver

Nadav Wilf

Nicholas Wichert

Nick Tippmann

Nicolas Tognoni

Nikhil Thomas

Nikolaos Souris

Nina Alter

Nir Eyal

Norbert Schwagmann

Oana Calugar

Olaf Lewitz

Olaf Myklebust

Oleg Mysyk

Olga Pavlovsky

Olin Hyde

Olivier Verbeke

Oriol Pascual

Oskari Kettunen

Paolo Lorenzoni

Parul Singh

Patrick Buechner

Patrick Smith

Paul Connaghan

Paul Gomez

Paul Merino

Paul Reichman

Pedro Carmo Oliveira

Pedro Rocha

Per Sahlin

Peter Cooper

Peter Hargittay

Peter Hong

Peter Troast

Piotr Durlej

Prudencio Herrero

R Bowater

Rachel Willmer

Rahul Gupta

Rak Dheva-Aksorn

Rammohan Reddy

Randall Minchew

Ray Hallare

Reginald Niles

Regis Rehel

Reid Mcgregor

Rene-Martin Tudyka

Ricardo Dorado

Richard Ackermann

Richard Kroon

Richard Prest

Rick Perreault

Ricky Juarez

Rindranirina Ramamonjison

Rob Linton

Robert Bowman

Robert Fan

Robert Fenton

Roberto Magnifico

Rodney Rumford

Rodolfo Angel Lomascolo Szittyay

Rodrigo Ludwig

Roger Weber

Ross O'Lochlainn

Royce Hamano

Rukesh Patel

Ryan Fujiu

Ryan Poissant

Salim Virani

Samuel Goldberg

Samuel Parker

Sash Catanzarite

Scott Austin

Scott Gillespie

Scott Kurland

Scott Roehrick

Scott Steele

Sean Ammirati

Sean Crafts

Sean Taylor

Sean Tierney

Sebastien Arbogast

Sergio Marrero

Shawn Arnwine

Shawn Purcell

Simone Brunozzi

Son Thanh Le

Stephen Rhyne

Stephen Wood

Steven Craig

Steven Mcilvenna

Sunshine Makarow

Sylvain Montreuil

Takashi Tsutsumi

Tal Rachleff

Tanya Ross-Lane

Theodore Barnett

Theodore Shivdasani

Thomas Lin

Thomas Neiger

Thomas Pridham

Tim Kastelle

Timothy Lombardo

Todd Werelius

Tom Philip

Tom Yandell

Tomasz Rudolf

Tomer Sharon

Travis Mccutcheon

Trevor Owens

Veeral Shah

Venkatesh Rao

Vidar Brekke

Vik Chadha

Vishal Bagga

Vivek Raman

William Loeber

William Mcbride

Wiro Kuipers

Young Lee

Yuki Sekiguchi

Yves Hanoulle

Zoiner Tejada

Foreword

When I first started blogging in August of 2008, I had no idea what to expect. Startup blogging was hardly "cool" back then. Plenty of venture capitalists advised me against it.

My personal background was as an engineer and my companies had been web-based startups, so that is what I wrote about. Struggling to explain the successes and failures of those companies, I discussed principles like continuous deployment, customer development, and a hyper-accelerated form of agile. When I delved into lean manufacturing, I discovered the concepts and terminology dovetailed. The result: a new idea I called The Lean Startup.

I started with some basic theory: that a startup is an institution designed to thrive in the soil of extreme uncertainty; that traditional management techniques rooted in forecasting and planning would not work well in the face of that uncertainty. Therefore, we needed a new management toolkit designed explicitly for iteration, scientific learning, and rapid experimentation.

At the time, I viewed it as incidental that the theory might be tied to a particular industry, such as high-tech startups or web-based environments. Lean, after all, emerged from Toyota, a huge automobile manufacturing company. I simply stated my belief that Lean Startup principles would work in other types of startups and in other areas of business where uncertainty reigned.

Boy, was I unprepared for what happened next. I was hopeful that we would change the way startups are built—but I didn't *know*.

Fast-forward more than four years and I'm astounded by what has emerged. A nascent community has blossomed into a full-fledged movement. Entrepreneurs, both new and experienced, proudly share their Lean Startup learning in case studies, conferences, and many, many blogs. Books, workshops, and courses authored by passionate practitioners relate experience, share insight, and create tools to teach students ways to make Lean Startup principles their own. Many investors, advisors, mentors, and even celebrity entrepreneur icons speak the Lean Startup language.

It's a big tent. We stand on the shoulders of giants: customer development, the theory of disruptive innovation, the technology life-cycle adoption theory, and agile development. Complementary lines of thinking, such as that of user experience professionals, design thinking practitioners, and the functional disciplines of sales, marketing, operations, and even accounting, come together to share practices that lift us all.

Lean Startup has gone mainstream. I wish I could say that this was all part of some master plan, that I knew all along that companies of all sizes—even those far outside the high-technology world—would embrace Lean Startup. I wish I had foreseen that within a year of publishing *The Lean Startup: How Today's Entrepreneurs Use Continuous Innovation to Achieve Radically Successful Businesses,* many large organizations, including such monsters as the United States Federal government (!) would have recognized that to cope with today's world—faster, more competitive, and inundated with data—new methods are needed to keep up. The truth is that all of this change has happened faster and more thoroughly than any of us imagined. And—as you're about to see—we're just getting started.

That's why I am so excited by this book you hold in your hands. *The Lean Entrepreneur* is about these new methods. Brant Cooper and Patrick Vlaskovits are among the earliest adopters of new ideas such as Lean Startup and customer development. Their new work turns their lens on three primary focal points: how to interact with customers, run experiments, and use actionable data to move the needle of any uncertain business endeavor.

As with all of their work, theirs is not just a book of theory. Brant and Patrick provide great tactical depth in each of these areas.

They endeavor to answer the question: No matter where you are as an organization, how do you know where to focus your Lean Startup activities? The Lean Entrepreneur offers new thinking, tools, and activities that help organizations identify and act upon business model challenges in a waste-eliminating manner. Following the precepts of traditional lean thinking, Brant and Patrick introduce the value stream discovery process, which helps organizations hypothesize what they must do, including product development, marketing, and sales in order to create value. These business model assumptions are then ripe for testing, measuring, and iterating upon.

Further, the value you create is meaningless without a customer who needs, wants, desires, and, ultimately, determines the final value of your creation. Brant and Patrick spend considerable time helping you think through your customer segments. Cleverly, and in the spirit of the scientific method, they even help you discover where your customer theory is wrong.

Everyone likes a good story; Brant and Patrick interviewed dozens of entrepreneurs and documented numerous case studies both inside and outside of high-tech, in both startups and large enterprises. There's even a classic Wizard of Oz minimum viable product that dates back to 1998!

Make no mistake: Brant and Patrick have been here since the beginning. They self-published *The Entrepreneur's Guide to Customer Development* in April of 2010.

From the outset, they were both practitioners and mentors, urging entrepreneurs not to follow a paint-by-numbers approach, but rather to think lean: fast, agile, and continuously learning. Over the last two years they've traveled around the world speaking, advising, and teaching Lean Startup.

The Lean Entrepreneur is an important addition to the growing library of principles and practices designed to improve how we tackle innovation and uncertainty, be it in high-tech startups, Fortune 100 companies, non-profits, or government offices.

I consider myself lucky to count Brant and Patrick as friends and colleagues. It is my hope that from this book you will gain valuable insights, make Lean Startup your own, and—much more importantly—that you are successful in changing the world for the better.

Eric Ries
San Francisco
January 2013

Introduction

What Is *The Lean Entrepreneur?*

It's hard to know where you live on the curve. As far as we can tell, the arrow of time moves in one direction. You can never step in the same river twice (Heraclitus) and all that.

Change isn't constant. We change constantly, but at different rates, depending where we are on the curve. Fast change comes in times of cheap experimentation. Massive new life emerged on Earth during time periods in which a convergence of foundational platforms, like the different aspects of Earth's biosphere, favored the emergence of diverse species, most of which failed. Massive new technologies emerge when the discovery and extraction of massive amounts of resources (water, minerals, fuel) provides low-cost industrial experiments, most of which fail.

Although our narratives of the past reveal eras of big change, those who lived during those times likely didn't see it that way:

"Hey bro, pretty cool, we're living in the Age of Renaissance, yeah?"

"Beats the Middle Ages, dude."

"Word."

The life you live defines normalcy.

Is change big or little? Dramatic or incremental? Permanent or cyclical? Disruptive or sustaining?

No one can pinpoint where we exist on the curve. Is change over or just beginning? Are we at an inflection point? Up or down? Is the end nigh, or is the Age of Aquarius approaching?

A broken clock is right twice a day.

How can we know when we are amid big change? Listen to experts and incumbents. If you hear a lot of this, then be forewarned—"The times they are a-changin'":

- "Don't worry, it's just the business cycle; or, in other words, the next bus to pick us up will be by in five minutes."
- "Will x be ubiquitous? Oh that's ridiculous; x is exactly what is already consuming your market. 'It's just a normal cycle, we'll be back.'"
- "Piracy is killing us!"

The Lean Entrepreneur is about navigating big change.

Whether what's emerging is considered the postindustrial age, an information society, or an experience economy, *The Lean Entrepreneur* aims to help you create products people want, innovate with new ventures, and disrupt markets. With big change comes big opportunity. We'll provide you with grounded ways to market test your ideas with the right market segment; we'll give you real, tangible examples of how successful entrepreneurs are doing so; and we'll get you started right now and get you up to speed quickly.

We think of *The Lean Entrepreneur* as a field guide because it is designed to be brought into the field, whether that is your office, the local co-working space, your client's place of business, or the local coffee shop as you surf cyberspace, planning your conquest. Whereas a traditional naturalist field guide helps outdoorsmen identify the plants and animals of a certain geography, our field guide will help you identify concepts and ideas in the geography of innovation. At first blush, some of these ideas may not appear to be applicable to your business, but with an open mind and a spirit of creativity, we will demonstrate how these concepts can and will radically reshape how you bring products to market and, ultimately, to your business.

The Lean Entrepreneur is a book of synthesis, of recombination, and, we hope, of inspiration. It is a synthesis in that we will show where several pre-existing ideas about how to innovate, which initially appear to be virtual islands strewn across a sea, actually share connections and complement each other. And if we have done this well, a larger, more complete, and more comprehensive map of the changes coming and how to innovate now will have emerged for you.

As Henry Ford recombined existing technologies from different domains (interchangeable parts, the assembly line, the electric motor) into a wholly novel and disruptive set of innovations resulting in the manufacture and distribution of the first durable, mass-market automobile, we hope to inspire vis-à-vis our interpretations of several big ideas, which will result in a new approach that scales well for disruptive innovators and entrepreneurs, from small, value-producing businesses to the Fortune 500.

The product development methodologies and innovation frameworks espoused by *The Lean Entrepreneur* are heavily influenced by truly big thinkers, such as Steve Blank and Eric Ries, creators of *Customer Development* and *The Lean Startup*, respectively. However, other, rather similar, innovation methodologies such as design thinking and discovery-driven planning also exist.

All the aforementioned frameworks tend to be driven by principle, rather than by a set of cut-and-dried tactics, and are typified by iterative, customer-centric, data-informed approaches resembling the scientific method; and we, as natural-born bricoleurs, happily borrow from ideas that we deem appropriate as well as discard or ignore what we deem unhelpful.

We urge you, the reader, to do the same with ideas and approaches presented in this book.

Why Read (Be) *The Lean Entrepreneur?*

Our mission in writing *The Lean Entrepreneur* is threefold:

1. To describe why our economy is primed for a new wave of entrepreneurship using new methods of disruptive innovation.
2. To provide you real-world examples of how entrepreneurs are creating new markets and disrupting others.
3. To show you how you can get started *creating value.*

The context of *The Lean Entrepreneur* is an iterative, customer-centric, data-informed business development approach in the face of market uncertainty. Although, to some degree, all businesses operate in conditions of market uncertainty, all such conditions are not created equal. Market uncertainty can be described by an innovation spectrum stretching from lesser market uncertainty when undertaking sustaining innovation to greater market uncertainty when pursuing truly disruptive innovation.

Uncertainty and innovation are a duality. Without the former, there is no opportunity for the latter. True disruptive innovation can only happen in environments in which the final product, and its value proposition, price, marketing, sales channels, and, most importantly, its customer are, at best, educated guesses but, more than likely, almost completely unknown.

The inverse is also true: If one is developing products for which the value proposition, price, marketing, sales channels, and market segments are known or very likely to be known; then iterative, customer-centric, data-driven approaches as espoused by *The Lean Entrepreneur* may be suboptimal.

Suffice it to say, when the value proposition is known and successfully delivered by a business to a known customer, the methods of execution used by its owners and employees are good enough, at least for now. Perhaps they could become more efficient or less wasteful, but to instruct successful businesses on how to be more efficient is not our ambition.

As you read *The Lean Entrepreneur*, we'll make the case that innovating in uncertainty requires a highly iterative approach. We'll also make the case that a disproportionate part of your business model is ultimately determined not by command-and-control

diktats from the executive offices of your company or even your own personal desires but implicitly by the market segment you hope to provide value for. The sooner you grok that your customers have significant de facto control over the destiny of your business, the better for you, your customers, your employees, your colleagues, your shareholders, and other stakeholders in your business.

To belabor the point, it is your market segment, not you, that determines how you distribute your product, how much they are willing to pay, what sort of messaging they respond to, and for what job they are in need of hiring a product. In other words, other than the fact that you can choose whether to serve a particular segment, it is up to the segment to decide whether you should be given a shot.

Since iterative, customer-centric, data-informed product development approaches to creating value predate this book, is this simply a gussied-up rehash of previous thinking?

Short answer: No.

We hear time and time again that the greatest contribution made by Eric Ries and the Lean Startup is the lexicon. It provides a language for anyone practicing entrepreneurship to talk about how to do *meaningful*

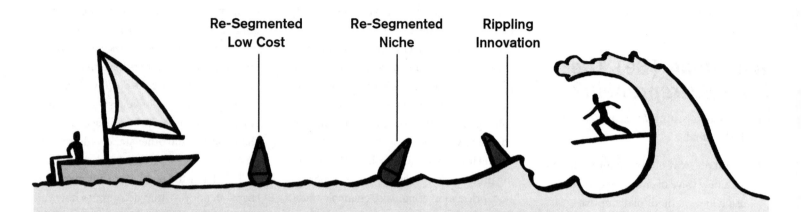

Re-Segmented Low Cost

Re-Segmented Niche

Rippling Innovation

Sustaining Innovation

Problem is well understood

Existing Market

Innovation improves performance, lower cost, incremental changes

Customer is believable

Market is predictable

Traditional business methods are sufficient

Disruptive Innovation

Problem not well understood

New Market

Innovation is dramatic and game changing

Customer doesn't know

Market is unpredictable

Traditional business methods fail

innovation. The point has never been about who came up with what, but, rather, how can we learn from past successes to make future endeavors more predictable.

We feel that we are now witnessing a phase marked by radical disequilibrium and fundamental changes in innovation and entrepreneurship enabled by a juggernaut of technological and cultural trends.

The best way to navigate the near future is to hyperfocus on creating value for customers and moving at the speed of the Internet. We'll show you how.

Who Is the Lean Entrepreneur?

We'd like to answer that question like most entrepreneurs who are asked to define their market: Everyone! However, in order to demonstrate that we drink our own Kool-Aid, we have spoken to and worked with many different individuals as we wrote this book. Here are our market segments:

- Scalable startup founders—If you are hoping to build "the next big thing."
- Lifestyle business founders—We don't think the term is derogatory in the least. If you're trying to build a *real* business that provides value to customers, we're talking to you.

- Intrapreneurs—If you are trying to change your business, whatever size, to move at the *speed of the Internet* read on.
- Educators—You recognize that entrepreneurship needs to be taught differently.
- Government Change Agents—If, like entrepreneurs trying to drive change inside big businesses, you are trying to drive change in how governments operate, we're here to help.
- Investors—If you could use help finding and providing assistance to the *right* startups.

Although we'd like to think this book will benefit everyone to some degree, this book is likely less than optimal for these market segments:

- Small-business founders who are starting companies for which there is already a known model—Typically these are the types of businesses found in malls: dry cleaners, retailers, franchises, and so forth.
- Lifestyle business owners—If you've already built your business and are generally satisfied with what you've achieved, congratulations! You probably don't need us.
- Solo practitioners—If you're trying to generate a personal or family income stream

via "projects" or small-scale products or services we think that's great! There are probably better books for that.

Generally speaking, if you've read Eric Ries's *The Lean Startup* and are looking for more tactical application of the principles espoused there, this is the right book for you. If you haven't read it and need convincing that a lean startup is the right thing for you and your organization, we will make the case—but you really should read Eric's book.

If you've read *The Four Steps to the Epiphany*, our *Entrepreneur's Guide to Customer Development*, or Blank's *The Startup Owner's Manual*, you will find new tools and methodologies for applying the principles you already believe in. There is not a lot of duplication here.

If you are well into the lean startup movement, a heavy reader of Ash Maurya, Cindy Alvarez, Sean Murphy, and others, we firmly believe we have exciting new material you can use to grow your business.

How to Use *The Lean Entrepreneur*

This book hopes to not only teach you and inspire you, but also to show you some fun along the way.

To that end, we've engaged a talented entrepreneur and artist who goes by the name of Fake Grimlock. Fake Grimlock has created an expressive set of illustrations just for *The Lean Entrepreneur*. The illustrations tell a story and serve to amplify concepts from the book.

You'll find them a bit whimsical at times, but be prepared to think deep thoughts as you take them in.

We've made them available for you for reuse and remix, subject to the Creative Commons license.

If you want to download the illustrations to use them in your presentations or blog posts or in other interesting ways, please do.* You can access them at **http://Lean Entrepreneur.co/illustrations** or e-mail us at **pics@leanentrepreneur.co.**

Our writing style aims to get to the heart of the matter quickly. Experts in specific domains will notice, probably much to their irritation, that we will intentionally gloss over some of the finer points we discuss. This is not because we don't think the details matter; they do, but they don't matter for the context of this book.

The Lean Entrepreneur is divided into 10 chapters:

1. Startup Revolution—A brief redux on what's going on now that makes lean startup the right methodology to apply to your business, regardless of size or sector.

2. Vision, Values, and Culture—We describe what a lean startup looks like in the startup world and in the enterprise.

3. All the Fish in the Sea—We help you figure out what customers to fish for.

4. Wading in the Value Stream—We explain how to posit the value you are creating.

5. Diving In—We introduce various methods of customer interaction to learn.

6. Viability Experiments—We talk about various methods of running experiments to de-risk your market.

7. Data's Double-Edged Sword—We help you not drown in data, while finding the information necessary to move the needle.

8. The Valley of Death—We guide you through the requisite ups and downs of traversing uncertainty.

9. Real Visionaries have Funnel Vision—We break down marketing and sales.

10. The Final Word—We end with a call to action.

Throughout, we include examples of real companies applying lean startup principles and succeeding. We hope you gain learning and inspiration from these companies, many of whom don't use the term *lean* to describe themselves.

Each chapter also includes exercises and templates you can use to help you think through your business model. Although we don't believe a step-by-step approach to success exists, we think many will find our exercises beneficial.

Learn the craft, then make it your own.

---

* We've licensed the illustrations with http://creativecommons.org/licenses/by-sa/3.0/. We'd love for you to use and share them, just remember to attribute "*The Lean Entrepreneur* by Brant Cooper and Patrick Vlaskovits with illustrations by Fake Grimlock" with a link to http://LeanEntrepreneur.co. Thanks!

1

Startup Revolution

The Myth of the Visionary (Take 1)

Visdorf feels summoned to the forest for unknown reasons. Alas, he is reluctant to go. The feeling has come upon him before but never like this, never so strong. He shakes his head and returns his gaze to the mysterious prose before him. He tries to focus on the bits of historical text requiring mental gymnastics and re-imagination. His mind blurs and the words spin up on the page as if in a magical vortex.

"Blast it all!" he exclaims as he slams shut the sturdy volume. "Curse this infernal vision!"

With a heavy sigh, Visdorf pushes himself away from the sturdy dining table and stands up. He turns to look out the window in the direction of the forest. The remaining daytime light is pulled toward the horizon; his dim shadow moves slowly along the wall until it is looming before him as the flickering light from the reading candle becomes predominant.

"Do not mock me, old friend," Visdorf says aloud to his dark visage. His mind made up, he strides purposefully toward the front door, grabs his pack and bedroll, and heads off into the early evening. His steps fall heavy on the dirt road leading to the edge of town. He walks with purpose, though his own mind is not leading. The last of daylight arcs across his back and the night envelops him. He leans forward.

* * *

As the edge of the forest nears, Visdorf hears merry music emanating from the last rickety building amidst the severed trunks of once massive trees. He stops before the path leading toward the revelry, and wishes nothing more than to join his comrades inside. One sonic voice rises in song above the others:

"Chant me the river of time flowing nigh!

"Betrayed by my lovers, the stars in the sky!"

"My sweet friend, TachNah," Visdorf says to himself, as he turns away toward the narrow trail that leads into the thickness of uncut Ancients, the source of all that sustains and severs life in this land of foreboding uncertainty.

Just then the door of the pub bursts open and out spills TachNah, and several other inebriated rabble-rousers. Visdorf doubles his pace.

"What clumsy goon goes there?" yells out TachNah. Visdorf stops, his large frame barely visible. "Why, it could only be one misshapen beast, I know," she says laughing.

"Le's go get 'im," says Klandor, one of the drunken men at her side. He stumbles forward, only to be sent tumbling to the ground with a heavy shove from TachNah.

"Shut your face, you dumb drunk. That's our friend Vizzy!"

Visdorf returns a few steps. "Yes, it is I, your friend Visdorf."

"You've decided then?" asks TachNah, suddenly lucid. "Heading to the Clearing by yourself. At night. Without your comrades?"

"You know as well as I, this is a trip I must take myself."

"You are a fool." She stares fiercely into the eyes of Visdorf, who looks away.

"Be that as it may." Visdorf turns.

"Wait." TachNah softens her gaze.

"It's decided. I . . . I must—"

"We will go too! Back together again!" says TachNah. The others: "Here! Here!"

Visdorf pauses. He stands tall, looming above them; a darker shadow than the night's. "Tempting as it may be," Visdorf spits while stepping menacingly toward them, "to drag you drunken sops into the forest and sacrifice you to the waiting Vekwolves, I shall not. If you wish to journey to the burning pits of Hell, then by all means do so. But not with me! Find your own damned swirling orbs of internal fire and torment! Follow your own raging beast. I shall fell Ancients if I must, slay wolves with their own bone!" Visdorf yells as he slashes the night with his glistening steel blade. He turns from his shocked friends and disappears into the dark woods.

* * *

Visdorf stares up into the night sky. He has found a small meadow and has made space for himself to rest. The stars above are dense. They move when his mind drifts, but are still when he looks carefully. He thinks of his friends. He knows he was too hard on them. He's not sure from where his vicious words sprang. "Fear, perhaps," he reasons. "I had to protect them. But felling Ancients? Slaying Vekwolves? With this?" Visdorf mocks himself, holding up his wolf bone–handled knife. He had walked for hours. The animal path he followed guided him to the meadow. This was not, however, the Clearing TachNah had mentioned.

"I am sure of that," he says to himself. Though he had never seen it before. The Clearing, as legend had it, was heavily guarded by Vekwolves and the living Ancients. No one survives the journey but the Ancients themselves and those who fight their way in. "And here I am and so . . . " Visdorf's eyes grow heavy and the stars dance again. "Their dance is familiar," Visdorf thinks as he drifts off to sleep.

* * *

Visdorf awakes with a start. In an instant he is on his feet, his blade drawn. The wind shifts across the meadow, as if undecided; an animal's warm breath, a pant. It is too dark, what light from the stars gone behind a low haze. He turns slowly, staring intently into the brush, his heart beating in his chest. He feels a low whoosh.

Visdorf is within himself. He is crouched, eyes closed and arms hanging loosely at his side. He turns from his feet, a vortex that begins with the ground. He pivots, his torso rotates, then his shoulders, and then like the tail of a whip, his arms rise up, his blade slashing through the air. The butt of the knife strikes the rib cage of a leaping Vekwolf, sufficiently knocking it off course, its teeth gnashing past Visdorf's head as it crashes into him. Visdorf falls to the ground and the wolf is instantly upon him again, locking onto his left arm, which Visdorf offers in lieu of his neck. Twisting and rolling to his left, Visdorf plunges his blade into the Vekwolf's side. The wolf lets out a disrupting cry and falls to the ground. Visdorf struggles to his feet, only to see two more wolves stalking him.

Again Visdorf hears the sounds of cutting air, but this time a quiet whistle and then a second, and a third. With quiet efficiency three arrows land, one at Visdorf's feet, and several moments later, the second and third cut deeply into the backs of the wolves' heads, pinning them unceremoniously to the ground.

While Visdorf is still trying to grasp what had just occurred, he looks up to see TachNah step into the clearing, bow in hand.

"Drunken sop? Really, that goes too far," she says with a plafyul grin.

"Hence the first arrow?" Visdorf quickly rejoins.

"Wanted you to wonder for at least a moment." They share a nervous laugh. The haze begins to break and the stars once again emerge. As if warned, Visdorf looks to the sky. "This isn't the Clearing, is it?"

"No, I don't believe so," TachNah says, examining his arm. "You are lucky."

"How so?" Visdorf asks angrily. He looks at her. "You call Vekwolves lucky?"

"You are lucky they all don't attack at once, but instead follow."

"This is the truth, I suppose," he says, wiping his blade on his pant leg.

"What's next, Visdorf? Where do we go from here?"

"We?" he challenges, but then softens. "We look to the stars."

They both look up again to the heavens. Visdorf rubs his eyes. "I am fatigued." TachNah doesn't respond, her eyes locked skyward. He looks at her and up again. "You see this, too?" She nods silently.

Like the vortex Visdorf saw when reading his mysterious history volume, the stars and galaxies and planets of the night sky turn; a magical light show formed from the past, but revealing something new. And then as quickly as it started, it is done. In a blink the stars are as they were. Or almost. A pattern reveals itself. A dozen stars Visdorf had never noticed before glimmer brighter than ever, forming a picture in the sky, like a map to the future.

"Are you seeing what I'm seeing?" Visdorf whispers.

"Yes," TachNah says, "and this is the way." She points across the meadow.

"I see now. I see what must be done." Visdorf picks up his pack and bedroll and together they start the long journey toward the Clearing.

The Myth of the Visionary (Take 2)

With brow furrowed and fingers callused from incessant scribblings and endless calculations noted in his weathered, leather notebook, and with the dim light in his workshop growing fainter, Henry sets down his well-worn nub of a pencil and leans back in his chair. He smiles wearily to himself. He has run the numbers for the hundredth time and they work. He is finally sure he has solved all the pieces to the product design puzzle he has been working on for months.

Closing his eyes and tilting his head back, he raises his arms and whoops aloud: "I did it!" Henry spins his chair triumphantly. "Now I can tell Susie," he thinks to himself. "We'll be rich!"

CUT!

Enough of this nonsense. If we promise to forgo our myth telling, will you forgo believing in them, at least for a short while? After *The Lean Entrepreneur*, you can return to your lonely albeit heroic genius, fighting his way through spasms of self-doubt, humiliation, and torment at the hands of the ignorant hordes of nonbelievers that surround him. We will set aside his *Eureka!* moment, and skip over his long, righteous fight to the top, his bounty of deserved wealth, and the adoring looks that are showered upon him. We will sheepishly ignore the tardy coronation of Visionary status.

Let's get real.

Man, being biological, follows biological patterns. So do man-made things.

Cycles exist in nature: water, seasons, phases of the moon, life and death, and so on. Human stuff goes through cycles, too: moods, business, life, and death. If you pull back far enough and don't sweat the details, you can find patterns in large swaths of human time. Humans love to label these time periods:

- The Stone, Bronze, and Iron Ages.
- Reconstruction, the Gilded Age, and the Progressive Era.
- The Machine Age, the Atomic Age, and the Postmodern Era.
- The Agrarian and Industrial Revolutions (here lives a myriad of postindustrial terms).

We limp forward, fall back, and then leap. Wash, rinse, repeat. Even in the best of economic conditions, millions are unemployed. It's worse elsewhere. Many have written about it before and will continue to do so. The economy is changing structurally, forever. White-collar jobs will follow the blue. Pundits everywhere have been competing for years (decades?) for what to call the postindustrial economy. It's the Third Wave, the Information Age, the Knowledge Era, the Services Economy; the economy is global, digital, virtual, and creative.

Meanwhile, manufacturing is not merely being sent offshore, it's being permanently displaced. Service jobs are deteriorating, too. High-end service jobs are sent offshore. Online marketplaces turn white-collar, college-required careers into commodities. Browsing the online workplace oDesk, for example, reveals the following jobs for which you can get competing bids from contract on-shore and offshore individuals or firms: engineering, accounting, marketing, sales, web development, design, customer service, technical support, administrative assistance, writing, editing, translating, HR, legal, recruiting, statistical analysis, and IT.

Furthermore, many other services jobs—retail, hotel, tourism, and the like—which often lead the recoveries, are often low paying, seasonal jobs. It's worth asking, *What are these people going to do?*

As Seth Godin writes, "The factory—that system where organized labor meets patient capital, productivity-improving devices, and leverage—has fallen apart. Ohio and Michigan have lost their 'real' factories, just as the factories of the service industries have crumbled as well. Worse still, the type of low-risk, high-stability jobs that three-quarters of us crave have turned into dead-end traps of dissatisfaction and unfair risk."[1] What's going on? It's pretty hard to get your arms around. Economic growth indicators that report on the past to help us plan for the future will be revised backward soon. Don't worry; experts will be on hand to explain.

Political institutions have never seemed so clueless. The media is completely flummoxed, having given up entirely trying to separate fact from fiction. Pundits are proven wrong on a daily basis, only to be trotted out before the masses for their opinions again. Economists run models based on assumptions that have no real-world bearing. *Ceteris paribus* is Latin for "on Fantasy Island." (Cue Ricardo Montalban.)

Yet, if you travel to tech hubs in San Francisco, parts of Manhattan, Santa Monica, Boulder, or Boston, you can't buy a hip, gourmet coffee without waiting in a queue of T-shirt- and jeans-clad entrepreneurs; the chosen fashion of the relentless.

Entrepreneurship is flowering globally. Chris McCann's *StartupDigest*, a startup-event newsletter, has over 200,000 subscribers and is published in 94 cities in 43 countries.[2] Lean startup meetups, which host startup speakers and offer mentoring, collaboration, and socialization, occur regularly in 185 cities in 37 countries.[3] More than 75,000 attendees have participated in over 750 Startup Weekend events in 325 cities in over 100 countries, where they form teams and build startups over two-day intensive workshops.[4]

The startup scene is so hot in Silicon Valley, entrepreneurs, investors, and the media are debating whether we are amid another investment bubble in the high-technology sector. Facebook went public at a valuation of over $100 billion. The same company acquired Instagram and its 13 employees for $1 billion. Valuations of hot, low-revenue (or in some cases, no-revenue) technology startups are reaching nosebleed levels. Engineering talent is difficult to find; competitive home buyers are overbidding on houses in the San Francisco Bay area. Sound familiar? Many commentators fear that Silicon Valley (and other tech clusters) is recapitulating the dot-com boom, bubble, and bust cycle of the late 1990s.

As in the past, there's no shortage of hand-wringing with regard to the types of companies being created. Copycat companies, feature-not-a-product ideas, entrepreneurs thinking too small, a lack of innovation, and so on are common complaints, especially among venture capitalists and page view–hungry bloggers. Even Silicon Valley cheerleaders implore entrepreneurs to stop making consumer iPhone applications and instead switch to building more efficient airplane wings, as if that's how entrepreneurship works, how innovation happens.[5]

We hear doom and gloom on one side and boom and gloom on the other!

Yes, this all moves in cycles. Human beings have witnessed similar trends before. But the cycles come quicker, and they even overlap. We're at the tail of one and in the eye of the storm at the same time! Cycles are moving at the speed of the Internet.

Although cycles mean what goes up must come down—and vice versa—the arrow of time means the world is different each time, and change, from the most macro perspective, heads in one direction. The long-term progress of humans has been overwhelmingly positive.

We argue that we now find ourselves amid a tremendous storm of economic, technological, and cultural disruption. We are experiencing massive waves of change, high tides of anxiety, and a tumultuous backwash of resistance, to put it dramatically. The disruption creates an odd mixture of extraordinary market efficiency coupled with volatility and uncertainty at levels equaled only by, perhaps, the quantity of information, data, and connectivity helping to cause it.

To prosper through these changes, whether as an individual or a business, you must be fast, efficient, and value-creating. You have to be lean.

Case Study: Disrupting Venture Capital

500 Startups is a global venture capital (VC) firm headquartered in Mountain View, California. Started in late 2010, it has invested in nearly 400 companies in 20 different countries. We spoke with principals Dave McClure and Paul Singh about how 500 Startups employs lean startup thinking in its investment decisions and how they, along with a handful of other investors, are disrupting the venture capital game.

Lean Entrepreneur: What is different about 500 Startups as opposed to other early-stage venture capital firms?

500 Startups: We think we are a good example of a venture firm that has adapted to the new nature of early-stage technology startups, which is being driven by a number of factors.

The first point is that it's becoming easier to launch a product and to get customers, and that's driven by rapidly dropping costs and access to these huge platforms like Facebook, like Twitter, like iOS and Android and others.

The second thing that is fundamental to our business is as the web gets bigger, the world is getting smaller. You can, very literally, be anywhere in the world, and start a global business.

Thirdly, access to capital for tech startups is getting easier as well. This capital is coming not only from VCs and angels, but governmental programs such as Startup Chile. We're seeing what is essentially a commoditization of early-stage money, as governments—regional, local, and federal governments—realize that sometimes their tax dollars are better spent creating entrepreneurs rather than trying to lure them from other regions.

LE: How has 500 Startups adapted to this environment?

500S: The process of due diligence on a potential investment has changed drastically. Ten years ago, the process to get to know a company or a startup was long. You really wanted to get to know the founders and the business, because you were probably going to write a quarter-million-dollar check. So all the drawn-out due diligence you were doing over two or three months was completely rational.

But because of those trends that we just mentioned, you don't really have to do that anymore.

Because, again, it's just so easy to start up, most people who get funded today have some sort of prototype already in place, even if it's a rough prototype of minimal use. That's far better than some of the ideas that were getting funded five or 10 years ago.

We are therefore able to deploy smaller checks. We are able to deploy these $50,000 checks, which in the bigger picture are not a big deal, but we make those decisions within less than a day, sometimes less than an hour.

So early-stage investors are increasingly realizing that for these early-stage startups, most of the meaningful due diligence happens in the rear-view mirror, after the first investment.

LE: Is large-scale venture capital dead?

500S: We don't think that's the case at all. In fact, we think what's actually happening is that though it's cheaper to start a startup, scaling a startup is more expensive. That's because as more and more of these startups exist, they start to saturate the best online distribution channels, driving costs up.

When customer acquisition starts to work and they want to plow more money into these competitive channels, they require a lot more money. The fact is it costs more to scale. So there certainly is still a place for the big VCs.

LE: How does crowd funding affect early-stage startups?

500S: We think that's going to be big. When people think about crowd funding they usually think about doctors and lawyers writing checks, but what's going to be interesting is that now founders can take a check, even a very small check, from someone who has functional expertise in an important area, say, pay-per-click. This means that traditional investors who simply wave checkbooks around are going to become increasingly irrelevant and we as an industry are going to have to adapt.

LE: What does it mean to call yourselves a lean VC?

500S: We think that being a lean VC is really about being the card counter at the blackjack table. Instead of being the traditional VC jumping around and doing big bets based on gut feeling, we think lean VC is akin to walking up to that table and placing the minimum bets possible, while we count the cards and as soon as we see the pattern, that's when we double down. It's really about putting a little bit in, watching how the founders behave, putting a little bit more in, watching how things go, and then putting a little bit more in.

That's much different than the traditional VC model, which is to take a lot of time to get to know the founders and then write a big check upfront, and then pat ourselves on the back and pretend we know that this is going to be a winner.

LE: Has the VC industry kept up with the meta-innovation recently?

500S: Our assertion is that venture capital is one of the only parts of private equity that has not innovated much over the last 10, 15, or even 50 years.

Here is a very simplistic example: If you are a public market trader and you bought one share of this one company, and the next day the price changes, if there was any pain in that transaction, you feel it on your books immediately.

Now if we look at venture capital, if you're a VC and you're writing a quarter-million-dollar or half-a-million-dollar check to an early-stage company, you are not going to feel the pain or the success for what, maybe a year, maybe two? Possibly even three years?

The point is that if you are a public market investor, you feel the pain right away, positive or negative. If you are a private market investor, you feel the pain measured in orders-of-magnitude longer amounts of time.

As fledgling companies are able to do more and work with less, we investors need to adapt our thinking and our processes, because as we write smaller checks, we are going to feel the pain sooner as well.

Venture capital hasn't innovated, because we never felt the pain as fast as we do today. Speed and feedback loops are paramount to the 500 Startups strategy.

On the one extreme, if we just take our time looking at deals, we are going to miss the deal because other lean venture investors are going to come in and write smaller, faster checks to those startups.

On the other side of it, even if we think that we are going to be able to deploy a quarter million or half a million into an early-stage startup, it's likely we will never see the returns.

The fact is that the amount of failure you see as a lean VC is no larger or higher than what you would have traditionally seen. It just feels more painful because if you are making smaller bets across more companies, you will perceive a higher percentage of companies failing. The reality is that it's actually the same as a traditional VC but simply more visible and the feedback is faster.

There are a number of converging trends and technologies that bring us to this point, summarized by (but not limited to, and in no particular order):

- Bytes eating the world
- Hype and hyper
- Crowds everywhere (feeling claustrophobic?)

Bytes Eating the World

In 2011, famed Internet-entrepreneur-turned-venture-capitalist Marc Andreessen described how technology companies are disrupting entire industries. He called this phenomenon "Software eating the world."

He declared, "Six decades into the computer revolution, four decades since the invention of the microprocessor, and two decades into the rise of the modern Internet, all of the technology required to transform industries through software finally works and can be widely delivered at global scale."[6] It's hard to argue with him, though some would prefer to think about it in terms of hardware eating the world, or the "cloud" eating the world. Of course, the Internet is software and hardware; hardware requires software and software requires hardware. Aside from the question of who's eating what, the line between technology companies and traditional-products companies is blurring to the point of making the distinction irrelevant.

Software is in everything: your car, phone, stereo, camera, and TV. Software is critical to any modern business. Customer management, logistics, resource planning, inventory control, human resources, accounting, factory automation—all are made up of software, software, software.

As Andreessen points out, you buy books, watch movies, listen to music, and play games created or distributed by software companies: Amazon, Netflix, Pandora, Apple, Zynga.

Innovative software coupled with new electronics results in new ways for computers and humans to interact (HCI), resulting in what investor Brad Feld of the Foundry Group calls "instrumenting human beings." We are at the very infancy of HCI and its natural progression toward a "symbiotic human computer future."[7]

The open software movement, which helped drive down development costs and drive innovation in the personal computer world, is now emerging in the computer networking industry led largely by Google's "G-Scale Network" and the use of the Open-Flow protocol.

Did we mention hardware? And materials science? Massively disruptive technologies like 3D printing are enabling the first wave of mass customization that will threaten manufacturing-based economies. Movements are well underway to open-source hardware development technologies and create hardware components that can be used across different companies, even in different industries.

"For the last hundred years and definitely for the last thirty years manufacturing has ostensibly been treated as a solved problem," says David ten Have, CEO and founder of Ponoko, a web-based platform for the manufacture of custom products. "The reality is that it is just a plateau that we've been sitting on and some technologies and some social forces have come into play that have caused us to push off the plateau."[8]

digital fabrication: Digital fabrication combines 3D modeling and additive

manufacturing technology to produce models, prototypes, and, most significantly, functional products.

Digital fabrication is giving small businesses the ability to manage inventories like Fortune 100 companies. Suddenly, experimentation with new products and disruptive innovation is not so risky.

This also matches up with the trend toward people producing products that are solving problems for themselves, their communities, and niche markets. More and more businesses are no longer developing for masses, but rather solving problems close by.

The culture of open-source software (which allows free use of the code under specific conditions) emerging in hardware is another death knell for the big-business-protecting patent system. (Not that this will be a quick death.)

The only way to thrive is to be what Steven Spear calls a "high velocity" organization. A high-velocity organization not only continuously produces higher-quality products, while increasing efficiency, but continuously improves *how to produce* the product. This, Spear argues, is the forgotten lesson of the Toyota Production System: that Toyota figured out "how to do the work in such a way that individuals and groups kept learning how to do that work better."

Current digital-fabrication technologies are at the state of the Apple I in 1976, estimates David ten Have, which, if true, means the effect that 3D printing and other digital-fabrication technologies will have on our economies and culture is potentially massive. Mark Frauenfelder, the editor-in-chief of *MAKE* magazine, points to the manufacture of components with significantly greater complexity than standard subtractive manufacturing allows for and to the largely unexplored applications in fine and custom art production.[9]

Hype and Hyper

Internet, mobile, mobile Internet, laptops, tablets, PDAs, GPS, 3G, 4G, IM, SMS, GPS, six degrees of separation, LinkedIn, Facebook, Twitter, the Matrix, you get the picture.

We're plugged in and connected, and, as some like to say, hyper-ly so.

Investor Mike Maples Jr. says, "Part of what we talk about with respect to hypernet is you're going to have billions of nodes connected to millions of clouds and that you're not going to think of it as one Internet anymore but you're going to have all kinds of different clouds and data feeds and screens and interfaces that don't even have screens talking to each other, sometimes overtly and sometimes behind the scenes."[10]

To a large extent, this has already happened, and we can see the ramifications, both good and bad. Hypernet means speed and reach. Data of any kind, from ads to zeitgeist, reaches further and travels faster. The implications are tremendous.

It took AOL nine years to hit 1 million users, Facebook nine months, and Draw Something around nine days in early 2012! How long before we see a pair of entrepreneurs team up to build a billion-dollar company?[11]

Coming is a world of worldwide, instantaneous connectivity. Machines talking to machines, data to data, decisions made by machines based on that data. The size

"That Wednesday, what had started as a series of bizarre, unexplainable glitches in quant [financial "engineers" who trade using brain-twisting math and superpowered computers] models turned into a catastrophic meltdown the likes of which had never been seen before in the history of financial markets. Nearly every single quantitative strategy, thought to be the most sophisticated investing ideas in the world, was shredded to pieces, leading to billions in losses. It was deleveraging gone supernova."[12]

Source: Scott Patterson, *The Quants: How a New Breed of Math Whizzes Conquered Wall Street and Nearly Destroyed It.*

and spread of demonstrations and protests across multiple countries in the Arab world, known as the Arab Spring, leveraged hypernet.

It's not just us, however; it's *them.* It's the machines!

Machines needn't have intent to assist in catastrophes like the financial meltdown of 2007. According to some analysts, 60 percent of equity trading is already done by machines. Not only are algorithms sometimes buggy (in other words, have coding errors that can wreak havoc); their effects are not predictable by human intelligence. Under unusual market circumstances, such as the unraveling of the housing market in 2007, for example, computer trading and the mathematically complex algorithms directing them had unforeseen and unforeseeable consequences. This phenomenon was, in fact, a leading cause of the market meltdown.[13]

Hypernet and hyperconnectivity disconnect us as quickly as they connect us. The 2011 power blackout in San Diego was historically severe, traversing several Southwest grids, leaving 7 million without electricity in 11 minutes. Tripping mechanisms, designed to protect the system, actually caused the rippling effect.[14]

When Amazon's computer-networked cloud service goes down, it takes major businesses down with it. Ditto with Facebook's open programming interfaces that other businesses use to connect to Facebook. Connectivity brings redundancy, but dependence also breeds fragility.

The same connectivity that passes useful and literally revolutionary information around the globe, just as quickly and perhaps more thoroughly passes mundane, brain-rotting drivel and, worse, manipulation, propaganda, rumor, misleading information, and outright lies. In fact, the fourth estate is now built on top of this page view–centric world.

Ryan Holiday exposes the farce in *Trust Me, I'm Lying*:

The link economy encourages blogs to point their readers to other bloggers who say crazy things, to borrow from each other without verification, and to take more or less completed stories from other sites, add a layer of commentary, and turn it into something they call their own.[15]

Ryan isn't referring to the blogs that the old-school media derides as pajama-wearing amateurs writing from their parents' basement, but, rather, the old media websites themselves. They depend on news that is first reported by blogs of all stripes, which then report on what people are saying without verifying any of the conjecture. Ironically, this is often called beta journalism and it is eerily similar to lean startup practices, though in a wholly negative way.

Feeling Claustrophobic?

All this connectivity not only affects individuals, businesses, and machines, but also creates a revolutionary crowd dynamic. That crowds wield tremendous power has long been known. See their impact on social upheaval, labor movements, or even John Steinbeck's phalanx theory, wherein he observers "with a drive, an intent, an end, a method, a reaction which in no way resembles the same things possessed by the men who make [it] up." Although Steinbeck noted the negative side of the mob mentality, it is also observed that the knowledge of the mob, as in a network, perhaps, can be greater than the knowledge of any of its members.

The organization of crowds is disrupting all sorts of disciplines. Scientific organizations, researchers, and private life-science businesses, including pharmaceuticals, use a loose network of private citizens to advance research. It turns out that smart people outside of corporate research and development departments can often break through scientific bottlenecks that internal researchers cannot.

Amazon's Mechanical Turk distributes simple tasks to workers worldwide who voluntarily perform the menial tasks for very small amounts of money. Although the Internet is littered with amateurish, horribly mundane, and ignorant user-generated content, the opposite also is out there. Much to the chagrin of professional photographers, writers, designers, and such, as well as stock pickers, political analysts, and members of other disciplines normally dominated by elites, there are legions of people in the great wide world who are their equals. The Internet and crowd sourcing brings that to light.

Crowd-sourced ad contests result in advertisements at least as entertaining as the best professional TV spots. Online news sites like Huffington Post leverage unpaid bloggers and yet produce copy that rivals that of traditional print stalwarts. Online graphic design and stock photography websites introduced market efficiency that approximates perfect free market conditions.

"If someone's going to cannibalize your business, better it be one of your other businesses," Getty CEO Jonathan Klein said after acquiring iStockphoto, a crowd-source marketplace for photographers.[16] Crowd-source networks break through man-made knowledge silos and break down thought-limiting hubris.

Crowd-funding sites like Kickstarter are currently used by entrepreneurs to take product orders before manufacturing to prove demand. Recent legislation in the United States will enable crowd funders to make investments, taking a stake in the startups they support. In the not-too-distant future, the investment bankers who arrogantly believe that their post-crash bonuses are justifiable will have their value tested as money flows like water downhill toward opportunity without them.

Investor Bill Gross says, "Crowd funding is going to have an enormous impact on entrepreneurs, impact on VCs, impact on the angels. It's just going to really, hopefully democratize fund raising, but it's going to have unintended consequences of some kind as well. Who knows what the pitfalls will be."[17]

Do we know if crowd funding will disrupt banking and venture capital? No, of course not. The way they are dismissing it, however, sure portends well.

Which Is to Say, Disruption Hurts

Globalization combined with online marketplaces resulted in offshoring and the commoditization of former high-margin businesses and occupations.

Disintermediation has disrupted multiple industries, putting creative people in direct contact with consumers. Increasingly, musicians sell directly to their fans, authors to their readers, filmmakers to their viewers, product producers to consumers via downloadable physical products! Intermediation

is transformative, too. The large studios, for instance, dominated their respective industries by curating content producers and owning distribution channels. The Internet brought democracy to these endeavors, but the democratization increases competition and drives down the price of the content, such as with Internet-based crowd-source marketplaces.

The Internet giveth and the Internet taketh away.

Black Swans, White Rats, Red Herrings

Predicting the future is a fool's errand, and so we may as well be first in line. All this talk about where we might be headed might be more persuasive if we knew where we were now. That being said, our brains work better when we have something to measure against. A baseline or a hypothesis allows us to create some sort of an experiment to determine how reality compares to our guess. Without the baseline, we are more likely to shape what we experience to match what we believed before the experience. It somehow matters little the size of the peg we imagine we can fit into whatever size hole.

If it's not bad enough that human beings are hardwired to suffer experiment bias, it's particularly disconcerting that our ability to predict worsens the more expertise we have in a particular domain.[18] It seems strange that this comes to light when our reliance upon experts has never been greater.

Our world is so complicated that we outsource our narratives. We seem to not care about the accuracies of the predictions, as long as we have explanations about things beyond our control that we can store comfortably in the back of our minds. It's what frees up our ability to cope with day-to-day life.

Truth be told, experts have been wrong for a long time, and by this, we mean all experts, including doctors, lawyers, scientists, and so on, to say nothing about the pseudo-scientific economists, psychologists, sociologists and less still of the self-aggrandizing and self-appointed pundit class, subject-matter experts, consultants, and think-tank denizens.

We are wrong before we are right. The very nature of learning presumes this to be so. You may have heard the one about how leading minds in historical times thought the world was flat because the beer was. Okay, we just made that up, but, truth be told, we are not smarter than they were. We only have more knowledge. Historical figures were every bit as fully evolved as we are.

As the news desk on *Saturday Night Live* once reported, "This just in, white rats cause cancer."

The sooner we give up the notions that we can, first, accurately describe the past; second, predict the future; and third, manufacture it, the better off we will be.

It seems reasonable that we as humans have an evolutionary-based predisposition to create narratives that explain the past and predict the future.[19] If our normal sensory filters were removed, if we could smell like a dog, see like an eagle, hear like a deer, we would need larger brains to process the data, not to mention look funny. The stories we tell, like our filters, create boundaries for our thoughts. It's easier for us to make sense of the world if we fit data into our existing model, rather than change the model to fit the data.

We are pattern-identifying machines. If you're hiking in the woods, you might glimpse out of the corner of your eye a dark object in the shadows. "It's a bear!" A direct look reveals a large rock. In terms of evolution, early warning is better than a 404 error: "That link no longer exists."

Remember the campfire game where you begin by whispering a story into the ear of the camper next to you and she passes it on until you've come full circle and the end story barely resembles what you started with? Well, memory is like that, only you're the only one at the campfire. How else to explain the difference between your memory and that of your partner with whom you shared that romantic experience? "Ah yes, I remember it well."

It's not actually true that victors write history; survivors do. Dead men tell no tales. The history told by losers, though presumably told by fewer people, is equally likely to be objectively true as the history told by winners.

One man's myth is, of course, another's religion. Although scientific research inexorably leads us in one direction, if we don't read the research, let alone conduct it, we are still left with the question of which story to believe: Should we favor the scientist or the preacher?

"Experts" theorize why YouTube succeeded so quickly. First mover! Or why Facebook beat out MySpace and Friendster. Uh, fast follower?

The more pseudo the science, the more personality-based the results. On we go, reshaping the theory to fit current circumstances or reshaping the results to fit the theory by manipulating variables. This is why TV pundits put personality first. You need to tell a convincing *story*.

The problem is when the story is false or when inappropriate lessons are drawn, as is often the case with visionaries and entrepreneurs.

Primordial Innovation Soup

All that being said, here's our analysis of the past and prediction of the future. *Caveat emptor*.

Throughout history, technological innovation leads to disruptive change, from the transformation of agriculture-based economies to manufacturing, and again to postindustrial. This has been so thoroughly analyzed and argued that we won't repeat the discourse here.

Patterns can be discerned within the changes. Patterns don't predict the future, but help describe the change, and help the understanding of why, perhaps, and provide a baseline to measure current changes against. If nothing else, it's an amusing thought experiment.

The transformation of the computer and resulting application breakthroughs over the past 50 years or so has been described in terms of Moore's Law. Moore's Law says that the number of transistors that can be placed inexpensively on an integrated circuit doubles approximately every two years. The specifics hardly matter, since the law has been extrapolated to describe nearly anything computer related that demonstrates greater performance, in smaller packages, at a minimum cost.

Oh yeah, and the performance needs to improve exponentially, too. In other words, if you're stacking pennies and double the number of pennies in each subsequent stack, the twenty-first stack will have over 1 million pennies!

The fact that you now carry a computer in your phone is directly attributable to Moore's Law. Personal computers, the Internet, and mobile technology represent wide swaths of technical innovation. Buried inside those swaths are thousands of technological advances that not only provide continuous, incremental improvement of the technology itself, but enable new technology and new applications and then set the stage for the next wave of transformation.

Each cycle lays a foundation for the next transformation.[20]

lifecycle adoption curve: Popularized by Geoffrey Moore, the technology

lifecycle adoption curve is a bell-shaped curve separated into five phases: innovators, early adopters, early majority, late majority, and laggards.

The next transformation, however, doesn't displace the prior one, but rather builds on top of it. Innovation comes so quickly these days that one transformation has not reached the mainstream in its *lifecycle adoption curve* before the next one is upon us. Developing countries, for example, are completely bypassing the personal computer wave to take advantage of ubiquitous mobile technology.

Today, technology innovation is finally about the individual. This perhaps surprises you, since we've all been talking about personal computers for decades. Up until recently, the computer revolution or digital revolution has been primarily about productivity and efficiency gains for businesses. Consumers played an important role, but it wasn't ever really about *them* and their *needs*.

Individuals don't want and have never wanted computers. They want to accomplish specific goals, get things done, be entertained, protect their interests, have a job, raise a family, and so on. They even want some of these things badly enough that they have been willing to put up with pretty awful solutions, including crappy computers.

Businesses didn't set out to solve these individuals' problems, because, well, because that's not where the big money was. The big money was in solving company problems. Individuals' concerns were only addressed as they were needed to solve company problems.

So, for example, businesses bought Windows computers in the 1990s and not the far superior Apples, because the IBM-based PCs were half the cost and no one cared that they had a horrible user experience. Medium and large businesses could still communicate more efficiently with partners and customers, while bypassing the need for each partner in the firm having his or her own secretary. Type your own damn letter on that computer! Business-level productivity gains (just barely) justified the incredibly expensive two- to three-year replacement cycle for computer and networking technology. The 2000s saw the rise of departmental productivity. *Software-as-a-service* emerged to dramatically reduce if not eliminate the pain of information technology (IT) departments owning the corporate applications. Suddenly, individual business units could acquire software available over the Internet, access it using a common desktop client called a browser, and improve departmental productivity without input from IT. It didn't really matter that the experience sucked.

software-as-a-service: Software-as-a-service is software used over the Internet.

Typically the software is run on computers in distributed data centers—in other words, "in the cloud"—and is accessed via a web browser.

The best indication of the rise in the significance of the individual is the concomitant rise in industrial design practices for high-tech companies. The last couple of years have witnessed a surge in user-experience design for software companies who are focused first and foremost on the product experience from the customer's perspective.

You'll know when human concerns have been addressed by computers when you don't recognize them as computers. People want appliances that do cool stuff.

What this means is that we're in a value-based economy. The businesses that *continuously* create the most value for a market win. This is true for big, established businesses, as well as startups.

One way to think about it: inside a tech-wave, the platforms are dominated by a few large players, an oligopoly. The platform enables other companies to create value for customers. Over time, competition on the platform drives down the price of the value created for customers. This is "value surplus," which is great for customers and society, increasing the standard of living across the board as more people have access to the value.

This pattern is true for all customers who participate in the relatively free market, including businesses on the consumption side and consumers. (Big businesses and governments don't benefit as much from less expensive value, because their inefficiencies prevent them from doing so.)

So, for example, because of market efficiencies, the cost of creating a new high-tech business has dropped dramatically. Cloud computing provides computer servers, network access, and storage as a service to businesses at a fraction of the cost of businesses building out the infrastructure and human resources to do it themselves. The service is likely to be faster, more available globally,

and more fault tolerant. Furthermore, you pay only for what you use and upgrades are a credit-card swipe away. It's very *lean*, since the service utilization is tied directly to customer demand.

The cost of producing product has also decreased. Free software is available to write the software that operates alongside the free web service and database programs running on all that cheap hardware. Furthermore, the software is easier to write, requiring less-skilled developers.

Internet and mobile startups are instantly global, to boot. Access to less-expensive resources and monetizable customers around the globe are waiting for you right this instant.

It's not surprising, then, that entrepreneurship is flourishing globally. It's a perfect storm. We have decades of technology foundation, an environment conducive to low-cost experimentation, and a need to create value finely tuned to customers' needs. We have thousands of startups, thousands of low-cost experiments, an evolutionary dream enabling an extraordinary opportunity for high market efficiency in the creation of value surplus for people.[21]

It's tough, though, especially on legacy businesses and the governments they bought to protect them. It's hard on everyone—all those who endeavor to create value, both young businesses and old, those inside and outside tech, those who want to grow big, as well as the solo entrepreneur.

shadow force: a core competency, operational excellence, or key differentiator internal to the business, which allows it to outperform the competition

Increased competition makes chasing value more difficult. Speed is of the essence in the hyperconnected world. Understanding and capitalizing on that special something, a *shadow force* allows you to outperform

the competition, as long as you continuously improve.

Over time, new disruption happens at the platform level, threatening the hegemony of the incumbents, forcing them to become

opportunistic or to consolidate around what remains of their core competency. Adoption of the platform continues along the technology lifecycle adoption curve, but rapid growth is behind them. Many are unable to respond to disruption competitively, that is, in value-creating ways, and so they seek other methods to maintain revenues, such as government regulation, patent hoarding and litigation, and crazy amounts of brand marketing.

A new wave of value-creating businesses ride on top of the new platform, killing legacy businesses, being acquired by them, or establishing new markets. The cost curve continues to decline, so these new businesses have less margin than their counterparts on the prior platform.

Apple's iPhone disrupted multiple industries simultaneously. Prior to the iPhone, Internet use on the mobile phone was following the same path as on a personal computer. The iPhone flipped that on its head, becoming, essentially, a parallel platform. Dozens of startups that were building mobile applications on legacy mobile operating systems were killed off, virtually overnight. Suddenly, their value was replicated at a fraction of the cost and made available for free (or nearly free) on Apple's App Store.

Similarly, the telecommunications giants' grand plans to monetize applications on top of their networks vanished. Telecoms went immediately back to their core competency: selling consumers access to bandwidth, selling the government access to users' private data, and buying off Congressional legislators.

What's crazy is that just because you have a mobile application with tons of happy users doesn't mean you have a business. The price of the value creation is almost zero. This is hypermarket efficiency, the likes of which we haven't seen since circa the 1920s, when the inability of family farms to make money led to agriculture subsidies that have lasted to this day (though the intended beneficiaries are long gone).

The value-creation economy comes on the heels of the collapse of the wealth-creation economy. It remains to be seen whether political leaders, big-business executives, and Wall Street regulators have heard the warnings with regards to motivating executives to maximize shareholder value rather than create value for customers (which, if successfully accomplished, should maximize shareholder value over the long term.) Both of the last two bubble meltdowns, recessions, major financial meltdowns—whatever you want to call them—can arguably be traced back to ill-conceived incentives rewarding non-value-creating activities in favor of speculative (and often illegal) short-term money making.

Entrepreneurship requiring little or no investment to get started and lifestyle, bootstrapped endeavors that will succeed or fail based on real value creation seem to have emerged as if in response to the prior hedonism.

linchpins: A term coined by Seth Godin to describe the "indispensable employee" who "brings humanity and connection and art to her organization."

What Chris Guillebeau refers to as the "microbusiness revolution"[22] is a calling to the "unexpected entrepreneurs," who are Seth Godin's *linchpins*.[23] Don't wait for corrections from Wall Street and the Washington, D.C. village, but forge ahead and create your own value.

Similarly, for those who dream of creating tomorrow's big companies, perhaps of being acquired, of creating a sustaining business that employs dozens or hundreds of people, or even of being the next disruptive force, the time to get started is now. Finally, for those large businesses that are committed to creating customer value, companies like Procter & Gamble, O2, and Intuit, as well as those contemplating how to disruptively innovate in order to stay relevant, a new way to compete is required.

The Value-Creation Economy

There are two sides to the value-creation-economy coin. On one side is customer empowerment and on the other is employee empowerment.

The nature of being hyperconnected, where access to your global customers is nearly instantaneous and 24/7, means that the more highly attuned to your customer you are, the more likely you are to deeply understand them.

There's an entire mythology that has grown up around Steve Jobs's dismissal of customer' concerns, such that he supposedly showed them disdain. Success was due wholly to his "visionary" capabilities. We would argue, however, that the mythmakers have the story wrong. Jobs's genius was not in his product vision or vision of what the world would become. As we've described, we believe there is no such thing as such a visionary.

Jobs's genius was in his deep understanding of his customers. He knew them so well, he needn't ask them what they needed! Perhaps this was innate; perhaps it was learned. Putting aside for a moment the graveyard of mistakes he made, the Apple retail stores are nothing if not a customer lab, where "geniuses" study customer behavior. It is a honey pot of sorts to lure customers to a place where they can be studied experiencing Apple products, so that other "geniuses" can make products that provide value to customers. Apple's first real sale, for the record, was to a customer who told Jobs exactly what he wanted to buy.

In the value-creation economy, customers are empowered by:

- Having a product experience that exceeds their needs.
- Having a relationship with the company in which the company treats them respectfully.
- Having a voice in the product.

The value-creation economy is defined by eliminating barriers between those who build a product and those who experience it.

To accomplish this, employees are empowered to:

- Make decisions.
- Continuously learn.
- Continuously improve.

This is obvious to some, sacrilege to others.

You might be surprised where it's happening. Consider this: U.S. Army General Martin E. Dempsey said, "We've gone to outcomes-based training. . . . What we've learned in this fight is that soldiers really need to be able to figure things out."

Donald E. Vandergriff, Maj. U.S. Army, Ret., believed the U.S. Army was stuck in the Industrial Age. Their personnel system created soldiers "who are not craftsmen who master their art, but instead are considered mere technicians who perform rote tasks," like factory workers.

As the world changes, so does the style of conflict and, in turn, the structure of the armed services. Without commenting on the wisdom, the United States is engaged in multiple armed conflicts around the world. The methods of deployment, as well as the length and style of engagement, is in conflict with the top-down Mission Command system that grew out of the World Wars.

Vandergriff argues for a more decentralized system capable of deploying an army that "embraces creativity, risk-taking, and flexibility while encouraging professional service." Over the past five to six years, the Army has adopted what it calls Outcomes-Based Training & Education (OBT&E) with the objective of developing soldiers who are adaptive to conditions on the ground.

A simple example that demonstrates the difference in training is to look at "SPORTS" (slap, pull, observe, release, tap, and shoot), a task taught to soldiers for clearing a jammed weapon. The traditional approach is a skill-training drill that adheres to task, condition, and standards (TCS). This is akin to memorizing best practices. In this example, the soldier must correctly perform the six steps in five seconds.

In the OBT&E approach, soldiers are presented with a jammed weapon in a specific combat scenario. When the weapon jams, the soldier only uses the taught process to clear the jam if the circumstances call for that action, and considers other tactics as well, such as taking cover or communicating with fellow soldiers.

The emphasis is on teaching the soldier how to read the situation and empowering the soldier to think and make decisions that reflect the environment. The soldier's ability to execute best practices is more reflective of the ability of the trainer than the ability of the soldier. The soldier's ability to find the right solution to specific problems increases their accountability, and, in return, the soldier is empowered.[24]

Good physicians know that understanding their patients deeply helps them diagnose illness. Family history, nutrition, exercise, stress, and other daily routines and quality-of-life conditions have an important impact on health. That being said, specialists can lose sight of the impact medical procedures and pharmaceuticals might have on quality of life and other factors that impact long-term health. So relying solely on the science of disease, medicine, and cures, it's possible to lose focus on the idea that analyzing the quality of life shouldn't be separate from the discussion about life itself.

Dr. Stephanie Cooper,[25] cardiologist and assistant professor at the University of Washington says:

> In the past, a doctor may begin interaction with a patient with an open-ended question, but research has shown that doctors often interrupt the response. The ensuing discussion is directed and manipulated by the physician, who often has preconceived notions about what the patient needs. Patients leave without having all of their questions answered, often feeling disrespected and not fully understanding the treatment plan. This leads to decreased compliance,

and in the worse situations, to increased likelihood of litigation if things go wrong. It may also result in worse outcomes. In recent years, there has been an increasing emphasis on patient involvement in medical decision making in which all the possible treatment options and outcomes are outlined and the patient and doctor together make a decision based on patient preferences. This is in direct counter distinction to physician patriarchal autonomous decision making (telling the patient what treatment comes next) but also is not an open-ended choice given to the patient, who cannot possibly understand all of the consequences of treatment options without guidance from their medical provider.

This is patient empowerment.

Not only are major universities like MIT, Stanford, and Harvard putting course work and lectures online; education startups like New Charter University are filling in education gaps for underemployed or career-transitioning adults. As in other sectors undergoing disruption, New Charter operates outside standard educational practices, such as not participating in government loan programs. So whereas government regulations are often intended to serve social good and often continue to do so, they also typically slow innovation that is necessary to help students adapt to the changing economy.

Director of User Experience Tim McCoy says:

> So essentially the government says, "Look we're going to give you $15,000 to pay for this student's year of education. In exchange, you have to do certain things so we feel that money is going to good use." So, for example, students are required to spend a certain amount of time in the learning environment. But it's really a *vanity metric*. What often happens is you end up with 10-week courses where students must sit through lectures for the entire 10 weeks regardless of how much you already know. It's time considered busy work for a lot of folks. By not participating in the loan program, we can run with a competency based model.[26]

Students are empowered.

Case Study: **Customized Value Creation**

Five years ago Bespoke Innovations founder Scott Summit set out to explore new possibilities made possible by developments in the digital-fabrication world. Here's his story.

I set out thinking: "Where can you create things that (1) are very complex and (2) will be meaningful in changing the quality of somebody's life?"

As it happens, I was always interested in prosthetic limbs. I saw an opportunity waiting to happen or a solution that is waiting to happen because existing products represent an unsatisfied need. Regular prosthetics are an engineering solution to a problem and not a design solution.

I thought, "Okay, here is an opportunity to fix that. Maybe I can combine 3D printing, which is the ability to make a unique thing for a unique situation, and prosthetic limbs, which are not very well suited for mass production since that makes generic the complexity and nuance of human individuality."

So that became the foundation for Bespoke. We started with prosthetic limbs and that's still what we

do as kind of the flagship, but now we have a number of other opportunities that follow a similar mentality.

Ultimately we want to show as much respect for an individual as we possibly can. We use technology tools and the design tools as our vehicle. I think it shows people tremendous disrespect to lump them all into the same category and say, "Okay, you're all amputees—you all get this part, this collection of titanium machined parts because you're all that similar."

So we rethink that and say, "How do we speak to a person's individuality and their taste and their uniqueness?"

The process we take is multifaceted. There's the "get to know us" process, where we explain to them what we do. We attempt to elicit their tastes and preferences in design aesthetic out of them and that's actually very difficult to do, harder than I had ever imagined.

Outside of people who are designers at heart, it's very hard to thrust somebody into the role of designing something for themselves, something very personal like a prosthetic limb. It's like the extreme version of telling somebody to design their own tattoo. We all generally don't do that because we're not used to doing that in our daily lives.

So we typically show people the art we have, the patterns, the designs we've done in the past and we use that as a kick-off point. We say, "By the way, we can change this material. We can add details if you like. If there are patterns that you like. . . ." We try to tease that out of them because ultimately we don't want them to simply select from our preexisting work. That doesn't take what we offer to its fullest potential. So we encourage people to cut loose a bit and look inside themselves and see what would make it the most personal and give them the most connection to it.

Then there's the technology part of the process. We do a 3D scan of their body and turn the images into usable data by running them through software that uses different cleaning algorithms and meshing algorithms. From that data, we actually mirror the person's sound-side leg and superimpose it over their lost leg. We align it by eye; there is a lot of craft involved. We line it up until it looks like it is in a natural location on the body based on the scan. That will be the reference for the rest of the process because now the body will be symmetric no matter what we do and it will be unique no matter what we do. The process philosophically goes to the heart of what we do because it generates what we think are the most important elements we offer: symmetry and uniqueness.

We have a number of templates that we've developed, which are partially mechanical and allow us to attach elements to the substructure of the prosthesis. The templates might create the design pattern, for example, herringbone tweed or a lace or a lattice, and we start mixing these templates into the computer files, playing with them to create the aesthetic we're striving for.

The final step is that once we have the data, we do a lot of communication with the client. We send them images of the prosthetic, which are photographically accurate even though they're virtual. When they're ready to pull the trigger we send the files out to a third party who three-dimensionally prints the parts. We have a few post-processing steps we can apply depending on what the person is looking for and then we're ready to send them to the person.

How they use them and how their life changes is up to them. We encourage them to communicate back to us when they're ready, because it's exciting for us and rewarding. We hear of stories where women all of a sudden are buying clothes to match their fairing. We recently had a case where this woman wore a beautiful dress and shoes that really brought out the best in the fairing we created for her.

The woman said she had been creatively hiding her prosthetic for eight years under stockings with foam pads and suddenly she's wearing skirts that show it as it is and it just looks great and she doesn't care about people seeing it and knowing that she's an amputee.

We've had soldiers, guys who don't express emotion readily, say they feel naked without it or they wouldn't walk out the front door without it. We've had people come to us and they have a gym sock pulled up over their prosthetic limb and they have three or four other socks stuffed into it to approximate a calf shape. People are mostly not comfortable with the fact that a part of their body is a bunch of skinny little titanium pipes; it's disheartening. So this process gives the prosthetic a dynamism, a suggestion of life. Even though intuitively we know better, it suddenly imbues the prosthetic with a sense of life that it wouldn't otherwise have.

We look at our business as a fundamental departure from the traditional thinking, which is to do a ton of research up front, market-research the hell out of it, focus-group it, throw in a ton of investment hoping that you're going to capitalize on the backside with a huge return on investment.

We're saying let's turn the whole thing on its head. Have a very nimble process where we can print one thing and if we think it's valuable and compelling, it can become an entire product line, because we don't have inventory; we print to order. If the next person walks in the door and says, "Hey, I've got this thing, my neck muscles gave out," we're ready to go and can do a quick scan and before they leave we can have a custom product created or at least in the process of being created. You can't do that with traditional manufacturing.

When a disruptive technology comes along it doesn't just change the way you do things, it changes the entire culture of the way you look at doing that thing. Online travel sites, for example, like Travelocity and Expedia, didn't just change the way we book a flight; they changed the way we approach traveling as a culture.

For the past 20 years, I was able to look at people with amputations and think, "I would love to do something about creating a better prosthetic leg." I could think about it and think about it and I wouldn't get anywhere. It wasn't until the technologies matured to the point where they became viable that I could start putting different elements together in the right way. Then I could start thinking differently and say, "Okay, now we look at prosthetics and don't think of them just as technology solutions, but think of the problem of a missing limb and whether there is a way to incorporate design and the arts and human emotion into the solution. It invites us or it challenges us to see problems and solutions in an entirely different light.

And Cue the Lean Startup

Whether you are a startup or a big business trying to revitalize growth or save your business or protect against the future; whether you are high-tech, low-tech, or somewhere in between; whether you are business-to-business, business-to-consumer, or business-to-business-to-consumer, you are at the mercy of the value-creation economy.

To succeed, grow, thrive, you must be focused on creating real value for known customers. You must be fast, agile, quick thinking, and quick acting. You must not only continuously improve your output; you must continuously improve the process of outputting. You must be a leader *and* a fast follower. You must be like a basketball point guard defending your counterpart, anticipating moves, and reacting fast. You must be the mirror image of a butterfly, mimic an octopus, be your customer's shadow.

You must be able to innovate sustainably *and* disruptively.

Clearly, this is no small task. The methods and processes differ greatly at opposite ends of the spectrum. Although lean startup principles can be applied across the spectrum, they are geared toward entrepreneurial endeavors tending toward the disruptive side. Most how-to business writing, academic research, and business school instruction tends toward the sustaining side.

The lean startup is a method developed by Eric Ries to increase the success of entrepreneurial endeavors wherever they might be attempted, but that is focused primarily on the disruptive side. Ries describes five core principles:

1. Entrepreneurs are everywhere—anyone creating new products or services in the face of extreme uncertainty.
2. Entrepreneurship is management—one can use processes to navigate uncertainty, and so these processes must be managed.
3. Validated learning—startups exist to *learn* how to build a sustainable business.
4. Build-measure-learn—a feedback loop used to validate in the marketplace that business activities (including but not limited to product, distribution, delivery, marketing, sales) are the right ones.
5. Innovation accounting—how to measure the progress of learning.

Based on our experiences—entrepreneurial quests, advising and mentoring, interviews with countless entrepreneurs past and present, friends, academics, and investors—we have developed how to think about and implement the lean startup. The *principles* of lean startup aren't new. You can find similar elements in "design thinking," user experience (UX) design, discovery-driven planning, to name a few. This poses problems for some. But to reject lean startup is to reject principles that have led to huge, successful businesses. To reject lean startup is to accept the *Myth of the Visionary*.

SUSTAINING ————+————+————+———— DISRUPTIVE

Incremental Improvement · · · · · · · · · · · · · · Radical game-changing

myth of the visionary:

The cultural myth based largely on a narrative fallacy that suggests some can predict the future and then bring it to fruition. In reality, the visionary is likely someone who is NOT committed to a specific scenario, but rather seeks change and seizes present opportunities and relentlessly pursues the change.

You may very well ask, if not new, what's the point?

The power of the lean startup language should not be undersold. The language is what brings together first-time entrepreneurs and those with experience, those inside and outside tech, those who seek to make significant change in nonprofits, government, and big business, as well as startups.

What is also true, we believe, is that the meta changes we witness in today's world that we discuss above, make these principles more learnable, applicable, and measurable than ever before. Furthermore, lean startup happens to arrive at a time of great need.

Lean Startup, Please Meet the Lean Entrepreneur

Our goal is to help entrepreneurs apply lean startup. To do so, let's take a quick step back and make sure we're starting from a common point.

The *lean* in lean startup does not mean small startup, or a startup with no money or no vision.

It comes from *lean manufacturing* as represented by the Toyota Production System. Basically, lean manufacturing is about optimizing efficiency in all value-added activities and minimizing or eliminating all non-value-added activities, where *value added* means providing value to customers.

Customers include both the final user of the product and internal customers who link activities through the lifecycle of product development and delivery.[28]

Critically, optimization that adversely affects value being provided is not *lean*. Also inherent in the Toyota Production System is the concept of continuous learning and continuous improvement.

Many discussions about lean fail to capture several key points:

- You cannot deliver value without marketing and selling it.

- The complexity of value creation means lean processes are often more efficient than traditional methods.
- Aiming at perfection is not a fluffy or spiritual platitude.

It's interesting that, whereas most lean discussion and implementation focuses on product development processes (manufacturing, for example), if you look at the product from the customer's point of view, they couldn't care less about the product development process. Hopefully the customer's experience is improved via lean methodologies, but the fact that lean led to that is irrelevant to them.

Marketing, sales, services, support, aspects of operations, partners, and so forth often have a direct relationship with the customer and a direct effect on their experience. The experience might look like the diagram below.

In long form, if everything goes swimmingly, a customer becomes aware of a product, goes through a courtship process during which he or she decides whether to purchase the product, makes the purchase, receives it, and then has an experience with the product.

Moreover, there are infinite activities a business might conduct that both directly and indirectly affect the customer's experience above and beyond their relationship to the product. This is called the company's

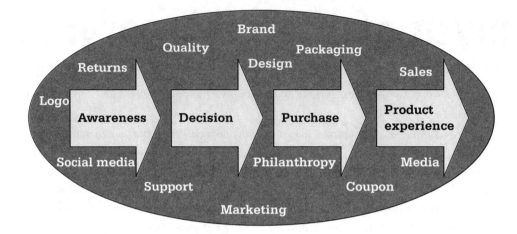

brand. (Yes, when it comes to brand, you must think beyond branding elements such as company name, logo, and tagline.)

In existing successful businesses, the value being created for the customer is *known*. It has already been validated that product x solves problem y for customer profile z. The business has already grown or is growing

rapidly. Dilemmas facing such companies belong in Steve Blank's third customer development epiphany, *company creation*.[29] The chaos that reigned in the startup phase needs to quickly turn into orderly execution. The better and more efficient the execution, the faster the growth, limited only by the values of the founders or investors and the number and size of distinct customer profiles for whom value is being created. The dilemmas that such a business faces are numerous, difficult, varied, and, to the point, fundamentally different than those faced by startups.

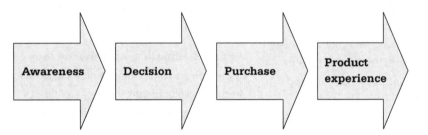

company creation:

The third part of Blank's *The Four Steps to the Epiphany*, when companies seek to prove they have a scalable business model.

Those that choose to be high-growth businesses aspire to be monopolies. If they are to accomplish this objective using free market tactics, many of the branding activities will be employed. Once you leave the comfort of manufacturing or other product development methodologies, which activities are value-added activities and which are not?

Traditionally, as growth accelerates, multi-hatted early-stage startup employees are organized into silos based on function. Whereas startup marketing and sales were once tightly integrated or even one and the same, they are now separated with carefully controlled integration points, as are manufacturing and testing, legal and financial, facilities and operations, and so on.

Value to the final customer is often lost when managers attempt to optimize efficiency inside the silos. Integration points between the silos grow into bureaucracies as silos seek to protect their members. The objectives of the silos often dwarf those of the company as a whole. Silos can turn into fiefdoms in which power and prestige are measured by size of staff and budget. Management team meetings devolve into departments competing with each other over vision, strategy, budget, and ego.

Lean attempts to offer solutions to this siloing inefficiency. Organizing activities into groups providing value to the end customer reduces activity-based silos. You do not measure waste by looking at what people are *doing*, but rather what's wrong in the *process*,

from product demand to product delivery to passionate product experience.

What lean uncovered was that there's likely a lot of waste if it takes two months to deliver a chair needing only two days (of actual building) to make. The early manufacturing belief that batch-and-queue activities are the most efficient process is turned on its head.

The batch-and-queue process is where a product manufacturing process is broken down into stages of production. Each stage will typically have an input queue, which was produced by the upstream stage, and an output queue, which is produced for the downstream stage. Each stage can be optimized so that theoretically, the product itself can be produced more efficiently.

The idea of a division of labor has been recognized for centuries and was fundamental to industrialization. The idea of comparative advantage, which refers to the ability of one country to produce a particular product at a lower marginal cost than another, is

SUSTAINING ———————————————— DISRUPTIVE

Problem is well understood
Existing market
Innovation improves performance,
Incremental change

Problem not well understood
New market
Innovation is dramatic,
Game-changing

dependent on the division of labor and is a fundamental precept of modern international trade.

The thing is, although what's good for the goose may be good for the gander, what's good for the gander may not be good for the gander's descendants.

In what may be another sign of the changes coming, increasing product complexity combined with increased demand for customization limits the benefits of organizing production around the specialization of labor. Batch-and-queue processing is more optimal when:

- Customer is known and established. Value being created is known and established. Value created is less varied.
- Production requires fewer parts, fewer stages, and less labor. Complexity is low.

Although the trend toward increasing complexity and customization has been going on for decades, advances in factory automation and workarounds have masked some of the inefficiencies of organizing company operations around batch and queue. Painting cars different colors does not pose much of a problem. Changing equipment

to produce different car models turns out to be a huge inefficiency, which the Toyota Production System overcomes.

That nonengineering departments are organized around the same batch-and-queue principles strikes us as insane. It's no wonder that corporate efforts to build teams, align objectives, optimize, streamline, innovate, <insert management consultant buzzword here> have failed dismally.

Lean Startup and Disruption

What does all this have to do with disruptive innovation? It's not hard to imagine how building product systems based on division of labor does not lead to profound new ideas that might change the world. The process is meant to increase productivity and lower costs in the production of a known product for a known customer.

Lean advances the cause, but not sufficiently. Lean talks about employee empowerment, learning about your customers, cross-functional teams, and increased agility, but the system remains focused on producing a known value for a known customer.

This is where lean startup comes in. So although lean manufacturing presumes value and that the customer and product are known, this isn't the case for startups. Startup founders have plenty of hypotheses regarding their startup idea and the products necessary to solve problems for specific market profiles, but these are only *known* to be true to the extent they've been validated in the marketplace, as measured by paying or engaged customers. In other words, they only *think* they know.

It bears repeating: A startup does not *know what value it is creating or for whom.* Put another way: if the innovation you are bringing to market has a predictable effect

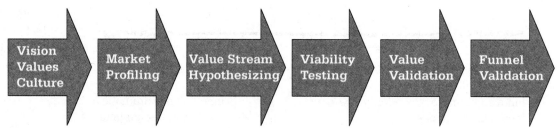

on a known market, you are sustaining an existing market and are, therefore, not disrupting anything.

This begs the question: If in a lean startup you don't know what value you are creating and for whom, how do you know what's wasteful and what isn't?

To measure waste in a lean enterprise, you can't look at things like unused raw materials, unused product features, inventory, and the labor to produce, test, release, and market all that's not purchased, used, or desired by your customers.

To measure waste in a lean startup, Ries introduces the concept of *validated learning*.

Waste in a lean startup are those activities that do not produce learning.

Since what the startup is all about is *unknown*, one can't organize let alone optimize employee activities around *executing* the creation of customer value. Instead, one must organize around *learning*. One must *learn* what the core value is; what solution provides that value; to whom it provides value; and how to market, sell, and deliver it so that the value is realized.

We propose and, therefore, lay out for you in the pages ahead, a path you can take toward discovering the value you are to create and for whom.

Although the customer experiences a product in the order shown in the diagram previously this isn't the order in which a startup discovers the value. It's important to note that there is not one way to learn such things, nor is the process of discovery linear. Also, before finishing the discovery and validation of the value and its delivery, one shouldn't be overly concerned with process optimization. So we're not going to spend as much time trying to make sure each learning activity is efficient as we will on eliminating or reducing activities that are nonlearning.

2
Vision, Values, and Culture

Vision and Values

Most successful endeavors start with a big Vision, capital V. The end success rarely matches the initial vision exactly, and sometimes the end result is hardly recognizable at all. The vision simply becomes part of the ex post facto narrative that makes us feel good about the visionary-turned-billionaire.

When corporate consultants and coaches insist you write a vision statement, they want you to project where you will be in five years. This is the sort of thing that leads to those horribly mundane opening lines in "about us" statements—"Industry leader in blah, blah, blah."[1] Those are the businesses with the management teams full of pre-billionaire visionaries.

The vaguer the vision, the more likely it will be true. "A broken watch is right twice a day" and all that. Did you know that the number 11 has special powers? If you open yourself to its energy, you will be drawn toward looking at a clock precisely 11 minutes after the hour. This is one way to become a visionary.

Irwin Jacobs, founder of telecommunications giant Qualcomm and certified billionaire, purportedly once told a room of skeptics (in other words, venture capitalists) that the brick of a cellular phone he was holding up would one day be used for credit-card transactions. Based on our own experiences with a room full of business experts, investors, and rotary-phone users we can well imagine the hilarity that ensued. That vision, however, is not *that* extraordinary, and we don't even know if the story is true. We never saw *Star Trek*'s Captain Kirk have to *buy* anything (heck, there's no room for a credit card in those pants, let alone a wallet), which leaves either his communicator or phaser as a means for making purchases from the *Enterprise*'s vending machines. We're guessing communicator.

In the mid-1990s, we published a letter to the editor in *InfoWorld* magazine, wherein we warned those complaining about 73 cable channels and no good TV to just wait and see how bad it gets when there were 3 billion channels.

Yep, we predicted YouTube and Internet TV. We're not saying we were the only ones, mind you. That's really the point.

The vision is not as important as the drive to achieve it. Jacobs's genius was not the vague prediction of what might become of cell phone technology, but rather his drive, his relentless pursuit to see the change happen.

Alas, we never invented YouTube or Internet video streaming or Internet TVs. Jacobs stopped at nothing, removed obstacles, ignored detractors, and likely changed the assumptions underpinning his vision numerous times on his way to building a multibillion-dollar company that built a winning platform that hosts cell phones that are used to pay for products.

It's not the vision that makes the visionary; it's the *driving force* to make *change* happen.

Driving Force

Mark Cuban once said: "'Follow your passion' is the worst advice you could ever give or get." Leave it to Cuban to come up with pithy anti-clichés that don't really say what he means. There's some truth in it, we suppose. His point is that the stuff you're willing to work hard at *is* your passion.

So, in other words, you may really like hot sex and cold ice cream, but they're not passions you should be following for your career. Or something like that. Don't follow your passions; follow your effort. It will lead you to your passions and to success.

Where we all want to get to is what drives you to do the things you do. What motivates you to work on a particular project?

When it comes to starting a business or perhaps seeking to reinvigorate an existing business, it's helpful to understand your driving force. Which element are you committed to?

- Segment—you want to bring any kind of product for a specific group (or groups) of people.
- Problem—you want to solve a particular issue or address a specific passion.
- Product—you have a singular product vision.
- Technology—you have an invention you wish to productize.
- Sales Channel—you are great at selling or are committed to e-commerce.

There are other drivers, too, like distribution. Amazon and Dell both disrupted markets through new distribution methods. Telecommunications companies, as much as they have fought to extricate themselves from the fact, are a pure distribution play.

The key insight as articulated by Sean Murphy and others is that all these elements of a business model form a system of simultaneous equations, in which there are multiple right answers for any variable, but changing one variable's value changes the others.

When you can simultaneously satisfy all variables, you have a business model figured out and are ready to test scaling it.

When entrepreneurs first look for their big ideas, it's likely they will start with a problem they have or something they have passion for, like helping a certain group of people. One of these may end up being the *driving force* of their business and so may be a variable that's held constant.

Nevertheless, the other equations still have to be figured out. If you decide to hold one constant, because this is where your core competency is or this is your driving force or your vision, fine, as long as you are aware of it and cognizant of the effects on your business.

Note, even if you do solve all the equations, it doesn't mean your business can grow big.

Segment-Centric

A company committed to a specific segment will build or deliver potentially any product or service required to solve a myriad of problems faced by an identifiable group of people or businesses. A startup starts by solving one problem and grows larger as it discovers and addresses additional needs. You might be committed to solving all information technology problems faced by hospitals or you might supply all new moms with products to keep their babies safe and healthy.

To figure out your business, you proceed from the inside out. In other words, you seek to understand your segment deeply, figure out what problems they face, and work with them to devise the solution, using a technology that best suits the customer's environment.

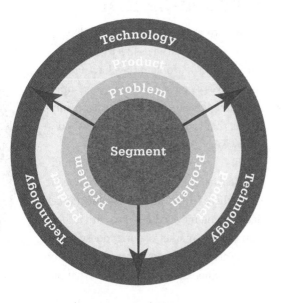

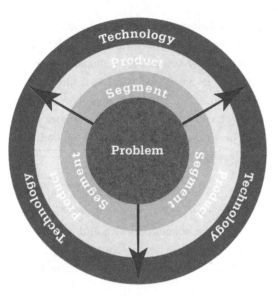

Problem-Centric

Many entrepreneurs start out by identifying a problem they'd like to solve. Often, this is a problem they have faced themselves or have witnessed close-up. It's a natural place to start, since the presumption is that the customer is understood pretty well.

This can also be a trap, however: First, just because you have the problem doesn't mean there truly is an addressable market. Second, you may be biased toward a solution that the market majority doesn't want.

In this scenario, you start with the problem, and then define the segment that has the problem most acutely, and then work to define the solution the market segment is willing to use to solve the problem. If you are truly aiming to solve the problem, you should be solution and technology agnostic.

Product-Centric

If, come hell or high water, you have a product idea and you will see it built, it can safely be said that you are product-driven. This is perhaps the most common driving force we see among entrepreneurs and it is perhaps the most dangerous. Your product is only as good as the problem it's solving and its suitability to the segment.

Products gather dust on shelves, both real and virtual, and businesses spin for years trying to match the value the founders thought they were creating for market segments that may or may not even exist.

If you start with the product, you have essentially chosen the technology. If you are building a high-tech product and are following the expert advice du jour, then you have chosen to build a mobile product rather than a web-based product. (Good luck finding a business model around your 99-cent app.) Regardless, you had better quickly find that problem you are ostensibly solving.

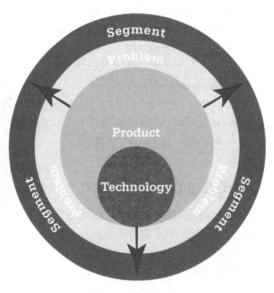

Technology-Centric

Technology is a platform or an invention that needs to find an application. Platforms can be sold separately or launched after an application has established some sort of a foothold. Facebook is both an application and a platform. The same can be said for Twitter. Apple's iPhone is both. New chemistry, plant extractions, genetic manipulation, new manufacturing means, and new materials can all be platforms for new applications.

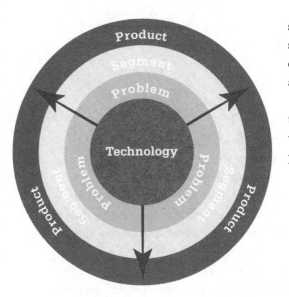

Entrepreneurs with technology are in search for problems to solve. They can develop products themselves or they may license their technology or sell access to the platform.

Your driving force isn't necessarily the most important part of your business, or what you need to focus all your energy on. It's a way to understand how you're attempting to shape your business. No matter what the business, you still must identify a pressing problem to solve, understand the segment most eager to solve it, and provide a solution that works for that segment.

It is a problem, however, if you don't know what your driving force is and so your strategy changes. One day you are keen on solving all problems of a particular customer and the next you are all about building and selling a specific product.

You can think of your driving force in terms of a pivot. If your product were to fail, what aspect of your business model would you be most likely to keep?

- Would you keep the product and change the market segment?
- Would you keep the segment, but look for a different problem to solve using the same product?
- Would you keep the same segment, but try a different product?

It's paramount that you take your values into consideration. Social entrepreneurs—in other words, cause-oriented businesses—are often committed to solving a specific problem or serving a specific constituency, and we think that's great. But they are, at the same time, likely limiting the size of the opportunity. Similarly, those entrepreneurs solving a problem that they themselves face, like, say, how to organize where they're going to hang out on Friday night, are not likely to take their companies to a stock market listing.

We hear a lot of complaining from certain sectors in technology about a supposed lack of innovation and about entrepreneurs thinking too small, but that, to our minds, is small thinking itself. With change, both good and bad, coming fast and furious, opportunities and fear abound. Big vision paired with the drive to make change happen is great and we're all for it.

Make the world slightly better for millions or dramatically better for hundreds, or change the course of human history.

Venture capitalists whining about too much money being thrown at small startup ideas are like Major League Baseball team owners complaining that player salaries are too high—these bastions of capitalism decrying free markets. Small visions are all right, too. Make a career by providing value to others. Employ tens and not thousands. There are life-changing experiences in small packages, too.

At some point your vision will be tested. The tough part will be to stick with the original vision or allow it to be shaped by what the market is telling you.

Your vision is about what drives your business to success. It is the change that you hope to make. No matter if you start with the segment, problem, product, or technology, the vision is less about *how* you change, and more about *what* you change.

Case Study: Is the Problem Really Solvable?

Admittedly, we have a bias toward entrepreneurs who are trying to solve real problems. What's not to like about eager, passionate people trying to make the world a better place? These are often more interesting projects than, say, falling in love with a solution or technology and searching for a problem to solve.

There's a trap, however, and that's when one tries to solve human problems. These are problems that the best technology in the world cannot solve; problems for which symptoms can be addressed, but not the actual cause; problems caused by the tendency of imperfect humans to do very human-like things.

One of us, for example, has an e-mail inbox that resembles the mythical Hydra. Perpetually overflowing with unread e-mails, the inbox stands to worsen when acted upon. When he answers one e-mail, he receives two more in response. In a pathetic attempt to stem this multiplication of urgent calls to action, he enables an auto-responder that warns recipients that he will be slow to reply. He hears constantly (via e-mail) how annoying these auto-responders are. His friends helpfully suggest multiple e-mail inbox management software services that promise to automatically filter, sort, defer, and magically resurface only his important e-mails for him, ostensibly harnessing sophisticated technology to manage his e-mail inbox better than he ever could himself, buying him time, freedom, and peace of mind. Gmail, for example, helpfully places Google+ notifications into the "priority" inbox.

There's something missing from the solution, however.

His problem is himself. He simply overcommits himself to too many interesting but time-intensive projects. His problem only *manifests itself in e-mail*—his fundamental problem isn't likely to be solved by a technology solution. When his well-meaning friends suggest e-mail inbox management software, they are treating the symptom (overflowing e-mail) and not the disease (the tragic inability to say no to interesting projects).

Although our hero in this story is at least reasonably aware of the problem, a savvy entrepreneur undertaking customer development to figure out solvable problems for a certain market segment should never assume his customers are so clever, and he or she should take care to avoid getting pulled into the human-problem miasma.

We once provided customer development help to a startup that was building an order-management software system for restaurants. The startup's cross-functional team got out of the building, visiting with the manager of a particular restaurant at length, multiple times.

As the startup team spoke with the manager, they also observed the activity in the restaurant and how the staff currently went about their business. It became clear to the team that the manager had a problem not easily helped by better technology: She didn't have a set protocol for how her waitstaff took phone orders and how the kitchen processed them during peak hours. Sometimes whoever took the order made sure it was fulfilled; other times it was handed over to someone else to fulfill. The manager didn't see this as a problem as she proudly described her non-management technique as "empowering everyone by keeping them on their toes."

From the startup's point of view, it appeared that Thursday, Friday, and Saturday nights were simply chaos and that diners were as likely to have a bad experience as they were to have a good experience. Their order-management system would not likely affect the experience.

While the team discussed this internally, the restaurant manager insisted that the vendor's software would be a good fit and would translate into more orders. With some trepidation, the team reluctantly agreed to a live beta test. What could go wrong, right?

Actually, a lot can go wrong. The software was deployed to the grumbling waitstaff, who reluctantly agreed to use it within their current non-system of order taking. Within a few days of increased missed orders and user complaints, the system was put to bed. Everyone politely agreed that the software hadn't been helpful, and both the manager and the startup team could point to the metrics showing noncompliance of waitstaff in using the software. Although the experience didn't prove fatal to the startup, the experience was a tremendous waste of time, money, energy, creativity, and morale. Nothing was learned from the process that hadn't been known in advance.

This all could have been easily avoided had the startup stuck to its guns and clung to its initial learnings that this manager was not a true early adopter because she had a human problem that she was not only unaware of, but also complicit in creating! Trying to solve such problems makes you a therapist, not an entrepreneur.

What Do You Want to Be?

We once worked with a company that decided to change its focus from being a small software company dedicated to building a suite of low-end IT products for one specific market segment to an enterprise software and hardware company serving a completely different segment. Both were built on top of the same technology. The problems being solved in the two segments were completely different.

The company succeeded until one of the executives decided that they hadn't really agreed to the change and wanted to return to the original business, whose margins had long since vanished in the face of open-source software. Further, during their growth quest, the founders motivated new and existing employees with a stock-option plan. They insisted that they were looking for a liquidity event, having missed out on the dot-com era. (Red flag, anyone?) In reality, however, they would never pull the trigger. Venture capitalist term sheets and acquisition overtures were turned away.

What they had were high salaries and a nice lifestyle business, and perhaps a simultaneous case of founder midlife crisis syndrome (FMCS). There's nothing wrong with lifestyle companies. We believe they are the backbone of the U.S. economy. However, there is a problem when founders don't understand their own values and they're not synced up with the corporate vision.

The big (or small) problem you commit your business to solving is your vision; your values describe what you hope your business to be. Do you hope to generate a personal revenue stream? Are you satisfied with earning a decent salary or profit to support your family? Do you hope to employ a couple dozen people? A couple hundred? Do you foresee an acquisition? IPO?

When you look at financing the company, do you plan on growing through revenues? Are you willing to max out credit cards? Or will you seek financing from professional investors like angels or venture capitalists?

Values might determine who you buy from and sell to. Social entrepreneurs commit their businesses to serving a particular cause. Of course, these business owners are well aware that the choices they make affect growth, the ability to sell the business, and so on.

Other business owners may choose to not sell to specific market segments, perhaps for perceived ethical reasons that go against their vision, or there may be another segment that the founders are passionate about serving. Again, that's all well and good, as long as these values are in concert with the vision.

Perhaps the bottom line is value creation. The Toyota Production System is not about efficiency for efficiency's sake. Value creation is at its core. The same is true of lean startup. Create an environment, practices, and processes that include empowering employees to empower customers, to move the business to be as close to the customer as possible.

The proximity is what allows the business to understand the customer deeply, to zig when the customer zigs, and to zag when the customer zags; to predict the customer's needs and always be creating value so that the customer remains passionate about the products and loyal to the business.

Lean into It: The Lean Startup Culture

Arguably, whether you are launching your own startup or trying to create an internal startup in a big business, it's the culture that will dictate success. Culture doesn't mean that your offices are in an up-and-coming neighborhood, on the wrong side of the tracks in a cool 100-year-old building that was once the home of architects, with a retractable roof, Nerf guns strewn about, free soda and beer, and weekly Halo network gaming competitions. (Of course, you can have all that if you want and if you do, we'd certainly appreciate an invite.)

Culture does mean that you create an environment that reinforces your values and aligns the company toward achieving your vision. It does mean that you create proximity to your customer as part of the fundamental DNA.

There is no defined lean startup culture. We identify a few core philosophies and then recommend other factors you should consider implementing. First, be a learning organization.

Sounds easy, but it is more difficult in practice. Somehow the Myth of the Visionary and the concomitant *Eureka!* moment are so ingrained in our culture that many entrepreneurs and business leaders believe their visionary abilities apply even to the most minor tactical decisions. All those we consider great visionaries, however, learned their way toward achieving change. They made mistakes, they reacted to the market, and more often than not they performed multiple business-model pivots.

A learning organization puts data before rhetoric, testing before executing, customers before business plan. It runs experiments to reduce risk, uses data to resolve conflicts, and interacts with customers to understand them deeply.

Key question: With the least amount of effort, what will move the needle of the business *right now*? If customers love the product, engineering new features is not optimal; look at your conversion funnel. If customers love the product and the funnel is optimized, maybe it's time to blow up your customer acquisition channels. If some customers like the product and others don't, it's likely not time for engineering or marketing or sales, but rather for understanding your customers better. Do you have a product, positioning, or segment problem?

Use data to resolve conflicts, measure progress, and inform decisions. An organization drowning in data is little better off than one without data. Those who fear the overhead of implementing data systems are missing the point. On the other hand, decisions by data only risk missing the big decisions by automating the small ones.

Data is used to *inform* decisions, not make them. Data tracked must be actionable and should mirror an objective tree that drives all organization activity and will vary at different phases of the business.

For example, at the top is a high-level objective; perhaps your growth is based on subscription revenue. Churn (customers canceling subscriptions or not resubscribing) is anathema to your business.

A high-level objective might be to reduce churn. What reduces churn? Increased product passion, which might be measured by the percentage of users who successfully refer the product to others. Maybe that metric is fine. What next? What about satisfaction as measured by specific product engagement metrics? How do you increase engagement? Try improving x, as measured by customer use of x over time period t.

A learning organization runs experiments to reduce market and technical risk, test new ideas, and optimize results. It interacts with customers to assess whether customer-problem-solution assumptions are correct.

Before building product, one learns whether the proposed product has a market. Before one follows the advice of Internet-social-media-marketing-ninja-gurus, one learns whether suggested tactics work with a particular market segment.

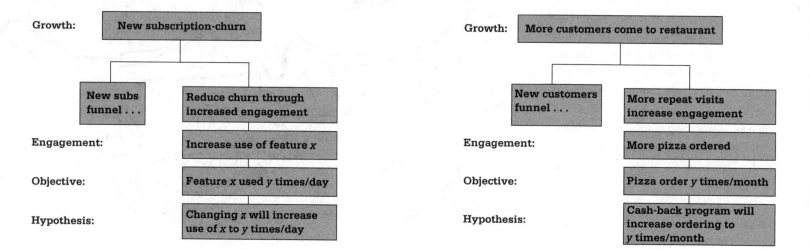

Case Study: Experience-Driven Jumpstart

PayPal™

We spoke to Bill Scott, senior director of User Interface Engineering at PayPal, about how embedding startup culture into large organizations requires commitment to change and new DNA. It's a challenging endeavor, but when undertaken thoughtfully, it can provide tremendous velocity to innovation.

Lean Entrepreneur: How did you approach taking over the UI engineering role at PayPal?

Bill Scott: One of the first missions I had was to figure out: How do we turn these web developers into true engineers? How do we get them to be user-experience focused and work closely with product design and engineering? How do we move away from a siloed environment?

Within PayPal itself, when I joined in late 2011, there were pockets of innovation. Groups were trying to do things in a more rapid sense, but I didn't really hear anybody talking about this in a shared, universal lexicon.

LE: What in your career convinced you that being especially customer-centric was a key to success?

Scott: Previously at Netflix, we were zealous about understanding customers through build-test-learn principles and I came to see huge value in having customer input at all times in our processes.

LE: How does that affect the internal teams?

Scott: You got rid of politics; you got everybody moving in the same direction, a shared understanding and a real reason to collaborate.

The other thing that became part of my DNA at Netflix was just how much of the user experience changes when you're doing lots of testing. You tend to probably throw away 90 percent of the code for the very specific tests you're building. It acknowledges that change is constant.

That is a different mindset than: create some software, put a big team together, and march towards the delivery. When the delivery is done, disband the team and go do something else, which is sort of the mode PayPal had been in.

LE: What did the change in mindset stem from?

Scott: When I came to PayPal, the guy who became the CTO, James Barrese, had just moved over from eBay and he had learned a lot from both successes and failures at eBay. He was part of the team who recruited me and gave me a carte blanche to change whatever I needed to in my arena. When David Marcus, who came over when PayPal acquired Zong, became president of PayPal in March, he called James and said, "I want to get a skunks-works together and I want to do this in a lean manner, and I want to reinvent the way we do our core business." James reached out to me right away and said, "Put a team together and let's grab a war room and we'll start with these skunk-works." It was great because it was led by the president of our company being like our project manager.

Hendrik Kleinsmiede took the lead from the design side, and I took it from the user interface engineering side.

Hill Ferguson became the head of product. Both of them were recently at startups. So, this is how all this new DNA came in.

LE: What was driving this change at PayPal?

Scott: From a financial perspective, you could say the ship was running great. But I think we had all experienced how start-ups function and we knew PayPal wasn't like that.

We thought, "Wow, look at all this revenue we have and these great products solving real problems, but with really less than stellar user experiences. What if we create great experiences, too?"

The other major reason was that the competitive space had heated up incredibly.

So in the course of a week, two more mobile payment startups would pop up. Most of them will fail, but it only takes one of those to catch enough wind in its sails, with enough venture capital backing and hiring the right talent, to become the next market disruptor.

LE: The previous disruptor being disrupted?

Scott: David and Hill and others in the organization who came in recently had this very keen sense of how fast you can move

as a startup and how fast our competition can move and knowing that if we can marshal our forces, we can easily, in our estimation, beat the competition and simultaneously create the best experience for our customers.

I should note, David's language, our language, is all the same. Our language is not about killing the competition or defeating the competition. That's not really our focus. Obviously we keep them in mind, but it's really, how do we have the best experience?

That means re-evaluating our risk models, our security models, without messing the business up. We're not going to sacrifice security.

LE: What were the challenges in getting buy-in?

Scott: My impression when I first got here was that there's a lot of smart people at PayPal, but because the company had grown so fast and there was so much going on, it was hard to function because PayPal had gotten so big and bureaucratic. This is obviously a big challenge.

If anyone wanted to do something different, the basic posture was to say no.

So what we've done with the lean initiative is that we have brought all those teams into the discussions up front. For example, we are working on new products that push the envelope in some areas with some of our risk models.

So at that very beginning, the head of risk, Tom Keithley, was in the room and saying, "We're going to make this work because we want the best experience."

Obviously we have to balance the user experience with our risk and security models. But having the head of risk take the view of the customer was really different than what was done in the past.

LE: How deep is this transformational mindset?

Scott: In every part of the company, from the executive staff down, we're looking at how we can transform PayPal.

You have to rethink how do you do your financial planning, how do you do your talent recruiting, how do you do your incentives, what are the roles of the team when your teams are all lean and agile?

All that has been looked at, every piece of the organization, without exception. We're going through this now and hope to roll it out to the complete organization in 2013.

Empowering the Edge

All employees, founders, and management-team members should be involved in improving processes and getting closer to the customer. The lean manufacturing practices at Toyota included empowering factory-floor workers to stop the production line any time they saw something out of whack. The core lean principle of continuous improvement—kaizen—teaches the importance of skill, problem solving, and self-improvement for factory workers.

Consider the following phenomena, which at first glance appear disparate but have something in common:

- Leading lean software development proponents like Mary Poppendieck urge that engineers be allowed to engineer solutions—in other words, that they not be kept separate from the customer problems they are ostensibly tasked to solve.

- Zappos doesn't try to shorten call times in their call centers, or up-sell customers, or use scripts. "We just care about whether the rep goes above and beyond for every customer. . . . [W]e trust our employees to use their best judgment when dealing with each and every customer."[3]

- The U.S. Army restructures training to emphasize in-the-field decision making by soldiers.

- Sales leaders teach salespeople consultative sales techniques such that they continuously learn in order to be domain experts and thereby become value creators, not just value communicators.[4]

- Doctors increase emphasis on patient involvement in medical decision making whereby all the possible treatment options and outcomes are outlined and the patient and doctor together make a decision based on patient preferences.[5]

- MIT, Harvard, Stanford, and other institutions of higher learning make their courses available free online.

- Seth Godin declares, "Now, the only way to grow is to stand out, to create something worth talking about, to treat people with respect, and to have them spread the word."[6]

So what do they have in common? They are all pushing power to the edge. The structural changes and the coming transformation are shifting power from hierarchical, centralized systems to decentralized, edge-based systems; to students, patients, and customers.

Kill the Silos

Teams divided into departments by function are a byproduct of mass-production thinking. The idea was to maximize the economies of scale by reducing the cost per manufactured unit. So one would build machines that reduced capital costs and try to run the machines at 100 percent utilization.[7]

Second, you might organize labor to be as machine-like as possible. Increased specialization allowed a labor pool that was predictable, easily scheduled, and essentially used like swappable machine parts.

This thinking works well when the demand for a product is well known, such as in production of airplanes during wartime, and when the process doesn't have too many cells. The more cells you have, the more in-process inventory you have, as well as a greater chance to make a mistake that affects the whole line.

In today's information-centric economy, the same holds true. Departmental silos were created as the management response to specialization of trade. But just as with manufacturing, the more complex the process and the more people involved, the less efficient is white-collared, batch-mode processing. We have only served to create distance between customers and the people making decisions that have a direct effect on them. You don't get great economies of scale by having marketers sitting with other marketers or engineers with other engineers.

There may be benefits, for sure, but there are costs, too.

Hierarchical structures have a difficult time measuring productivity in a way that aligns with corporate objectives. Staff objectives are often counts of activities, or hours working on specific activities, or even results that equate to the worst of online vanity metrics!

Internet vanity metrics include things like page views, or app downloads, or clicks—data that is not actionable. Research and development (R&D) might be measured by number of patents; engineering and manufacturing are measured by lines of code or quantity of parts or features per product; marketing is measured by PR hits.

It's almost amusing that organizations undertake huge strategic initiatives to align departments and ensure that departmental metrics tie back to business objectives, such as revenue growth, yet don't *structure the business around business objectives*. The silos are sacrosanct! They are assumed to be the most efficient structure.

Some organizations are doing it a different way, including O2, Intuit, and lean startups like KISSmetrics and Meetup.com. They break down objectives into actionable targets.

In traditionally siloed businesses, corporate objectives are broken down into departmental sub-objectives. Resources, budgets, schedules, and deliverables are analyzed, negotiated, and promised. Silos protect their borders. Senior managers measure middle managers, who manage producers. By the time you get to the lowest rung on the ladder, you cannot draw a line back up from employee objectives to corporate objectives.

How would you organize your business if it were not organized by traditional departments? Try forming cross-functional teams directed at overcoming clearly identified roadblocks.

Obviously this doesn't work in all businesses or any business in all scenarios. It's worth a thought experiment, however, to uncover areas in which such teams can solve problems quickly, rather than waiting for departmental queues to free up.

Case Study:
KISSmetrics

Like many companies today, KISSmetrics is a distributed team, and like most distributed teams, communication can be difficult. Having 25 people distributed across four time zones and hindered by e-mail and conference-call inefficiencies and a lack of serendipitous face time typically results not only in productivity problems but also in morale issues. KISSmetrics management, including CEO Hiten Shah and Neil Patel, recognized that communication issues were having a significant, negative impact on the growth of the business.

"The left hand didn't know what the right hand was doing," Shah says. "Remote people didn't feel like they were connected with the rest of the company or even with their team. They felt like they were in their own little silos, yet we were only a 25-person company. We were having difficulty getting things done, and as a young company, that can be devastating."

Management decided to implement a process they named the "Golden Motions," which would break through the inertia. The basic idea was to pick a single metric important to the business and then have an internal competition to improve it. Being an analytics firm, KISSmetrics is well versed in benchmarking and tracking actionable metrics—in other words, data that directly impacts the success and growth of the business.

As one example, they arduously track the percentage of people who come to the site, the number who sign up for a trial and talk to the sales team, and then there are several steps to go through, culminating in the percentage of people who end up purchasing.

This is a pretty standard funnel, though one that encompasses both online and offline steps.

The first step in Golden Motions is to find the funnel bottleneck. Where was the greatest drop-off in converting customers from initial interest to satisfied customers?

"We noticed that we weren't getting enough people who actually complete the implementation of the product. We'd get a ton of sign-ups but a very low percentage of people would end up integrating the product, and you need to complete integration to get value from it."

The second step was to establish teams to achieve a specific objective. They formed three cross-functional teams with a target to improve that particular metric by 25 percent in three weeks. Nearly everyone in the company was distributed across teams, including sales, marketing, designers, support, and engineers.

The third step was for each team to come up with its own hypothesis and then work aggressively toward invalidating it. "Usually they start by talking to customers, micro-surveys, and user research like usability testing before we actually run an actual experiment like split-testing features. If the team disproves the hypothesis in the process, they don't run the experiment, but develop a new hypothesis."

The cross-functional nature was critical to success. Neither design nor engineering could have resolved the problem on its own. For example, one team had a hypothesis that when people sign up they don't fully understand what the product can do for them, so there was no urgency in getting it deployed. To test the assumption, a salesperson started asking why the person had signed up and recorded the answer. It was not a typical question that sales would ask. It turned out, however, that the hypothesis was false; customers seemed to understand the product's value proposition.

So after the first three-week cycle, they made some modest progress, but, through surveys and interviews with the teams, management decided to improve the program. What they found was that the competition format didn't work that well. Multiple teams trying to tackle the same problem was problematic. There were limited resources to test hypotheses on actual customers by using split-testing, for example. Plus, teams came up with similar ideas.

For the second cycle, they decided to create problem and solution teams. One team's sole responsibility was to analyze the business and identify problems. The other teams were responsible for testing solutions for different problems.

For the lack-of-integration bottleneck, the hypothesis that turned out to be correct was one that had to do with a desire for faster integration. The resolution was to provide options during the sign-up process, so new users could pick the path they wanted, including a basic fast integration, an advanced self-service option, or a free consultation request. By making them choose up front, their integration rate increased.

"We ended up blowing away our 25 percent improvement objective," says Shah. "Not only has business grown significantly since implementation of 'Golden Motions,' communications, morale, and the feeling of connectedness has as well."

Implementing processes by hierarchical rules or tools as a means of improving communications is akin to treating symptoms. Siloed problem solving results in communication only at the connection points defined by high-level processes. Creating a common goal across business functions naturally improves communication.

It might be helpful to look at lean startup practices from the perspective of a traditional departmental organizational structure.

Product Development

Flow in lean circles means that manufacturing is pulled through the product development process so that each component is built only when demanded by the next step in the process. In other words, Step C tells Step B, "Don't build your part until I need it." This results in no excess inventory and the elimination of wasteful activity.

It's important to understand that flow begins with customer demand, not the product manager, vice president of engineering, or the CEO. In an ideal, web-based product scenario, lean development would result in features being developed, tested, and released only as the customer has indicated desire or need for specific functionality.

When still learning what value is being created or how to improve value, development is synonymous with experimentation. Continuous deployment is an optimized process whereby a cross-functional team will work on a specific feature hypothesized to move the needle of the company. The functionality is released to a subset of existing customers and its use measured against the test hypothesis.

At IMVU, Ries's team deployed 50 changes to its product every single day.[8]

There's actually a danger in continuing to develop without concrete demand. It's very difficult to random-feature your way into product-market fit, but you certainly can random-feature your way out of it.

So what does product development work on if not new features? Plenty of resources exist to help build agile development teams and implement lean software processes—and this book is not one of them, but we can think of a few things to do:

- Pay off technical debt.
- Live the life of the customer.
- Run experiments.
- Search for new innovations.

technical debt: *Technical debt* describes problems or unaddressed product development issues that accumulate due to other priorities, such as concentrating on new features.

What moves the needle of the business is not the number of lines of code, features, or products but the amount of customer passion. What is inside your product-development processes that drives customer passion?

Marketing

To be glib, marketing can be thought of as having two flavors:

1. Fluffy branding activities, graphics, images, and messaging that appear on TV and radio, in magazines, and on the web that magically create buzz, build awareness, and hopefully lead to increased revenue.

2. Specific campaigns and business activities that get users into the top of a sales funnel and through the funnel resulting in sales and sustained engagement with the product.

The first is generally considered a black-box endeavor that requires creative people and pseudo-psychologists to leverage consumer emotion to create need for a product.

Not incidentally, the world's non-Internet advertising model is a house of cards built upon this black box, currently being disrupted by Internet advertising. It requires sophisticated data analytics and a plethora of hidden assumptions, focus groups, and consumer surveys that demonstrate justification for, among other things, millions of dollars spent on Super Bowl ads, and tens of millions of dollars spent by a TV network for the rights to broadcast Super Bowls.

The second requires a Google Analytics account.

A lean startup uses neither approach until it can demonstrate that the market segments being pursued are already passionate about the product and that the method of converting prospects to customers has been optimized.

A lean startup is not ready to scale until the product itself is the best marketing tool.

The objective of the second type of marketing described is to develop a series of known steps that merely requires their competent execution. Yet there is an infinite number of possibilities for each step, and new ones are invented all the time. Wouldn't it be prudent if, for example, before you took the advice of that Internet-social-media-marketing-ninja-guru, you understood if it is going to work? Or before you paid that PR agency a costly retainer?

Are all products right for infomercials? Of course not!

The fact is that not all marketing activities are right for all products and all customer segments. If someone is selling you—whether an agency, consultant, or presumptive full-time employee; whether ninja, guru, or rock star—a toolkit, a bag of tricks, a black box, or a magic formula, walk away.

The bottom line is that there is no reason why you can't apply an iterative learning process to marketing the same way you might when developing a product. For each phase of your business, your marketing team's learning plan might look like this:

Employing the wrong salespeople or sales channel has the same deleterious effect as hiring the wrong marketing person. Months go by and you have little to show for time, effort, and money.

Pro tip: Revenue is sometimes a vanity metric.

Or you could have the opposite problem, where you sell more than you can deliver because:

- Wrong product decisions were made.
- Sales overpromised product capability.
- A shotgun sales approach resulted in a nonscalable business.

You need to learn how to sell your particular product before executing. The right sales engagement sells what you already have, but also helps establish what the product must have in order to be sold. Best to learn this prior to releasing the product, but, if late to the game, still best before building out the sales team.

The right sales engagement also establishes which market segments are the best to pursue and how to pursue them. In other words, early sales calls should establish the pattern of selling into a particular segment and what marketing is required to quicken or even automate the process.

Legal and Accounting

If your business isn't a law firm, then legal matters do not create value for your customers. Typically, they are non-value-creating activities: most likely necessary, but not value-added. (We suppose there are instances in which legal does add value to the customer, perhaps through a granting of certain rights, but generally this isn't the case.)

Legal activities are necessary to protect the business, and without them, there's risk that the value-creating activities will not survive. Legal activities must remain aligned to the value creation, however, or they are wasteful and harmful to the business's vision and values.

The legal task becomes more difficult when we look at larger, established businesses seeking to imbue startup culture. In these cases, businesses should proactively set up legal protections with respect to the

Marketing learning	Deep understanding of customer segments	Messaging, positioning, buying process	Conversion funnel	Acquisition channels

startup-like activity. The same can be said for accounting. Accounting-department activities that are misaligned with the business's value creation are wasteful. Businesses with a primary focus of reducing cost have little chance of being lean. They might achieve "skinny," but not lean.

Root-Cause Analysis

Root-cause analysis is a set of methodologies used by organizations to establish underlying causes of specific issues. The goal is to use objective thinking to figure out why something went wrong or why something is not possible, instead of blaming individuals or believing the it-can't-be-done naysayers.

Truth be told, the blame may rest with an individual, but how did the person get hired? Did the new hire get proper training? Maybe overcoming a specific obstacle is not currently possible, but what then are the alternatives?

Since put into use as part of the Toyota Production System, the 5-Whys method has remained primarily focused on manufacturing and engineering processes. Toyota figured that there was a puddle of oil on the shop floor because a parts purchasing agent was motivated to lower costs of parts purchases.[9] At IMVU, Ries figured that a new product release made existing customers unhappy because corporate didn't emphasize new-employee training enough to managers.

One key to root-cause analysis in the lean startup is that the resolution costs less than the cost of the issue being resolved. If training mishaps are minor and few and far between, then a huge investment in training is wasteful. During rapid growth, however, the lack of training may lead to more costly mishaps and warrant investment.[10]

We're happy that engineering teams are living in a state of blissful harmony, but meanwhile sales is blaming marketing for a failure to sell, marketing is blaming engineering for a lack of features, and engineering is blaming sales for selling vaporware. Can't we all just . . . get along?

There's no reason why root-cause analysis can't be used in the rest of the organization, with the same rules:

- Identifiable issue.
- No blame game.
- Actionable solutions.

Case Study: **Root-Cause Analysis on Sales**

A new media company we'll call NewCo is developing a platform to enable customers to create highly interactive presentations and training. Customer targets are large corporations and the military.

NewCo scaled quickly through investment capital based on revenue projections. Because the company was developing a platform, investors knew they had to be patient while the sales pipeline was built, but of course they were not infinitely so.

Two years into the company and six months after their first investment round, the management team and board of directors recognized an obvious issue with the sales pipeline. Potential customers were falling out early, sales conversion rates were low, and the sales cycle was taking too long. The issue was brought to a head when a prospect that was labeled a 90 percent positive, $1 million-plus deal collapsed just before a board meeting.

The analysis of what had happened was typical of most business-to-business startups. The management team was locked in a room for a couple of days with no real direction apart from playing the blame game. The conclusions from the meeting included the following:

- Sales needed to be more honest reporting pipeline status.
- Sales needed to be more conservative on the deal size, the likelihood of closing, and the closing date. The executive team needed better policing of the pipeline.
- Sales needed more stringent prospect qualification.

The CEO, putting his leadership hat on, urged for a commitment to work harder, faster, and so on. Putting on his I-report-to-the-board hat, he added subtle threats that "If the sales executive and staff can't do their job, then maybe some restructuring is in order."

No real causes were identified; hence there were no actionable solutions.

The results were predictable: The pipeline became smaller and was managed better, resulting in better predictability, but not better results.

Six months went by and it was time for another roasting by the board of directors followed by another team meeting. A couple of key things changed, however:

First, the brainstorming process was formalized based on root-cause analysis as practiced by Stephen Davies, the VP of business development. Second, a new CEO was in place who fully backed the new approach. Davies began with a clear problem-definition statement: "Inappropriate sales opportunities are created as part of the sales funnel process." There was nothing inherently wrong with the tracking process once there was a potential in the pipeline, but the process for qualifying the initial potential was problematic.

The next step was to brainstorm causes and categorize them. For this, NewCo used an Ishikawa, or fishbone diagram.

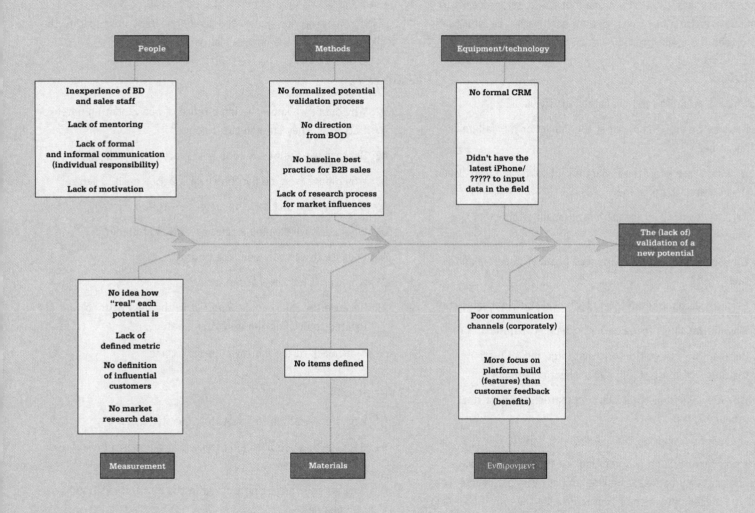

The key is to start at the same point as the Ishikawa, but then follow the causal path until one gets to the point where one is no longer in control; that is typically where the root cause is. In virtually all cases, there is more than one root cause, so one needs to repeat the exercise a few times, one for each path. The Ishikawa is used to keep the team focused on each potential cause.

Version 1

Q1: Why are we failing to adequately qualify leads?

A1: Because we didn't know what the impact of this failure might be.

Q2: Why didn't we know the impact of not validating leads when they entered the pipeline?

A2: Because we have an inexperienced board of directors and sales staff.

Q3: Why do we have an inexperienced board of directors and sales staff?

A3: Because we focused on hiring technical staff, not sales staff.

Q4: Why did we solely focus on hiring technical staff?

A4: Because the assumption was that large sets of platform features would attract inbound sales from promotions.

Q5: Why did we assume that platform features would attract inbound sales?

A5: Founders' assumption/inexperienced founders.

The first time through was very high-level. The results make sense, but are very backward looking and not very actionable. Looking at the preceding, which answer represents the root cause? One

could blame the inexperience of the founders, but that is not very helpful. The kicker is the assumption that large feature sets will automatically drive inbound sales. There is a lesson everyone can learn from.

Many organizations would stop there, but NewCo returned to the Ishikawa, following the next causal path.

Version 2

Q2: Why didn't we know the importance of not validating potentials when they entered the pipeline?

A2: Because we had no baseline best practice for B2B sales.

Q3: Why did we have no baseline best practice for B2B sales?

A3: Because we didn't develop a sales execution strategy.

Q4: Why didn't we develop a sales execution strategy?

A4: Because it was not seen as a priority.

Q5: Why was it not seen as a priority?

A5: Because the salespeople were out in the field with no time allocated to develop the execution strategy.

And so on. Back to the Ishikawa for path three.

Version 3

Q1: Why are we failing to adequately qualify leads?

A1: Because they are not being tracked in the most efficient and effective manner.

Q2: Why are they not being tracked in the most efficient and effective manner?

A2: Because we didn't invest in a real customer relationship management (CRM) system.

Q3: Why didn't we invest in a real CRM system?

A3: Because the executive team did not understand the impact that a real CRM system has on the sales organization.

Q4: Why didn't the executive team understand the impact that a real CRM system has on the sales organization?

A4: Because we have an inexperienced board of directors and sales staff.

Q5: Why do we have an inexperienced board of directors and sales staff?

This is sounding familiar. The root cause for this leg might be at Answer 3 because recognizing the lack of understanding might push the organization toward getting some training to get it up to speed on sales best practices. Stopping too early might result in a great CRM system, but if the executive team still doesn't understand the need for it, then there's not much chance for real improvement.

So the solutions from the full analysis include:

- The development of a sales-execution strategy with emphasis placed on learning and validation.

- Mentoring for all executives, especially in business development and sales.

- Investment in an appropriate CRM system.

- Performing a full-feature review on the product, distilling the 10 percent of features that actually have benefits, and integrating them into the sales-execution strategy.

- Pushing harder on military sales. It's a longer cycle, but once a need is established, then validation is straightforward.

Big, Old, and . . . Lean?

It's pretty easy for us to sit back and declare that large, successful—even dominant—businesses should act like startups in order to maintain, regain, or protect their success. But there is truth in the idea.

The point isn't to be critical of large businesses; heck, they've achieved more than most. There's also truth, however, in the observation that the tactics, strategy, and branding that made them big aren't the same as those that launched them in the first place.

The idea is to put a startup culture in place in order to find that completely new value proposition that leads them to huge growth again.

It sounds easy, right? Build a startup inside your existing business. Charge it with the clarion call "Be innovative." Hold meetings where employees ideate. Give everyone a bit of autonomy. Big businesses know they need to innovate. Without some amount of innovation, it's unlikely they will compete successfully in the market at all.

The problem is that the term *innovation* has ceased to have real meaning. It's a buzzword. To many, *disruptive* innovation and *sustaining* innovation have come to mean the same thing. You can't go a day without hearing how company *x* is innovating, is the innovation leader, or is discovering new ways to innovate. It's innovation by branding. *Invention* has become the measure, rather than finding a market for an application of the invention.

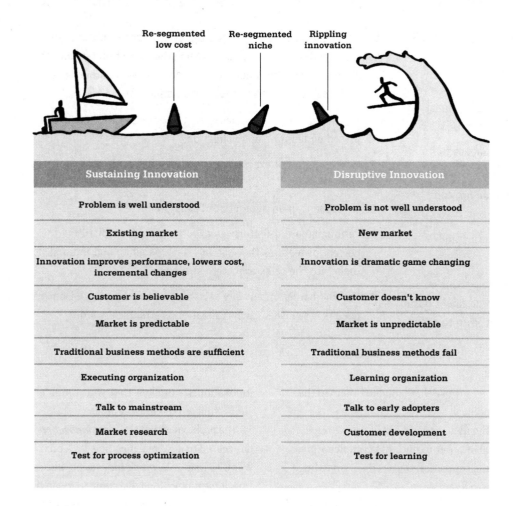

Re-segmented low cost | Re-segmented niche | Rippling innovation

Sustaining Innovation	Disruptive Innovation
Problem is well understood	Problem is not well understood
Existing market	New market
Innovation improves performance, lowers cost, incremental changes	Innovation is dramatic game changing
Customer is believable	Customer doesn't know
Market is predictable	Market is unpredictable
Traditional business methods are sufficient	Traditional business methods fail
Executing organization	Learning organization
Talk to mainstream	Talk to early adopters
Market research	Customer development
Test for process optimization	Test for learning

The number of patents held receives more attention than the number of loyal customers.

Universities have a similar issue: lots of research and few applications. Lab-to-market programs teach the 4 Ps (product, place, price, promotion) of marketing and how to write business plans, but not how to discover a market.

When that fails, technology is licensed to big businesses to bolster their patent portfolios. More often than not, the new technology never sees the light of day.

Governments that get involved often exacerbate the problem, doling out money to startups comprised only of university researchers occupying space in an incubator. The researchers research; they don't create marketable products.

Part of the issue is the old idea that scientists, researchers, and engineers who invent must partner or turn over their inventions to the business side of the house. If this is what they prefer, then so be it.

We believe, however, that things would be better if the inventors were taught to be entrepreneurs. In order to build things that matter, inventors need to be closer to the market, closer to problems their technology might solve. Second best is to find domain experts, perhaps other scientists, who are entrepreneurial. The last resort is to use local business experts. This will all but kill the disruptive portion of the innovation.

The business side of the house is used to asking two fundamentally disruption-killing questions:

1. What is the return on investment to the organization?
2. When will the organization realize the return?

It's not that business executives are wrong in asking these questions. They are very rational to do so. In large, successful organizations particularly, money is invested in projects that have the highest likelihood of generating significant revenue. Additionally, executives are often compensated for short-term thinking. Bonuses for protecting the business a decade from now are of limited use. In short time horizons, the projects most likely to produce returns are those that address the needs of existing customers.

Existing customers' needs are well understood, marketing and sales channels are proven, and business processes exist that close the circle between learning what customers need and delivering that value. This describes sustaining innovation to a T. All innovative endeavors will be sucked into the sustaining vortex, because they will be measured against the performance of existing (or recent) products.

Startups and startup-like ventures cannot be held to the same measures, which is not to say they aren't.

It's a good way to send a startup into a death spiral, however, wherein execution of best practices is favored over learning and one moves with great efficiency toward failure.

When Steve Blank suggests that accountants not run startups[11] and Eric Ries talks about "innovation accounting," they are demonstrating how to track a startup's progress toward finding a scalable business model. A startup must learn its way, and a large organization that seeks to find new revenue opportunities must learn its way, too. It's simply not going to cut it when a team of managers is allowed to nix ideas because of their pay grade. Management hierarchy is not structured based on ability to predict the future. Yet, that's what we're doing, only we use *analysis* as a euphemism for "reading tea leaves."

A large, hugely successful communications company in southern California made two impressive moves toward improving internal innovation:

First, they formed (and funded) an organization to create internal startup teams to create products that would, if successful, generate demand for core products.

Second, they adopted lean startup principles with the aim of finding working business models versus formulating a presentation with impressive spreadsheets and pie charts representing crystal ball planning.

Early in the process, we led the teams through a workshop to posit market segment assumptions and problem-solution hypotheses, and to identify core business risks. We established how the teams should get out of the building to learn through customer development, what viability experiments they might run, and what data they should track as they moved through the learning process.

In the end, the teams presented to an internal venture funding group. The problem is that like many of their venture capital firm counterparts, the group evaluated the startups based on their own mythological ability to envision the future, rather than the real-world learning presented by the startup teams.

In fact, the whole program was scrapped. It was a repeat of an oft-told story: When the core business needs resources, both capital and human, the internal startups are the first sources to be tapped.

Creating a startup culture is, in our view, the right way to create truly innovative products inside large organizations. There also needs to be a fundamental shift toward long-term thinking. Many U.S. businesses seem to have a cyclical, love-hate relationship with long-term thinking. When the economy is going great—or at least is bubbly—short-term shareholder value is revered, coinciding with stock-option-based executive compensation plans.

To succeed in today's economy, businesses must be focused on creating real value for customers, not paper value for executives or investment bankers.

The issue remains: How to do that?

Over the Horizon: A Framework

In 2000, McKinsey & Company management consultants Mehrdad Baghai, Stephen Coley, and David White introduced a "3 Horizon" framework to help break this pattern.[12]

1. Horizon 1 is the core business, accounting for most revenue. The business model is well understood and is executing (for now) with all cylinders firing. The primary focus is on near-term performance.

2. Horizon 2 represents *internal* businesses on the rise: products that have customers, have perhaps achieved product-market fit, and are ready to scale. These businesses have the potential of becoming core to the business—in other words, a Horizon 1 unit.

3. Horizon 3 contains early-stage startups. They might include research projects, prototypes, inventions, products in pilot phase, and strategic investments in external young companies. Most of these startups, for a variety of reasons, will fail.

This, it seems to us, is a reasonable way of looking at things. But how these groups are funded and how they interact with each other (if at all) are critical to their success. The three horizons should be seen as a pyramid, with a greater number of smaller investments on the bottom and winners bubbling up to the top, the same way the innovation economy works.

Geoffrey Moore, author of the marketer's bible, *Crossing the Chasm*, sees a problem in the application of horizon planning whereby Horizon 2 teams are often tossed Horizon 3 projects that are little more than "prototype-stage products" developed by "lab-centric inventors." Additionally, Horizon 1 marketing and sales organizations are often assigned to push Horizon 2 products that are unproven.

Horizon 1 business units have no real incentive to prove the viability of Horizon 2 products rather than making money on proven Horizon 1 products.[13]

Here, once again, we see products that may very well be the company's future salvation being held to account by existing business metrics.

"Thus," Moore concludes, "innovations are better off in bootstrapped startups, because at least there they can get access to the market and suppliers, and their investors will use fairer standards of measurement." Although we're not sure the latter is (yet) true, the prescription seems pretty close. The key is to combine lean startup methodologies with horizon planning to properly define the horizon boundaries. Businesses should use startups to prove product ideas and business models, before integrating core resources such as sales and marketing. Furthermore, labs and research centers should be considered pre-startup. In other words, experimentation in the development of technology is separate and distinct from the experimentation done in Horizon 3. Horizon 3 startups are for experimenting around developing the right application of the technology for a specific market segment. Research centers live in Horizon 4!

Case Study: Lean Startup Horizons

Intuit is a great example of a company adapting the horizon planning model through the application of lean startup principles. Of course, Intuit is no ordinary company. From its inception, Intuit has been focused on creating new value for its customers. That Intuit can be seen as a poster child of Moore's *Crossing the Chasm* in the early 1990s to a leading practitioner of design thinking in the late 2000s and now a shining example of Ries's lean startup is a tribute to the early vision and leadership of co-founder Scott Cook.

Thirty years of success means overcoming several periods of computer-based disruption from the era of shrink-wrapped software to modern mobile apps. Today, with the portfolio approach of horizon planning, Intuit continues to deliver on current-term commitments while purposefully setting a foundation for future growth through experimentation and continuous learning.

Here's how Intuit defines its "3 Horizons":

1. Horizon 1 extends and defends the core. In other words, it continues the growth of current proven products and improves profitability.
2. Horizon 2 builds emerging offerings. Product teams validate their business models or emerging products and prove the ability to scale.
3. Horizon 3 creates viable options. It proves the startup's concept by validating that users love the product, and it has a compelling business-model hypothesis. As part of an ongoing refinement,

Intuit has evolved away from using revenue numbers to determine horizon-level status and instead looks to *validated learning* metrics.

Where many companies get off track is that Horizon 3 products are seen as lab toys, non-market-testable prototypes—in other words, something that's not yet been tested in the market.

Intuit's Hugh Molotsi says: "Part of testing a user concept in Horizon 3 is putting it in the market and seeing what actual user behavior is. Therefore, it didn't feel right to call something that's launched in a scrappy way a Horizon 2 product. It's still Horizon 3 because we're still experimenting with it."

Revenue numbers simply hark back to the traditional style of measuring all new endeavors by return on investment. Instead, Intuit turned to the following three love metrics:

1. Net Promoter Score, which measures the willingness of a customer to refer a product to others.
2. Active usage, which measures customer engagement with a product.
3. Customer benefits, which measures whether a product's promise is achieved.

As Molotsi further states:

For each product you define the benefit provided to customers, such as saving time or saving money. So one of the things we measure is: Are you actually delivering that? So when you are a Horizon 3 you're trying to run experiments to prove those things.

Horizon 2 is experimenting with the business model. You've found a set of users who love the product, are using it, and are benefiting from it, but is there actually a scalable and sustainable business there?

You have some hypothesis—you're going to charge subscribers a monthly fee or you have an advertising revenue model, whatever the case is—you have some business model hypothesis that you're going to try to prove.

Protecting the Core Business

In large organizations, fear is often the cause of failure to disruptively innovate. Some of the fear is well founded. As discussed earlier, it's critical that internal startups are protected from standard, core-business operating procedures, but protection cuts both ways. Core business units have legitimate concerns regarding their young startup siblings:

Sales: For value-based organizations, salespeople's compensation is dependent on the ability to sell products that provide value. Forced to sell unproven or mediocre products, salespeople will find workarounds or leave.

Marketing: New products that are perhaps incomplete or don't jibe with existing core products might confuse existing customers, adversely affecting brand image. Furthermore marketing activities that support an unproven or mediocre product or service will prove wasteful.

Legal: Privacy, compliance, and intellectual property are a few legal issues that big businesses must concern themselves with.

Human resources: Some people are drawn to chaotic, wear-many-hats situations, whereas others prefer orderly, well-defined roles. This needs to be managed.

Job security: Anyone working in a business being disrupted by an internal startup will understandably feel vulnerable. Ultimately, you *hope* that your startup cannibalizes your core business. If the internal startup doesn't do it, an external organization will. This points to a number of potential cultural issues that will need to be addressed as well.

Intuit helps business units deal with these issues. Using cross-functional teams and defining the Horizon metrics as learning rather than revenue means each business unit's core business (H1) sales and marketing teams are not tasked with executing with unproven products developed by the H2s and H3s.

Employees are empowered to participate in innovation, and they can move between horizons. "We often have programs where we rotate engineers that are H1 engineers through the H3s and H2s, just because they have either personal interest or they just kind of want to see what it's like or just to bring in fresh blood all the time," says Intuit's Bennett Blank.

Additionally, Intuit has an unstructured-time program, during which employees can spend up to 10 percent of their time working on projects they're passionate about. "That's actually been really powerful as well because a lot of our new ideas are coming out of that," says Blank.

To protect the brand, Intuit deployed a sub-brand called Intuit Labs to let customers know that products released within it are still in the experimental stage. To address the legal component, Intuit developed a core set of legal documents and processes, which, if followed by H3s, do not require involvement by corporate counsel. This approach can simplify and speed up the H3's progress.

Intuit has a number of in-market wins, including H3 graduates SnapTax and GoPayment.

Lean startups are not just for Horizon 3s and 2s.

H3s do lean startup to find a product that results in passionate users.

H2s do lean startup to find a scalable business model.

H1s can do lean startup, too. The lean startup processes help existing, core businesses become more effective by moving closer to the customer, becoming a continuous-learning organization, being more agile, and relentlessly improving internal processes.

Startups can apply Horizon ideas to their planning, as well. After nailing product fit for one segment, it could be beneficial to start exploring alternative products to sell to the existing segment, in addition to searching for additional segments.

Work to Do

A long time ago, we promised ourselves we would never suggest to someone that they write a vision statement. We will keep that promise. So, instead, you know those fun personality quizzes in airline magazines? We ask you to get in your favorite yoga position—c'mon, admit it, you do yoga—and answer the following questions as honestly as you can. You don't have to show it to a life coach or anything. There are no *correct* answers.

1. Where does your product or idea fall on the innovation spectrum?

   Idea:

   a. Adds functionality to existing product category.

   b. Dramatically lowers cost of new product for an existing product category.

   c. Highly tailors functionality for an underserved market.

   d. Is an existing product category for new large marketplace.

   e. Is a new product category, new market.

   f. Is flipping an existing market completely on its head.

2. What's your philosophy on taking money to fund the business?

   a. Bootstrapping, baby!

   b. Friends, family, and fools.

   c. Cash, credit cards, coupons.

   d. Accelerators, angels, a**holes.

   e. Venture vampires (We're kidding!).

3. What is most important to you?

   a. There's a specific (large or small) market segment I'm committed to and passionate about serving.

   b. It's important that everyone get ahold of my product.

   c. My technology is game changing. I just need to find the right application for it.

   d. My vision is radical and I will see that it is made real.

   e. My vision isn't as important as the fact that I will do whatever it takes to change the world.

3

All the Fish in the Sea

Ask first-time entrepreneurs who they plan on selling their product to, and the most likely answer you'll hear is an enthusiastic "Everyone!"

Those a bit more savvy back off from global hegemony by proposing a vertical slice, such as "financial services companies," or horizontally, "the Fortune 1000," or by product, as in "people who buy milkshakes," or even a specific demographic, such as "women between the ages of 18 and 73." Unfortunately for new businesses, these ill-defined *segments* are neither realistic nor helpful.

segment: A defined group of people who share the same problem or passion and speak the same language.

Products likely do exist that are purchased by both those 18 and older and 73 and younger, but not by *all* women between 18 and 73. Why do those who buy, buy?

Imagine you were a commercial fisherman. Your livelihood depends on catching and selling fish. If you are asked, "What sort of fish do you plan to catch?" and you answer, "All the fish in the sea," you are surely doomed as a commercial fisherman.

It turns out there are not only many fish in the sea, but they have different forms and different ethologies. Methods of fishing that work well for some species don't work so well for others.

Battle-tested entrepreneurs know how to fish, and when asked who will buy their product, they respond not by reciting demographic characteristics, but by speaking about specific buyers and their particular pains, passions, and needs.

Who will buy your product is as important as the gloriousness that is your product. Although the customer chooses the product, when building a new business it's up to you to choose your customer. In fact, depending on your values and vision, the choice you make may be even more important than your product idea.

If the most important element of your business idea is the particular market segment you want to serve, and you think you can serve them in a way that matches the vision you have for your business, then you may decide to treat your market segment as the fulcrum on which to *pivot*. In other words, you change your product idea, your distribution channels, and your marketing and sales plans to fit the needs of that segment.

pivot: To keep one foot firmly planted in one fundamental aspect of your business model, while changing other aspects.

If you are committed to solving a segment's problem (or addressing a passion), you should be solution agnostic.

Famed marketer Seth Godin says:

Great customers . . . will engage and invent and spread the word. It takes vision and guts to turn someone down and focus on a different segment, on people who might be more difficult to sell at first, but will lead you where you want to go over time.[1]

If the segment you choose is not one that resonates with you personally, will this adversely affect the passion you have for your business? Will the time and expense of a long sales cycle be difficult to overcome with your revenue model? Does the prospect, who has a budget, also have an adequate workaround to the problem you're solving? When discussing how a prospect is solving the problem now, has the prospect described the specific shortfalls of the existing method? What is the cost of those shortfalls to the segment in terms of time, money, market share, risk, or customer satisfaction?

Your solution must address one or more of these shortfalls. How does your solution do that? Be specific. What functionality or feature of your solution resolves which shortfall?

Does the passionate customer represent an impossibly small market to support a business?

Market segments drive your business model. Alex Osterwalder's seminal business-model book, *Business Model Generation*, breaks business models down into nine components:

1. Customer segments—who you aim to reach and serve.

2. Value propositions—products and services that create value for your segments.

3. Channels—how you communicate with and reach your segments.

4. Customer relationships—types of relationships with customers; for example, direct and personal, indirect, automated, and so forth.

5. Revenue streams—how you will be paid.

6. Key resources—physical, financial, intellectual, and human resources required.

7. Key activities—the most important things a company must do to make the model work.

8. Key partnerships—suppliers and partners that complete the model.

9. Cost structure—how much it costs you to run your business.[2]

If you look at the nine building blocks, you can see how your values and customer segments drive the business model: The segment determines the preferred method of payment and how customers would like to interact with the business—in other words, the "relationship." Conversely, a business that *chooses* a specific type of relationship is purposefully blocking segments from becoming customers. (There's nothing particularly wrong with this.) Specific segments determine sales channel, how much customers are willing to pay, what type of solutions they require and, therefore, cost structure of the business, as well as key partnerships and activities, and resources required to serve the chosen segment(s). Alternatively, a business can choose to commit to specific channels, revenue streams, or key activities that will, once again, purposefully eliminate some market segments from consideration.

Not to beat a dead fish, but this is a critical point in understanding your business model: Are you committed to certain business-model assumptions and, therefore, seek to find customer segments that may fit?

Or are you committed to addressing a specific problem or passion and, therefore, seek to find the customer segments that fit and will let the remaining business-model building blocks fall where they may?

Or are you committed to serving a particular segment and, therefore, seek to find their most pressing issues and work toward assembling a business model capable of addressing those?

Whichever way you choose, the process of segmenting your market is one of the most poorly understood concepts in today's business startup world, yet as we can see, it is one of the most powerful.

Case Study: The Ethology of the Fish

In the kelp beds off the coast of Southern California, one can find thousands of species of fish, but two of the most sought after by commercial fishermen are the California halibut and the white sea bass. Both fish are classified as demersal, meaning they live near or on the bottom of the ocean floor, and catching fish of both species in the 20- to 30-pound range is not uncommon.

Halibut are flatfish. They make themselves effectively invisible by nestling into the sandy bottoms between patches of eel grass, and when sardines swim by, they explode out of the sand to nab them. They have two eyes on one side of their body, which make them very adept at ambushing predators. Fishermen know that one of best baits for catching halibut is a fellow denizen of sandy bottoms, the lizardfish.

White sea bass are long and cylindrical, and have a much more typical fish form. They cruise the kelp beds looking for squid or mackerel to eat. White sea bass are very difficult to hunt with spear guns because they are very sensitive to noise, and the slightest inorganic sound will set them off.

Any amateur fisherman can throw a line off the end of the local pier baited with frozen squid and pull in a few mackerel, or maybe even a rockfish.

But commercial fishermen have to—day in, day out, in good weather or in bad—acquire their target fish and then sell it for more than the cost of catching it. To do that repeatedly and scalably, they must develop a deep understanding of the ethology of the

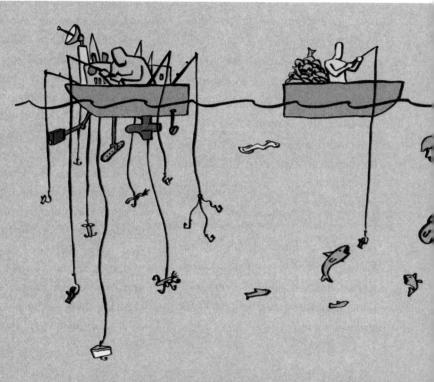

fish. They must learn what sort of bait to use with what tackle, the best time of day, and what environment will maximize the potential to catch the particular fish they are looking for. Fish can only be caught when they are accessible—it doesn't help you to know that there are fish 1,000 feet below your boat, if your line cannot get down to that depth.

The market segment you pursue is inextricably linked to the other aspects of your business model.

Segments determine how future customers expect to interact with the product, how they will be marketed to, and their method of purchasing. Differences in how people are reached, their expectations of the buying process, how their trust is earned, the price point they'll accept, what distribution methods are most efficient, the messaging that attracts them—all these factors (and more) may represent different subsegments.

What are the value propositions, the benefits and messaging (bait), the pricing structure and channels (tackle), and the length of sales cycle (how likely a fish will snap your line)? Will you need a big net (full-page ads in the *Wall Street Journal*) to catch lots of small sardines? Or will you need to staff and finance a whaling ship to be out at sea for months at a time to catch two or three whales (enterprise sales model)? Or perhaps you need to chum the waters a bit (*freemium*)? Maybe you'll be hunting on a reef with a spear gun for 20-pound groupers (B2B sales at a conference)?

freemium: A term used to describe a product offered in a "free" version, as well as in one or more premium account versions, requiring payment.

You can build a mobile app for senior citizens, launch a Facebook campaign targeting Fortune 100 CEOs, or charge $25 for a food-cart hamburger if you'd like, but the mismatch between product, tactics, pricing, and segment might delay that Hawaiian perma-vacation you've been planning.

As with many aspects of entrepreneurship, the practice of segmenting your market seems commonsensical, but is more complicated than meets the eye. The problem is that few take the time to truly master it.

Entrepreneurs carry market segments around in the back of their minds, relying on gut feel to determine whether the customers they are seeing are the right customers. The problem is, when you're chasing revenue, any and all customers will seem like the right customer.

Common mistakes in segmenting:

- Dividing groups of people by firmographics or demographics.
- Dividing groups by arbitrary characteristics, like early adopters or Facebook users.
- Dividing by product category, like fine-dining restaurants, or electronics.
- Dividing by vertical markets: healthcare, financial services, and so on.

Know Your Audience: Why Segmentation Matters

Lean thinking—for example, lean manufacturing—has a concept called *pull*.

pull: An arrangement in which nothing is done simply means that nothing is done in product creation or delivery until the customer (including internal customers in the design and manufacturing process) expresses a need or a demand for the product or for the intermediate "deliverable" from the downstream process.

Product-market fit can be thought of as massive pull.

Pull has two primary characteristics:

1. Demand demonstration. We're not building the product, part, or feature because we *think* the product is wanted; it has been ordered.
2. No overproduction. We're building just in time (JIT)—in other words, no inventory. The product, part, or feature is created only when pulled by the next downstream process.

Combined with lean's concept of *flow*, *pull* means that not only is the final product not overproduced, but neither are all intermediate parts, so that from design to delivery, a product flows from raw materials to the customer's hand without waste: no wasted activity, time, or materials.

Product-market fit can be thought of as *pull on a large scale*. So many customers are demanding your product (and product features), that a clear market signal has been sent saying your product is needed. Marc Andreessen, when first describing the concept, used the term *pull* without referencing lean: "the market *pulls* product out of the startup."[3]

This is different from normal market pull. Remember, in a nonstartup environment,

product-market fit: A match between product and market segment that results in high growth or high demand. This isn't an assumption, but rather describes a significant change in the number of customers based on having achieved the fit.

the customer is known, as is the value being provided to the customer. The company is in execution mode, having already figured out how to build, market, sell, and distribute the product. Lean helps the business do that better.

In a startup endeavor, however, we seek to discover the customer and the value. Pull in this context means two things:

1. Demands demonstration: Value has been discovered.
2. No overproduction: Only features contributing to value are built.

Product-market fit represents this discovery for one or multiple subsegments.

Defining and understanding subsegment pull is the only way to measure progress toward product-market fit. Product requests from engaged customers may be a good indication that you've nailed—or are close to nailing—the core value proposition, but if these requests are scattered across multiple segments, it's easy to misunderstand the signal.

On the other hand, if you understand your subsegments well, you can measure pull coming from a specific group of users with a common need. The same applies to other measures of market signal—in other words, what the market is telling you about the demand for your product. Looking at

month-over-month growth rates across all users is not as effective as month-over-month growth rates *per segment*.

Better to understand which segments are growing fast versus those that are, perhaps, not growing at all.

If you measure user satisfaction, it makes a lot more sense to know a lot about who is satisfied and why, rather than monolithically

knowing that most customers are happy (or not).

Without proper segmentation, you are left in the dark about who is testing your value proposition. As businesses achieve some measure of positive market signal, customers will provide feedback: what they like, what they don't like, what works, and what doesn't. They will do this solicited or

unsolicited. Some of it is valuable, some of it isn't. All of it indicates market signal, but how do you know what to listen to and what to ignore?

In their quest to achieve the oft-stated ambition of "thinking big," entrepreneurs express the desire to have access to huge markets, and if they convert a conservative percentage of them, the revenue is so huge that investment is a foregone conclusion. When discovering the value you're creating, however, it's virtually impossible—from the outset—to discover a core value proposition that suits this whole market en masse. Instead, successful solutions evolve over time to attract more and more subsegments without losing the early adopters, or the early adopters are used to attract the mainstream customers, after which the early adopters are abandoned!

This is arguably the case with Apple's iPhone and iPad. Having watched and learned from (and participated in, to some degree) the early entries in the tablet/microcomputing device industry for over a decade, Apple leapfrogged the early adopter market with the first iPhone release. *Early adopter* is the name coined by Everett Rogers and popularized by Geoffrey Moore to describe an early customer of a particular product or technology. These customers are often willing to put up with unfinished or imperfect products for a variety of reasons:

- The solution solves a problem or pain just enough.
- The buyer likes to be seen as a leader.
- The buyer is a tinkerer in particular areas.

Note that one common misconception is that an early adopter is strictly a personality type—that is, a particular person who is an early adopter generally will be the first buyer of *anything*. This is certainly *not* true, even by industry.

Those who must have the latest electronics gadget don't buy the early versions of all new electronics product categories. Additionally, someone who buys products to play with and quickly discards them is a tinkerer, not an early adopter. It's important that an early adopter understands and needs your value proposition.

We often see this misconception lead to problems in the high-tech industry. Startups seek coverage for their product on online media sites like TechCrunch, assuming that readers tend to be early adopters. Unfortunately, the bump in traffic they receive—even that which results in conversions to product sign-ups—is misunderstood as product-market fit and can wreak havoc on young companies.

The TechCrunch bump, as it is called, literally can kill a company by sending them off on a wild goose chase once the first wave of (non) early adopters subsides.

The would-be early-adopter crowd for Apple's first iPhone (who were not fierce Apple brand loyalists but tech junkies) decried the limited feature set and lack of customization available—functionality that they desired as early adopters but that would have hindered the usability by the mainstream adopter.

Ironically, the way to go big is to focus small. You are more likely to discover what will go big by focusing on individual use cases.

One of the biggest entrepreneur traps is to be all things to all people. Big companies get big by being a few things to a large number of groups of people. Although a plethora of feature requests might indicate a positive market signal, they are potentially fatal without knowing who they come from or why they are being requested.

A Southern California startup we spoke to was recently shuttered by its CEO after he had an epiphany during a meeting with a large, influential partner prospect:

I was sitting in his office and the potential partner asked the rather simple question: "What is your core value proposition?" I sat there, mulling over the features upon features we had added to the product over the prior few months based on in-depth customer interviews, automated feature requests, and conversations with prospects, and I realized I couldn't answer the question.

I went home that day and sent an e-mail to my list of 1,500 customers telling them that regretfully, the product would no longer be available.

If you haven't done the proper market segmentation, categorized feature requests by segment, and made the effort to understand *why* the customer asked for a particular feature, then you are no closer to product-market fit than if you were receiving no requests at all.

This isn't to say that you will not pursue additional market segments. The point is that it's very difficult to pursue many at once, especially if they're particularly divergent. GroupMe, the group messaging service acquired by Skype in 2011, had explicitly rejected a corporate segment that was willing to pay for its service. For several reasons, it chose to pursue the free-user route instead. Sometimes saying no to a segment means saying no to immediate sales, but yes to building out a long-term business model or, in this case, an attractive acquisition target.

When you catch a fish you didn't mean to catch, it is called a by-catch. This can be serendipitous—for example, if you were fishing for mackerel (a small fish) but you accidentally hooked and landed a white sea bass (a large and very delicious fish). Generally speaking, however, you do not want to hook a leopard shark when fishing for halibut.

As you have no intention of eating the shark, you need to get the hook out of its mouth so you can let it swim free, but in the meantime, the hooked shark is aggressively thrashing about in your boat, destroying your equipment and tangling your line. You also aren't terribly thrilled about getting your hand near its teeth to remove the hook.

You didn't want to catch this fish. You aren't set up to catch or even eat sharks. Yet, you got one on the line and you and your fishing buddies have to deal with the consequences. Accidentally hooking a leopard shark is a total buzzkill.

On the other hand, if, upon learning how to catch halibut, you found that the methods also led you to catching lingcod, you might have found the next segment you could pursue. Lingcod and halibut have overlapping ethologies. Halibut like sandy bottoms near what fisherman like to call structure, for example, rocks with eelgrass, or reefs, or maybe even piers, whereas lingcod actually live in the rocks. They're both ambush predators that feed on bait fish.

As you start to dominate the halibut segment, you might send an additional boat and cast into deeper water to find the sweet spot for lingcod with little change to gear, bait, and existing processes.

Market Segment

An IT manager and CIO may face the same problem—network security—but they don't speak the same language. Although the IT manager is actively fighting a breach, a CIO might be estimating the potential risks of exposed assets. The CIO doesn't look to IT managers in other organizations to find solutions to network security issues. Neither do IT managers look to CIOs for the best products to solve their immediate issues. They do not look to each other as a reference for resolving the problem, so they are said to not speak the same language.

The benefits they hope to receive from a solution are different. Therefore, the product requirements will be different. They also tend to get information from different sources and their methods for approving solutions will differ, and will require different marketing and sales methods.

Clues that people are in different segments:

- Their depth of pain or passion is markedly different.

- They hang out in different places—for example, Facebook versus LinkedIn.

- They expect different solutions—for example, fast food versus a sit-down meal.

- They expect different distributions—for example, online versus brick and mortar.

- They expect different sales methods—for example, field sales versus e-commerce.

Clayton Christensen asks, "What job is your product hired to do?" The same product is hired to do a different job by different customers. In his now famous (among marketers) example, a researcher for a fast-food restaurant found that a large portion of milkshake purchases in the morning came from commuters:

> They faced a long, boring commute and needed something to make the drive more interesting. They weren't yet hungry but knew that they would be by 10 A.M.; they wanted to consume something now that would stave off hunger until noon. And they faced constraints: They were in a hurry, they were wearing work clothes, and they had (at most) one free hand.[4]

Proposed changes to the product to increase market penetration of this company's milkshake focused on maximizing its utility to this particular use case for a specific segment—the commuter. Although this exercise—answering the question of what job your product performs—is a clever one, you don't want to ignore the customer when answering the question.

Perhaps if you have the marketing budget of a fast-food restaurant it's not an issue, but to startups, the fact that your customers who are hiring the product are identified as commuters tells you a lot about how to reach them and convert them into customers.

Market segmentation isn't only about how to design a product for them, but also, just as importantly, *how to market and sell to them*.

As an aside, we should note that it has been known for many years that segmenting along demographic traits does not prove to be terribly useful,[5] nor does it a market segment make—yet for some reason market segmentation is still thought and taught to be synonymous with a listing of intersecting demographic traits.

Back to the milkshake example: Other subsegments were hiring, too. A thinner milkshake was developed for parents who were looking to hire a product for the job of rewarding a child, but who didn't want the drink to last a long time.

You can easily imagine the myriad reasons why different visitors to that fast-food restaurant hire a milkshake.

In fact, there were likely other subsegments who bought milkshakes in the morning alongside the commuters. Additionally, some commuters didn't buy milkshakes. What did they buy and why? Most commuters didn't even go to the restaurant. Why?

The more you know about your customers, the more you know about your segments and even your subsegments. The more you know about your subsegments, the more you know about attracting more of that particular group or alternative, and the more you know about which segments to ignore. Key aspects to the story include:

Problem statement: boredom on commute.

Existing workaround: bagels, donuts, milkshakes.

Solution: thicker milkshakes; add fruit.

Personas: Create a Fake Customer

A description of the customer with the job he or she wants done is called a persona. Popularized by Alan Cooper in 2004, personas are a description of pretend users and what they wish to accomplish. *Wish to accomplish* is another way of saying "job hired for." Originally conceived of as a tool for designers to ensure products were being developed in ways that would resonate with users, we believe the concept is useful to help you understand your customer deeply and drive all customer engagements, including marketing and selling.

So instead of just looking at how people will use the product and then treating sales and marketing as problems of distribution and exploring what magazines they read, you treat them all as a desirability problem of creating something wonderful that people want to buy, and you do that by identifying who is going to use it, what drives them, and what goals and desires they have.

Cooper says that these need not be real users, but rather archetypes of actual users. In our opinion, there's nothing inherently wrong with using a real user as long as the sketch is representative of others. The advantage of using stereotypical characteristics is that the sketch is readily accessible to others, but your primary goal is to be as accurate as possible. You want to be able to recognize them when you see them.

Vague descriptions tend to solicit broader feature lists and less understanding of your must-have use case. You are not going for an assemblage of different users to come up with a composite.

Rather, you're writing a character who has a specific goal and acts in precise ways. In B2B environments, you create a persona for all user types and even those who influence the purchasing decision. Every market has multiple personas, and each persona might have multiple use cases. Ideally, you design your product around one persona with the most compelling use case. Think of compelling along a continuum. A product is considered a painkiller if it is a must-have product, in contrast to a vitamin product, which is nice to have. We think of a shot of adrenalin as like the painkiller, only addressing a passion rather than relieving a pain.

Alan Cooper talks about a higher level of compelling—that which evokes *desire*. "People's desires always have a way of emerging after their needs are satisfied. When a person needs something, she will do what is needed to get it, but when she desires something, she is loyal to it."[6]

If you find a use case that evokes desire, you are ahead of the game. Your business, however, depends on evoking desire somehow. In the end, you may discover that it takes a combination of business qualities that go beyond solving a problem: product plus support, customer service beyond the call of duty, addictive gamification, off-the-charts ease of use, massive return on investment, and so on.

As with the other phases of building your startup, the way you determine your ideal market segment is by interacting with your customer (customer development), testing (viability testing), and measuring (data).

Case Study:
Salim's Fish Inventory

Our client, Salim, CEO of a company we'll call NewCo, is developing a mobile application for restaurants to automatically track ingredient-sourcing information in real time in order to maximize menu efficiencies in terms of dish availability, food prices, and recipe costing. If, for example, a restaurant offers fresh halibut on their menu, but the supply is low one day and prices double, the chef needs to change the menu or offer smaller portions in order to maintain dish margins.

Salim is a successful Southern California restaurateur who came up with the solution based on his own experiences. He's passionate, he hustles, he is personable and well connected in the restaurant industry, but does he understand the market from the right perspective to design a must-have solution to the ingredient-sourcing problem? Rather than focusing first on all the features Salim wanted to build, we focused on the six daily problems of restaurateurs that Salim told us he faced:

1. Food and plate costs—Getting an accurate food and plate cost is too complicated, so I just follow my gut and hope I don't lose money.

2. Master product list—I try to keeping a master list, but updating it is too time consuming.

3. Recipes—My profitability is a guessing game because I am not able to readily update plate costs and, therefore, menu prices.

4. Inventory—Because inventory takes so long, I only do it monthly when it would be ideal to do it weekly.

5. Reporting—The data I get from my bookkeeper/accountant are not detailed enough for me to determine the reasons for my food-cost variances.

6. Labor—I don't have enough labor hours to allocate in order to properly manage my food cost.

This is a good set of problems to work from, and we can begin to imagine what jobs a product needs to do in order to solve them, but which are the most pressing? What are the easiest to fix? Who decides whether to buy a solution to fix them?

When we asked Salim, this successful owner of multiple restaurants, a man with a tremendous amount of market knowledge, "Who is going to want this?" he answered like a typical entrepreneur: "Everyone will want it and will pay $99/month."

The implication is that everyone would want it because all restaurateurs look, feel, and smell like Salim, right? Wrong.

To get entrepreneurs to think about good segments, it's sometimes helpful to think about people or organizations that, at first blush—that is, superficially—look, feel, and smell like a good segment, but would never buy the product. So we started talking this through, and Salim came up with the family-collective persona.

The family collective is a family restaurant as represented by a one-location restaurant, perhaps a family-owned Chinese or Indian restaurant. It's a family affair: They want to make a profit, but it's just as important that the family is working together and that everyone has a role, and the main thing is keeping the restaurant going and the bills paid. The way they source their ingredients is not the same way Salim does. Their networks are different. They go to the same sources from within their community. They tend to do things by routine, the way they've always done it.

Quickly, Salim launched into another persona, the old-school independent. This is a chef/owner, maybe a small Italian restaurant. Joe, the owner, is a bit older, has a few employees working for him, already sent his kids to college, and owns his house. He's not really in it for the money at this point; he wants to pay the bills, stay in business, but he also enjoys hanging out with the regulars. He wants to be productive and happy in life. He likes talking to people—this is his life. The food is not bad, not complicated; the menu doesn't change much. The restaurant is an extension of his personality. You're not going to sell him an iPad application.

Thinking about these two antisegments—the people who look the part superficially, but won't buy the product—broke the ice on how to think about segmentation.

From there, we established several positive segments, like Jack, the solo independent chef: Jack is single and is chef and owner of a Newport Beach seafood restaurant. He currently has one location, but hopes to have more. His restaurant is his lifeblood and he spends virtually all his waking hours there. He is a college graduate, is technology adept, and keeps up to date with emerging restaurant trends. He considers himself to be a fine-dining chef, and serving fresh fish is a key to his restaurant's differentiation. It is important to him to be up to date on current inventory, and he is willing to update his menu daily to reflect current offerings. His biggest challenge is finding the time to call sources to keep up to date on available product.

The segmentation exercise includes not only the persona, but any other data that helps to describe the problem or relevant differences from other segments.

For example, the structure of the restaurant is important. Jack, the solo independent chef, doesn't have a sous chef employed, meaning he is solely responsible for the ingredient-sourcing decision. A solution must save Jack time or it's worthless.

Any details that affect how the business will be marketed and sold to are relevant, such as who influences the decision maker and what is the decision maker's source of industry information. Salim was able to establish several additional segments, including those labeled "Team Independent," "Small Corporate," and "Corporate."

Choosing a Market Segment

As we've discussed, the market segments you decide to pursue drive your business model. You can write a detailed plan on your product platform, how it will be distributed, what marketing channels will be the most efficient, and how the product will be sold, but all that depends on your market segment.

(Unless, of course, you choose your market segment based on one of those criteria. In other words, if you *choose* to disrupt the distribution model and only serve customers willing to buy computers off the Internet, then your distribution has chosen the segment that will behave that way.)

Notice, however, that we did say "choose." Yes, you get to choose your market segments. Not only will this affect the potential size of your business, it may also affect how you feel about it. It's important that your *vision* for the business align with your *values* and that the market segments align with your vision.

Case Study:
Carla's Dream Jobs

We were helping a social entrepreneur (we'll call her Carla) whose vision is to help out-of-work women find their dream jobs. Carla is passionate about changing the lives of these women in fundamental and meaningful ways. She wanted to create a marketplace that would match their dream jobs with real-life business opportunities.

One business model hypothesis that she and her team were exploring had the job opportunity side of the product provided by large businesses that would require an enterprise, B2B sales model. She lamented the possibility of needing to build the product to satisfy that segment, thereby threatening her vision as well as her relationship with the segment she wanted to serve. She questioned whether she would have the same passion for her business if she had to work too long in that vertical (niche) market.

We reminded her of several things:

First, she owns her vision. Ultimately, she gets to do what she wants. The size of her business will be affected by the choices she made.

Second, if she is to see the business through, she'll be at it for a long time. Many entrepreneurs have a tendency to dramatically squash time lines. If she chose to pursue this particular strategy and it was successful, she would be at it for years, not months. Moving on to adjacent segments, perhaps those more closely aligned with her values, would be a long way out in the future. Deciding early whether she wishes to commit to that path is important not only to herself, but to customers, employees, and investors.

Third, you are not ready to be in a startup if you can't do the things you don't want to do. Again, it's not about losing the vision, but about flexibility, listening, and doing things you don't want to do in the realization of the vision.

Our discussion ultimately led Carla and her team to choose a different segment for the opportunity side of the market, one that was more in line with her vision.

One way to help you narrow down which segments you should pursue is to create an opportunity matrix. List segments (or personas) as row titles and criteria used to evaluate segments as column heads.

For the restaurant example, we list the different restaurant segments down the left-hand column and the criteria we use to evaluate the segments across the remaining columns. We chose the following criteria:

- Depth of pain—how bad is the problem we're trying to solve for this particular segment?
- Budget—can the segment pay for a solution?
- Ease of reach—are they marketable through relatively easy channels?
- Ease of MVP (minimum viable product)—do we think the solution is relatively easy or complex?
- Values—how do we feel about serving this constituency?

Opportunity Matrix

	Depth of Pain A	Budget B	Ease of Reach C	Ease of MVP D	Size of Market E	Values F
Solo Chef	H	L	H	H	M	H
Team Independent	H	M	H	H	M	H
Small Corporate	M	M	H	M	M	M
Corporate	L	H	M	L	H	L

The criteria you use are up to you and your business. Be sure to choose characteristics that differentiate the segments. If all evaluations for a particular criterion are high, then that criterion is not serving a purpose for this exercise. Other criteria might be:

- Length of sales cycle—how long does it take to acquire a new customer?
- Cost of sales—does sales require people on the street or is it online conversion?
- Tech savvy—does the segment look for technology solutions to problems?

To be sophisticated about the approach, you can weigh each criterion. For example, depth of pain is most important, so the weight is 4 out of 1–4, but "ease of MVP" only weighs a 2. Then, you can score the criteria for each segment 1–4, 4 being positive, 1 negative. Finally, you can use a mathematical formula to determine which segment scores the highest.

The score for each row would be:

$$(\text{score}_A \times \text{weight}_A/(\text{Sum of weight})) + (\text{score}_B \times \text{weight}_B/ \\ (\text{Sum of weight})) + (\text{continue for all columns})$$

In our example, we took more of a back-of-the-napkin approach, whereby we simply ranked each criterion H for high, M for medium, or L for low, and eyeballed which segment(s) appeared to be the one most worth pursuing. This exercise helps you identify the segment characteristics you need to validate—in other words, the values you've put into the matrix. Are they right? Go out into the market and speak to customers to find out.

Does the solo chef really have the highest pain? Is the solution the easiest to provide?

As you prepare to validate the assumptions captured in your personas and market-segment characteristics, prepare a list of five people or organizations you can approach for each segment.

In our first book, *The Entrepreneur's Guide to Customer Development*, we go into detail on how to find, approach, and hold conversations with members of your potential market, but we won't repeat that here. In a world where the number of connections required to reach anyone on Earth has decreased from six degrees to just five in the last decade, avenues to your customers are all around you.

- Access your network through Twitter, Facebook, and LinkedIn.
- Use alumni organizations.

- Cold call.
- Use the friends and family of your friends and family.
- Visit online communities.
- Visit offline meetups.
- Use Craigslist.
- Send out surveys.

Although we eschew airport business books and motivational speaking, there is credence to the clarion call "Just do it." To be an entrepreneur you have to be willing to do the things you don't want to do, to do the things that you don't feel you're good at, and to take personal risks that make you feel vulnerable. You must.

The way to get started is by creating tasks that are of a doable size. Looking at the success of big businesses may be inspirational, but the tactics we see them undertaking right now don't represent how they got big. All big businesses started out small—by definition. You must start small, too! You can find your thousandth customer only *after* your hundredth, which came *after* your tenth, which came *after* your first.

You don't need to draw up big strategic plans to find the first 10 customers that care about your product; you just have to go out in the big, bad world and find them.

So, what do they look like? If you don't know, take a stab at describing one. Close your eyes and imagine them. This is the process of creating assumptions—guesses, really—that give you something to measure against when you go out into the real world. Then, go out in the real world and find them, and talk to them.

If You Get Nothing Else from This Chapter

Like most things in life, there's no one right way to do segmentation. You cannot understand the solution to the problem of a particular segment, however, without diving deep. So some prefer to choose one segment at a time, dive deep, and then move on to the next if the first one fails. Others prefer to go less deep across multiple segments until one becomes the leading candidate.

Still others align resources across multiple segments, for example, a 70–20–10 split where 70 percent of your resources are committed to learning deeply about one segment, 20 on a second, and 10 percent as opportunistic. Your choice may depend on resources, if nothing else.

The point *isn't* to fill out tons of templates like those included under "Work to Do" at the end of this chapter. The point is to document your assumptions and begin validating (or invalidating) them.

The path toward success begins by nailing the delivery of value to a narrow, well-defined group of people who share a pain or passion and who would look to each other to recommend products or services that address that pain or passion.

This group of customers can be defined by a description of an archetype. The archetype may have multiple use cases, but one is more compelling than the others. The use case represents a goal the customer has, or a *desire*, or put another way, it represents a job for which the user needs to *hire* a product.

You hopefully will encounter multiple segments, and you will likely need to focus your energy on one segment in order to nail your value proposition. In time, if successful, you will tackle your other segments too.

Documenting your segment assumptions, even if backed by market research, does not prove your assumptions; rather, it helps you think them through and establish what needs to be tested. Only the market determines the validity of your assumptions. Documenting your assumptions gives you a baseline to measure against when you get out of the building.

Case Study:
It's in the Name

ßetabrand

Traditionally, the clothing industry is seasonal. Two to four times a year, large clothing companies release products to the world and maybe, eventually, they make their way online. It's an old-fashioned industry that moves at old-fashioned speed compared to the ways people interact with companies on the Internet.

That's not what founder Chris Lindland had in mind for Betabrand, however, an online clothing company. Not an online clothing catalog, mind you, but a clothing company. Chris explains:

"What I figured is that an online clothing company has to abide by the rules of blogs or Twitter, which people expect when interacting with companies online. The idea with Betabrand is we're going to try to put up products as rapidly as we can."

Like Eric Ries's continuous deployment, whereby IMVU deployed changes to their web application 50+ times per day, Betabrand's aim is to put out a new product every day. They produce only a small batch of a particular product, but enough to come to a decision point:

"If there's anything that we've learned from our customers," Chris says, "it's that with the first hundred to two hundred pair sold, we can make minor changes on it to improve it and retest, we can turn it into an entire line, or we can kill it."

While admitting that they don't sit down and profile their ideal customers, in the end, they target very distinct segments by finding existing online communities.

"What we do is we look more at products that would appeal to very vocal communities online and then allow those people to chatter about our products and drive traffic to it.

"For example, we make pants for biking to work in. These pants have reflective cuffs and a reflective pack in back that you can pull out that reflects while the person is riding along. There really was no market for 'biker fashion.'

"There was only practical biking attire that you could find at bike stores. There was no one out there that was selling clothing that fit the biker lifestyle. So I made these pants to appeal to the biker subculture. As it turns out, there's an enormous number of biking blogs and an enormous amount of people who tweet about anything new in the bike world. We created a product that had a shamefully loyal audience out there. I think what happens is there are these self-appointed bike bloggers of every community and they need content so they all wrote about my 'bike-to-work pants.'"

Sometimes it works, and sometimes it doesn't.

"One product that we failed with was a collection we created called Harvester. We had been very successful with two products promoting them to the foodie demographic—successful because they were like the bikers. You give them a funny fashion story and every single food blogger will write about it, like our Cornucopia Bag or these pants called Glutton Pants. I was convinced that this was too easy—you just need to make a line of clothing for foodies and they'll promote it for you. So we went out and tried to make the most crazily hyperorganic locally sourced and dyed products possible. We decided we were going to put them out according to the harvest calendar and get foodies to really care about this. The thing is they just didn't care at all. The products were overly expensive; they didn't really have that much of a hook. I thought that the idea that you could put on a garlic shirt that literally came to market the day that garlic came to market would actually be a cool thing and nobody really cared. So we sold through everything but it just didn't go any further than the initial batch."

So the question is, how do you create a culture that embraces such experimentation? Chris has the answer to that, too:

"I used to work for a dot-com and it happened to be located near a friend's newspaper and I would go meet her to get lunch and I was amazed by how boring my workplace was compared to a good old-fashioned newsroom. Everyone was saying that the dot-coms are these hot, exciting, sexy things but it was just a bunch of cubes and people had quiet meetings and it was really just a quiet environment.

"Then you'd go over to a newsroom and people would be swearing at each other and it was just kind of chaos all day long because there was a deadline and in most dot-coms there aren't deadlines. So I said, 'All right, well what we're going to do is we are going to have deadlines. We're going to have two releases a week and it's going to be these grand, creative performances whenever they go out.' The result of that has been it's a very exciting workplace because everyone from our engineers to our production people gets involved in these events each week. They are incredibly exciting because you have a hunch that a product will be popular and you get to find out within 24 hours whether you're right or not. That's what makes that environment work. We have pitch sessions every week. It's like a writer's room for a TV show where you're just pitching ideas and now and then you have hits. So everyone's always submitting ideas. It really is an idea factory."

One Final Analogy

As we've discussed, attracting the wrong customer at best causes confusion and at worst wreaks havoc. Early on in your startup, you have to choose whom to let in.

Pretend you are a bouncer. You're working at a nightclub in Manhattan that is having an exclusive party. You understand well the style of person you want to attend. You can recognize potential party guests based on how they talk, walk, groom, dress, and spend. You know what their explicit (and, more importantly, implicit!) expectations are of what makes a great party: what sort of music should be playing (Thievery Corporation), who is playing it (local DJ), and how loud the music should be (very). You know that they like certain types of high-end cocktails (lavender jalapeno elderflower fizzes) and how they don't drink domestic beers (you couldn't give away Budweiser if you tried).

You know that they intuitively dress to look good in your dark nightclub environs, which include furniture and lighting all in line with your patrons' unspoken expectations.

As a bouncer, you have a great responsibility. Not only do you need to admit the party guests who will have a great time in your club, but you need to keep people out—the sort of people who have different expectations of what makes for a good party: people whose musical, sartorial, and culinary tastes lie elsewhere.

Inherently, this is patronizing. You, as the bouncer, will be making decisions on behalf of potential patrons who may want to get into your club, but don't realize they aren't a good fit, hence will probably not enjoy themselves and probably won't spend money. These people like cheap domestic beers (Pabst Blue Ribbon), and complain loudly and bitingly at drinking $14 lavender jalapeno elderflower fizzes, ruining the vibe for everyone else. With their vociferous complaints, they occupy a disproportionate amount of your staff's time as they make suggestions for features (playing the hit song "1901" by Phoenix) that you, your staff, and your passionate customers will never agree to. To add insult to injury, they don't spend any money.

The problem isn't these people. The problem is that you let them in. The fit between them and your club is wrong. Hence, you need to be vigilant. They like to go to well-lit hipster clubs that play French alt-rock music so they can enjoy their retro-Americana beers like Pabst Blue Ribbon or Yuengling. They have a certain sense of ironic humor that isn't shared with your customers. It would be a waste of their time and money if you let them into your club.

In a club, the problem likely fixes itself quickly. The hipsters leave. Often in the startup world, however, entrepreneurs will be quick to be all things to all people, and in doing so, they are without a solid identity or value proposition.

Work to Do

1. Create a market segment. When thinking about your customers, don't start with "Everyone who" or "Anyone who." Answer these four questions:

   a. What is the pain or passion? Ask yourself, "Why do they have this problem?" to get deep. This should not be a shallow response.

   b. What impact will solving the problem or exciting the passion have on the customer? If the impact is small, you don't have a market; you must find a deeper pain. How does your product change the customer's life?

   c. Where do the customers hang out? If you wanted to find them online, where would you browse? Which forum? Which blogs? What Twitter hashtag? Where would you find them offline? What stores? What meetings? What events?

   d. Who influences them? Which blogger? What personality? A specific author or celebrity? A spouse or partner? Parents?

2. Create a persona for the ideal customer. Who would be the *most passionate* about your product? Provide as much detail as possible. If you were to go where they hang out, you should be able to recognize them when you see them. It's all right if the description is a stereotype or even a caricature at this stage. It doesn't matter if you're unsure. Take a stab.

3. Create several more segments and personas for different use cases.

4. Create an antisegment. One who appears at first glance to be an ideal customer but will never buy. Why won't they buy? How does that help refine your ideal customer?

5. Create a segment matrix. Choose the most important characteristics with which to evaluate the segments.

	Depth of Pain A	Budget B	Ease of Reach C	Ease of MVP D	Size of Market E	Values F
Segment 1						
Segment 2						
Segment 3						
Segment 4						

To get this template and others, e-mail fish@leanentrepreneur.co.

4

Wading in the Value Stream

Articulating the Value Stream

In lean manufacturing, an organization's value stream is comprised of all activities undertaken to provide value to the customer. Activities include everything from developing the concept of a product to its design, engineering, manufacturing, and delivery.

As we've discussed, the value stream in a lean enterprise includes both value-added activities (for example, assembling part of a car) and non-value-added activities (for example, forklifting parts across a warehouse floor). The objective of *lean* is to eliminate as many of the non-value-added processes as possible (some are necessary) and to optimize the efficiency of the value-added activities, while maintaining the established value to the customer.

The value being produced should never be adversely affected by process optimization, the elimination of activities, or other improvements. Destroying real value is more *wasteful* than eliminating inefficient time, money, or raw resources utilization. An organization may or may not be better off becoming more efficient through elimination of waste independent of its effect on value creation. The latter may be the goal in some organizations, but it isn't *lean*.

In the context of a lean startup, in which the production and delivery of value hasn't been proven, you don't truly *know* either the value being created or for whom it's being created. You may *think* you know. You may believe what's between your ears; you may have faith in your idea and your abilities, but until you've successfully conducted transactions whereby customers have paid some currency for the value you've produced, you don't actually *know*.

This is why we say that, no matter what your startup endeavor is, your job is to *discover* the value, for whom it's being created, and whether there's a large enough market to support the business you envision.

This is true in large organizations as well as startups. If you are working on known problems with known solutions, you are likely making incremental improvements to your products, some based on true innovation. This is fine and good and is necessary to compete against your known competition. It won't protect you against disruption, however. For that, you must foray into the unknown, into disruptive innovation.

If history teaches us anything, it's that for your startup to succeed, or your existing business to flourish, you must be willing to experiment and fail in search of the right combination of problem, product, and market that results in big success.

Fundamental changes will occur in your thinking between concept and delivery. Your early assumptions will likely be proven wrong. This is true of all types of businesses that face uncertainty. There's nothing wrong with that—embrace it. Go ahead; we'll wait.

Case Study: Seeing from Customer's View

When Sight Machine founder Nathan Oostendorp set out to disrupt the $2 billion machine-vision industry, he assumed his solution would require a massive amount of hardware: cameras, mounts, brackets, and black-box appliances. Machine vision is a quality-control process whereby camera sensor equipment is deployed across a factory floor and image analysis is used to ensure that automated manufacturing lines are producing high-quality parts or product.

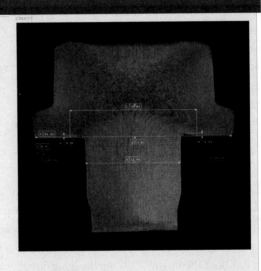

The existing practice typically required custom solutions for each customer and required massive amounts of professional services. Nathan's vision was to create a platform that customers could "order like they were purchasing a Dell computer. We provide you all the pieces and then we put them together to do very specific things." The value proposition was to dramatically lower the total cost of ownership of deploying and maintaining a machine-vision system, through lowering the costs of hardware, integration, and customization. The system could be installed "by anyone with an Allen wrench."

The trade-off would be flexibility. Once installed, the setup is difficult to modify. Sight Machine's choice to pursue this model was driven by the pain of the current high-price model and the assumption that customers didn't really want to have anything to do with the system itself. In Nathan's words, "We thought people didn't want to have to deal with the technology and so we were developing appliances that would process images into data, compare the data to given parameters, and then do something with the data, like trigger a light or send an alert."

As they were developing the platform, Sight Machine conducted pilot programs with early customers. But because the product was not ready for primetime, it required a lot of manual installation. It was this customer interaction that changed their perspective on what customers really needed.

"So when we actually started interacting customers with the technology we found that they were actually curious about the technology. We had to bring the operation of it even closer to them." In other words, flexibility was as much the driving factor as lowering the total cost of ownership. Customers wanted to be able to move the cameras and mount them in challenging environments, as well as create their own tests in the software. In other words, they wanted the flexibility of the high-cost, services-based model—but they wanted to be able to implement, manage, and customize the system themselves.

"Today, our goal is to show up in a van—like the Geek Squad—with a bunch of hardware in the back and mount a camera and have vision systems set up on the first visit. Unlike the way it works right now where you maybe have a four- to six-week lead time for all of your equipment; we really make it so that anyone can get something up and running very fast."

Value Assumed Before Deep Customer Interaction

- Low total cost of ownerships (TCO)
- Turnkey
- Customer doesn't need to touch system

Value Validated After Deep Customer Interaction

- Zero capex (hardware rolled into subscription)
- Software-as-a-service (SaaS) (no black box to maintain)
- Customization by customer required

We recognize this is not a traditional way to conduct business. Although many successful entrepreneurs implicitly understand that many of their ideas about their businesses are guesses and go about their own way of testing these, the Myth of the Visionary is the predominant startup meme.

When businesses cost a lot of money to get started, investors from bank officers to venture capitalists want to know as precisely as possible what the return on their investment will be and when they will see it. The opportunity cost of the investment was high. The business plan was an assurance document, despite its fictional quality.

Big businesses look for the same assurance. Despite their best intentions of encouraging disruptive innovation, the very nature of asking, "What's the ROI and when will I see it?" lures disruptive ideas toward sustained, modest innovation. To predict the market, you have to be in a known market. To disrupt, you must create new markets.

Reducing the cost of startup endeavors means a lower opportunity cost and the ability to fund experiments. It's actually rather ironic that we are willing to fund scientists to conduct research in new technology, whether in robotics, chemicals, materials, and so on, but the moment we wish to commercialize said technology, we abandon the scientific method.

In other words, it's perfectly okay to test, fail, iterate when developing a technology, but to test, fail, iterate to find a marketable application of the technology seems ridiculous to many.

Of course the technology is marketable; it's groundbreaking!

The result of scientific research is tangible, or at least factual. You put in money, you eventually get out a result. This works or it doesn't.

The entrepreneur who says, "Eh, this may work or maybe not," is not giving a very compelling pitch. It's not very comforting, but there's truth therein. As a matter of fact, based on the numbers, the entrepreneur would be the most truthful if he said, "We'll give it a go, but it most likely won't work."

If you were to look at the value stream of a lean manufacturer, you would, from a high level, understand the steps involved in producing and delivering value. If someone were to outline the plan from delivery of raw materials to its flow through the manufacturing process and on to the delivery of goods to a customer, you would likely be able to identify value-added activities and non-value-added activities without a lot of knowledge of the particular product.

But what about analyzing the value stream when value is not known? If our goal in a lean startup is to eliminate waste in the discovery of value, how do we know what's wasteful? The fact is you can't eliminate all waste if you don't understand the value you're creating. The process of discovery itself will include waste. If you build a prototype that flops, you arguably wasted your time building that particular prototype, but it's at least less wasteful than building the entire product before it flops!

This is why Eric Ries incorporates a different measure for lean startup. In lean manufacturing, you're wasting time, money, materials, and labor when creating unused excess or when performing non-value-added activities. In a lean startup, you're wasting if you're not learning. "The effort that is not absolutely necessary for learning what customers want can be eliminated." Validated learning is demonstrated by positive improvements in the startup's core metrics.[1]

Note that core metrics do not automatically mean revenue and, as a matter of fact, early on, they most assuredly don't. Core metrics initially relate back to the phrase *what customers want*, which, by the way, doesn't mean customers *know* what they want. We can hear you say that you can raise $10 million and build a product no one wants and learn a ton, too!

That's true. Which is why *lean* takes no stance on how much money you should raise. Arguably, one could learn a lot quicker with more money. In practice, however, we often see that (1) more money leads to more waste simply from a lack of discipline; and (2) more money often motivates investors to want more sooner (What's my ROI and when do I see it?) just as it does in a large organization. You've perhaps heard that nine moms can't make a baby in a month.

Your objective is to learn, but not all learning is created equal; quality trumps quantity. Your objective is to learn what is fundamental to your business success with the minimal amount of effort. Learn as if you believe you will fail. A prototype that fails helps point you in a better direction. A $10 million investment in product development and launch is one big failed experiment that leaves no room to pivot or learning to pivot around.

It's easy to understand big waste:

- Spending a year building a product no one wants.
- Spending six months looking for investors to fund a year's worth of development on a product no one wants.
- Writing a business plan for four months to convince an investor to fund a year's worth of development on a product no one wants.

Small waste is much more insidious, flailing through business-model ideas without direction:

- Opportunistic and shotgun sales.
- Product feature mongering.
- Great marketing for a crappy product.

So the question remains: How can you develop your lean startup value stream, which is measurable by validated learning?

In any successful business, a certain number of customers go through a series of steps to become aware of your product, experience it, become satisfied with it, and then finally feel a high level of loyalty to the experience. Through the process of customer acquisition and conversion, and then delivering on the product's fundamental promise, the successful business *learns* what problem it should be solving and what products and services it must provide, plus particular activities in marketing, selling, product development, support services, and so on, it needs to employ, in order to let the user most efficiently *flow* through the experience from beginning to end.

The process can always be improved. The sales process might be made more efficient so that it maps closer to customer expectations. Marketing can be expanded to automate part of sales and be more inclusive to adjacent segments. Engineering might reduce non-value-added steps in the creation of features and reduce "feature inventory." Manufacturers might adopt lean manufacturing! As long as value is maintained, these are *lean* practices, and continuous improvement is a core lean ethos.

Because we don't know what the value stream is in a lean startup, however, we're not so concerned with improvement but rather with learning and validating what the *internal business* processes are in the creation and delivery of value, such that the business is successful and growing.

Traditionally, the 50,000-foot view of a startup value stream might look like this:

Business Planning → Investment → Product Development → Marketing → Sales → Feedback

As we've seen, however, this has also resulted in a lot of failed startups and a lot of waste.

As the costs of building products has plummeted such that most entrepreneurs require little to no capital to get started, the value stream has not been rethought, but rather been shortened.

Product Development → Marketing → Sales → Feedback → Investment to Grow

In terms of sheer volume, it's not surprising that the number of startups failing has increased. It wouldn't surprise us if with a lack of real planning, the *rate* of failure had also increased.

Whether the product should be built is not seen as a question even worth asking. If it is asked, it is answered through persuasion born of charm and personality rather than through any factual element.

Can lean help us?

Through its evolution, lean has remained primarily an engineering endeavor. Design is sometimes included and internal representatives of the customer, such as product managers, are often added to the process, but in practice, direct customer interaction is poorly represented in the lean process. Data collected by the business is often tied back to efficiencies of business units, quality of code delivered by IT, customer satisfaction as measured by marketing, but there's little to connect product and product developers to customer satisfaction and product loyalty.

The Toyota Production System includes stories about engineers and design leads interacting with customers firsthand, in order to learn what to build. We know that Toyota salespeople sold cars door-to-door and considered this part of being *lean*. One hears of efforts to develop lean sales and lean marketing processes, but few lean organizations are truly completing the lifecycle of a customer's relationship with a business in one lean flow.

As long as everyone is being lean inside vertical silos, rather than as a horizontal team creating value, startups will fail and big companies will only be capable of sustaining innovation.

Unlike many engineering- or design-led lean processes, we include marketing and sales in the value stream. Many feel that marketing and sales are inherently evil and are non-value-added activities. In a perfect world, one would not need them.

Such people tend to believe that if you build the best product, the market will eventually find you. It's often referred to as the build-it-and-they-will-come philosophy.

We empathize. Your product *is* your best marketing. All marketing depends on word-of-mouth, so if people have good things to say about your product, you are a step ahead.

An inverted corollary is "Nothing kills a bad product quicker than good marketing." The bottom line is that if people have no path to your product or service, then you will not be able to provide value to these people. They won't become your customer. Assuming that you truly wish to provide value, the importance of letting potential customers become aware of the value shouldn't be diminished. The process of converting customers should be built around what the buyer wants the process to be. This is critical to delivering value and creating passion in the product.

The fundamental difference between marketing and selling products that deliver value and marketing and selling products to make a dollar is that the former is part of creating a lasting business based on repeat customers, long-term retention, and referrals. The latter (generally) is about maximizing revenue through as many one-off transactions as possible. The ambition isn't to maximize customer satisfaction that generates word-of-mouth marketing, but rather to simply maximize money coming in, while minimizing money going out. When the product has run its course, those businesses launch another product under a different brand.

"Now the only way to grow is to stand out, to create something worth talking about, to treat people with respect and to have them spread the word."[2]

—*Seth Godin*

What we are talking about is building businesses based on providing such extraordinary value that customers are willing to pay something valuable to them: money, time, a significant amount of attention. As Seth Godin points out, this isn't accomplished by a race to the bottom, but rather a race to the top. In other words,

doing what others are doing at a lower cost isn't where the value play is. You must provide something meaningful, something more.

This isn't always true, however. A "value surplus" can be created where increased competition lowers cost without destroying value. Customers that couldn't afford the value before, now can. This is clearly good for the consumer. It mustn't mean lower quality or lower value, but rather getting more for less. This is the natural result of true free market capitalism (the Adam Smith version, not the libertarian version).

New product → Company strives for monopoly → Competition enters market → Customer gets more for less

Businesses naturally strive to achieve or maintain a monopoly. In free markets, this is accomplished by relentlessly adding value. More value comes in many different flavors—higher quality, more features, support for social causes, environmental initiatives, better packaging, and so on. What Steven Spear calls the "high velocity" company is one that maintains its market lead by relentlessly leveraging some core competency. We call this the "shadow force," because this capability isn't necessarily visible to outsiders.

Eventually, you want to discover your value stream that encompasses everything from when someone first discovers your product through the end of the customer lifecycle. So what marks the end of the lifecycle? Many might say, "Duh, when the customer pays you." Not so fast! The customer lifecycle is a loop. It isn't complete until they contribute to the top of your acquisition funnel. They do this in two ways and both are important.

First, they continue as loyal customers:

- Resubscribe.
- Become regulars.
- Sign long-term contracts.
- Buy other products and upgrades from you.

> "People's desires always have a way of emerging after their needs are satisfied. When a person needs something, she will do what is needed to get it, but when she desires something, she is loyal to it. She knows that it is a discretionary purchase, and she will buy what makes her happy and will not necessarily judge rationally. When a consumer desires a product or a brand, his loyalty is one of the strongest forces in business."[3]
>
> —Alan Cooper

Second, they become product champions:

- Invite friends.
- Agree to a press release or case study.
- Provide a testimonial.
- Agree to act as a personal reference.
- Show off product to others.

There's a point we want to capture that goes beyond when a customer feels satisfied simply because your product delivered on its promise.

So what might a value stream look like that maps activities to learning, includes marketing and sales, as well as answers the question, "Should we build the product at all?"

Value-Stream Discovery

From the 50,000-foot view, your value stream might look something like:

Validate idea → Validate product → Validate marketing and sales → Validate growth engine

Planning and customer feedback are worked into each step. (Investment can be as well.)

Drilling down into a generic product, validating the idea typically involves testing three components: the problem you're trying to solve, the customer segment that has the problem, and the proposed solution.

Validating the product means figuring out the specific product functionality required to minimally solve the problem.

Validating marketing and sales indicates that you know what channels to reach out to in order to find the target customers and what's required to convert them into satisfied customers.

Validating the growth engine is determining how you convert satisfied customers into passionate customers, at a cost that will allow the business to scale.

Let's look at a normal user acquisition and conversion funnel. We might use Dave McClure's Pirate Metrics[4] as an example for web-based businesses:

Acquisition—How users get to your website, such as Google AdWords or Facebook ads.

Activation—Customers sign up and try the product.

Retention—Customers are satisfied with the product, so they come back and use the product regularly.

Revenue—You're paid by advertisers based on the quantity of users or customers who pay for the product.

Referral—Customers are passionate about your product such that they put new people in the top of the funnel through word-of-mouth or even by "showing-off."

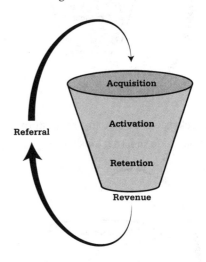

All businesses have such a funnel. A B2B funnel typically uses different labels, but it amounts to the same thing.

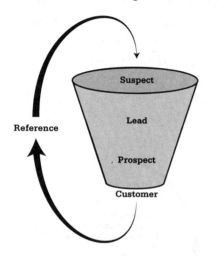

A packaged good sold in a retail store might have a funnel that looks like:

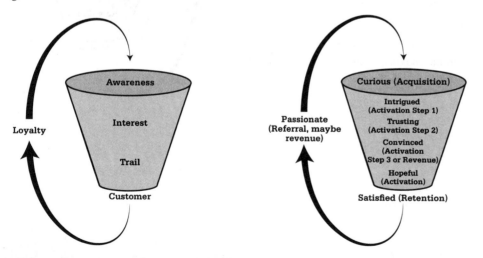

This might be a valuable way to understand how your customer moves from "aware" to "repeat buyer." You can visualize that the number of people who go through the funnel decreases from stage to stage. It's easy to imagine the activities you might perform to get them to move to the next stage. So the funnel is a valuable part of the stream, but it's not enough.

First, though the funnel purports to describe the state of the customer, it's really seen from the seller's point of view. A funnel from the customer's point of view is better described using emotional states. So, McClure's AAARR funnel might look like this:

We've drilled into the funnel to expose both the customer conversion process and the customer's product experience. Each step is indicated by the emotional state of the customer. You can rightfully quibble with the words, but this method can be a powerful way to empathize with the customer and to avoid the trap of thinking about the process you would like to implement versus the one the customer wants to experience.

To summarize:

- When customers first become *aware* of your product via advertising, social media, or from a friend, they will seek to learn more if they are *intrigued* (acquisition).

- If upon learning more, they like what they hear, they become *trusting*. They have started the path down the funnel toward activation.

- Once they have been *convinced* that the product and company are right, perhaps through references, they buy the product (revenue).

- After buying, they are *hopeful* that they have purchased the right product. They next try to realize the value proposition promised to them (activation).

- Only after using the product for some period of time do they become *satisfied*.

The value proposition has been realized and they are likely to continue to use the product (*retention*).

- Customers who are merely satisfied don't *refer* products. *Passionate* users do.

Note that for business models in which scale must be achieved before revenue is realized, revenue is not realized until after user retention, whereas in most other businesses, revenue is achieved prior to retention and, many times, prior to activation. To illustrate, Facebook doesn't charge customers to use the product. As some like to say, the customer (the user) *is* the product. Facebook had to nail the product to such a degree that people were willing to invite all their friends *and* a large enough percentage of those friends had to convert and be engaged enough to invite their friends. This is known as the viral coefficient. Viral coefficients greater than 1.0 result in exponential growth. Revenue is realized only after scale has been achieved.

In business models where there is a free component (often known as freemium) and revenue is achieved by up-selling to premium accounts, we treat the free component as a component of acquisition. Revenue happens when customers are convinced that the paid component is worth paying for.

It's worth reiterating here that free does not equal freemium. Free means there is no paid component for the product's use. Revenue is not made directly from users, but via other means, such as selling user data to third parties, selling advertising, or, in Facebook's example, taking a cut of revenue from for-pay applications that run on top of Facebook.

It's also worth noting that freemium is not really a business model. The business model is based on selling premium features beyond the free level. Free is a hook to get users to try the product, perhaps become dependent on it and pay for additional usage, or it's simply a marketing activity. Entrepreneurs should be careful about over-complicating their value proposition. As we have told more than one entrepreneur, if you sell hats and have identified a market that wishes to pay for hats, there's no sense in giving them a visor first and then upgrading them to a hat later.

Sell them a $&*@&! hat!

On the other hand, you may be able to disrupt an existing market by offering a free product in an otherwise for-pay business. Your revenue comes from consistently identifying and delivering value on top of the free version. Keep in mind that you can't disrupt a for-pay model with free if free already exists!

Back to our funnel. For each step, you wish the customer to move on to the next step. You want them to take a specific action. As a business, you must do something or have something that leads the customer to take that action. That it is easy to imagine a whole laundry list of activities a business might deploy for each stage, or product features it might build to deliver some value, makes discovery difficult. What's optimal? We want to be able to posit one best-case scenario and work to validate that scenario, hoping it will instruct us on how to capture the market.

Customer State

To develop one scenario for an entire value stream, we've found it helpful to begin at the end and work backward. In other words, we flip the funnel. It's actually a flipped value stream. We start with, "Why is your customer passionate?" and work backward:

- Passionate—your customer loves your business; your customer is loyal. Passion comes from something more than that the product met expectations.
- Satisfied—your customer's expectations have been *minimally* met. *Minimally* is not imbued with negativity. This is a positive thing; your product does what you've promised.

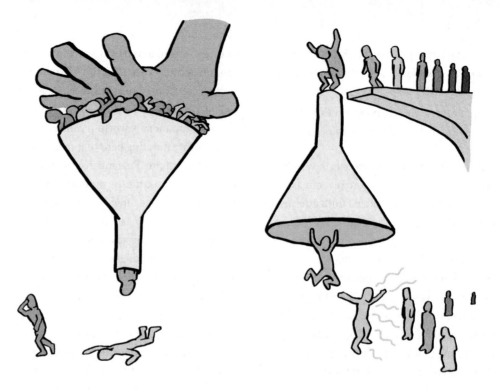

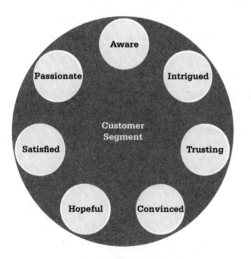

- Hopeful—your customer first *experiences the product* in order to realize the promise you've made. They are hopeful that their needs will be met, that they hired the proper product to complete the job.
- Convinced—your customer has become convinced your product is the right fit for the problem they're trying to resolve. The reasoning can be both rational and irrational and include reasons beyond the product itself.

- Trusting—your customer believes not only in the likelihood that the product will do the job, but also that the company is worthy of a relationship.
- Intrigued—your customer is intrigued when early investigation indicates the product will solve a problem important to them.
- Aware—your customer first realizes your product exists and purports to address a concern of theirs.

For some products the lines between convinced, hopeful, and satisfied are blurry, if not arbitrary. The goal is to measure the changes between customer states. If you have fewer states, then you have less to measure. Other products will have more states. If you're selling B2B, you could create a whole decision-making tree that includes all the champions, opponents, and deciders and the internal processes they go through to purchase a product. As a matter of fact, if you're selling to businesses you should create such a tree.

Customer Action

Next, we want to ask ourselves, what specifically is the customer doing that indicates the state they are in? We follow this working-backward process *all the way back* to the point when they first heard of you.

Emotional State of Customer	Customer Action (example)
Customers love your product and your company (*passionate*).	They continue their subscriptions and tell their friends about you.
Only after using the product for some time do customers become *satisfied*. The value proposition has been realized and they are likely to continue to use the product.	Log in daily, run report, view dashboard, create something. (What is the *specific* interaction with your product, and what is the frequency with which that happens that indicates satisfied engagement?)
Customers are *hopeful* that they have purchased the right product. They next try to realize the value proposition promised to them.	Log in, create something, upload something, configure something, view something. (What is the specific minimal interaction with your product that customers must do to try and realize the value proposition for the first time?)
Once customers have been *convinced* that the product is a good fit and company is capable, they buy the product, resulting in revenue.	They buy.
Customers *trust* that the product is a good fit and the company providing the product is worthy of their business.	They sign up for the product trial.
If upon learning more, customers like what they hear, they become *intrigued*. They have started the path down the activation part of the funnel.	They read more about product benefits on your website and in testimonials.
Customers first become *aware* of your product via advertising, via social media, or from friends.	To learn more, they visit your website landing page and watch a video.

Obviously, these are examples from a hypothetical software-as-a-service application. You must create your own set of hypotheses for your product.

Business Action

This value-stream discovery technique can be used with any business, with some tweaking for different products and services. As you flesh out the scenario, it becomes apparent that the business needs to *do something* or *provide something* for the scenario to work.

Customer State	Customer Action (example)	Company must do something like . . .
Passionate	Subscribes. Refers.	Something beyond basic product that delivers promise. • User experience? • Customer service? • Support cause? • Elegant product?
Satisfied	Uses product in specific way over specific time period.	Build minimum specific functionality that delivers on value proposition. • Feature *x* • Feature *y* • Feature *z*
Hopeful	Tries product in specific way.	Overcome blank slate? Drip campaign? Follow-up phone call?
Convinced	Buys.	Ability to purchase. Call to action.
Trusting	Demos product.	Provide trial. Get testimonials. Provide tutorial.
Intrigued	Reads landing page, watches video.	Provide website messaging and positioning; create video.
Aware	Reads third-party blog post; visits company website.	Reach out to third-party blogger who is a customer influencer.

What would your customers say about you? Let's look at the different possibilities companies might employ to affect the customer at each state, by imagining what the customer might think or say when feeling a certain way.

They're Passionate

- "The product is so easy, so beautiful; it makes me *want* to use it."
- "The product does what I want it to, and then so much more."
- "This game is addictive!"
- "I have to get to the top of the jackpot!"
- "When I called customer support, the CEO answered!"
- "They took the shoes back, no questions asked. Even paid for return shipping."
- "My replacement arrived *before* I shipped the defective one back."
- "For every pair of glasses I buy, they provide a free pair to someone in need."
- "The package is so cool!"
- "Their new packaging makes pouring so much easier."
- "I've improved my bottom line, month after month."
- "I don't know, the product just makes me feel good."

- "It found problems I didn't know I had. Now I'm a hero at work."
- "Not only do the jeans fit me, but the looks I get . . ."
- "The waitstaff went above and beyond the call of duty."

They're Satisfied

- "The food was delicious."
- "I was actually able to find jeans that fit me."
- "I am able to create and share new surveys in under 10 minutes."
- "The intrusion-detection system immediately and consistently reports accurate anomalies on my network."
- "The shoes fit and look good, too."
- "After I configured the system, I am finally able to track my marketing campaigns."
- "This game is fun!"
- "Using this product has helped me generate more leads."

They're Hopeful

- "I hope I chose the right product to solve my issue. Let's give it a try."
- "I hope this thing works as advertised."
- "It's rated as at the top of its class, let's see."

- "I've heard the prime rib is top-notch, I can't wait to taste it."
- "I hope implementation goes smoothly; this wizard looks helpful."
- "I'm nervous I won't know how to work it."
- "I wonder what I should do first."
- "It *says* no assembly required."
- "Wonder if it comes with batteries."

They're Convinced

- "Wow, Oprah recommends it."
- "Demo seemed to do what I needed done."
- "Worth a shot."
- "After 30 days, trial seems to be paying off."
- "Sample tasted good!"
- "Well, not too expensive."

They're Trusting

- "Feels like they're talking to me."
- "I respect the testimonials they have on their website."
- "Data analyst gave them a thumbs up."
- "Online customer reviews are positive."
- "Huh! Four out of five doctors recommend it."

- "Trade mag review was enthusiastic."
- "Not much to lose, satisfaction is guaranteed."
- "At least I can return it, plus free return shipping."
- "Looks like it's approved by the Better Business Bureau."
- "Case study example matches us perfectly!"
- "Friend said it was cool."
- "4 out of 5 stars!"

They're Intrigued

- "Cash back sounds good."
- "Sounds cool."
- "Whoa, this demo rocks."
- "Nice data sheet."

- "That's a clever video."
- "Sounds exactly like what I need."
- "Yep, that's my problem."
- "Who woulda thought, better, faster, AND cheaper."

They're Aware

- "Wow, those trade show boot babes were hot."
- "Sales guy was kind of pushy, but the product sounded pretty good."
- "Did you hear about that product thingy?"
- "Wonder if it's for real."
- "Yeah, we should check that out."
- "Huh, what's this?"
- "Cool packaging."

Measure

What is particularly helpful in the software world is that one can measure the customer's progress through the various stages. In today's software-eating-the-world environment, most businesses can figure out ways to measure much of their value-stream activity, too. Getting customers to interact with you online is key. You are only limited by your creativity.

Of course, you are encouraged to observe your customers and even speak to them, which are a couple of tactics available to everyone.

Your customer will do *something* that indicates they've moved a step through the funnel. In other words, you want to *measure the customer's state*. Sometimes this can be done with simple analytics tools. In other instances, you must be much more clever.

Customer State	Customer Action (example)	Company must ...	Posit Baseline/Measure
Passionate	Subscribes. Refers.	Something beyond basic product that delivers promise. • User experience? • Customer service? • Support of a cause? • Elegant product?	How disappointed would you be if product were no longer available? (MustHaveScore) Net Promoter Score Friend invites Agreement to act as reference
Satisfied	Uses product in specific way over specific time period.	Build minimum specific functionality that delivers on value proposition. • Feature x • Feature y • Feature z	"Customer will log in daily; view feature x, upload y, and share z once a week." Instrument product to measure.
Hopeful	Tries product in specific way.	Overcome blank slate? Drip campaign? Follow-up phone call?	"Customer needs to do x to get started, y to finish task." Instrument product to measure x, y.
Convinced	Buys.	Ability to purchase. Call to action.	Revenue
Trusting	Demos product.	Provide testimonials.	Demo sign-ups
Intrigued	Reads landing page, watches video.	Create positioning, create video.	Video views
Aware	First learns of product.	Reach out to third-party bloggers.	Website unique visitors by referral

Going through this process documents the business model assumptions you need to test first.

The value-stream stages can be divided into these categories:

• Growth engine
• Minimum viable product
• Conversion
• Funnel
• Acquisition channel

For each, you have assumptions concerning specific customer behavior and business activities required to induce the behavior. You have also thought about ways to measure progress.

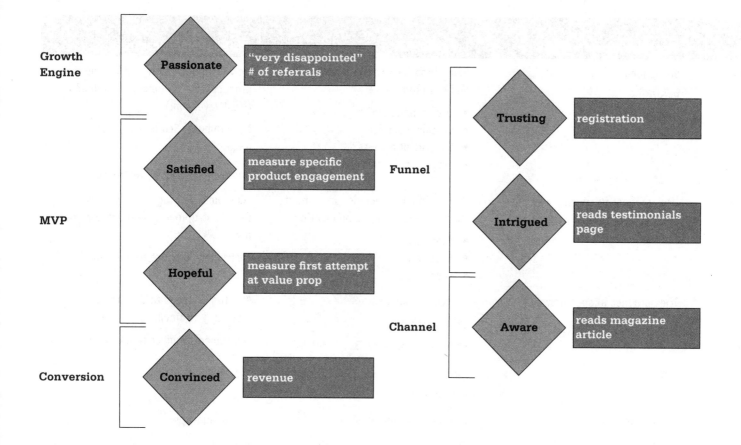

Growth Engine

What your customer does when passionate or loyal is the primer for your growth engine. For network effects businesses, passionate customers invite all their friends, colleagues, or whoever needs to participate to make the experience more valuable. A transaction business (both online and offline) relies primarily on some combination of case studies, testimonials, or referrals from existing happy customers; ongoing periodic transactions; and, sometimes, regular maintenance, support, or other services fees. Subscription models need referrals plus maintenance of subscription, in other words, low churn.

Minimum Viable Product

The MVP is your proposal for the minimum specific functionality required to provide the value proposition. The value proposition is the value you are hoping to deliver to a specific customer segment. The customer uses your product in a specific way in order to address a specific pain or passion. You want to nail the specific, not the general. At this stage, you aren't concerned with how many people download your product or like you on Facebook. Rather, you must figure out what *specifically* your customers do with your product to complete the *job* your customer hired your product for. There may be more (or less) to the solution, but there are two things you should keep in mind:

1. Overbuilding makes it more difficult to understand what is the must-have part of your product. You're not *done* building after the MVP. This is simply the first iteration.

2. Imagine the product from the outside in: Working backward from solving the problem makes you solution agnostic and architecture independent.

Conversion

How will you cross the penny gap? Getting customers to take out their credit cards is more difficult than it seems, no matter what the price. The act of paying money for anything is rarely a purely rational exercise. The steps of conversion happen between "I want to buy" and "I bought." What needs to happen in between? Proper pricing? Trust? Ease of process? Approvals?

Funnel

All sales have a funnel comprised of several actions taken by the customer correlated to several activities undertaken by the business. We use the word *activities* in a very broad sense, from packaging and obtaining retail shelf space to providing elements of trust, such as testimonials or secure shopping cart badges on a website.

Acquisition Channel

The acquisition channel is how you first reach your customers. The methods you use are dependent on the behavior of the market segment. This is what the "Where do they hang out?" question addresses. Eventually, this is how you scale. Once you've nailed the value proposition such that you become your own acquisition channel, you're ready to discover and validate and grow other channels, as long as the lifetime value of a customer is greater than the cost of acquiring them.

At this point it's not necessary to document all possible steps for a particular segment; we want to start by articulating one funnel and one acquisition tactic you think is promising.

Case Study:
AppFog's High Hurdle

Lucas Carlson is the CEO and founder of AppFog, based in Portland, Oregon. AppFog is a platform as a service that allows web and mobile application developers to deploy, scale, and run their applications in the cloud as easily as installing an iPhone app. The number of deployed applications on AppFog grew from 600 at the beginning of 2011 to 25,000 at the end of 2011. They recently raised $10 million.

Lean Entrepreneur: What caught my attention about you, Lucas, is when I heard that you started AppFog with just a landing page and it blew up pretty quickly. I'd love you to share your experiences.

Lucas Carlson: Yes, absolutely. As a quick background, I've been developing software since 1996.

I've been in the startup world for a long time, and I've always loved startups and I've always wanted to do my own startup. I always had plenty of ideas. I've often tried to do these little ideas, and my experience led me to realize two things that helped me when I started PHP Fog.

First, one of the biggest faults with my side projects was I didn't know how to get in front of the people that would use them or end up using them. So I dabbled in WordPress plugins, but I had no idea how to talk to people that used WordPress plugins or get in front of them.

Second, I viewed them as revenue streams that could augment my income, but not as businesses, so I would lose interest at a point because, to me, they were means to an end.

LE: So the passion really wasn't there about the products. We could call this founder-market misfit.

Carlson: Right, so I had been watching Heroku for a long time and I thought it was really cool. I started to move all of my side projects into Heroku. The problem was one night I realized I had a whole bunch of PHP projects that I couldn't move to Heroku because they don't support PHP. [PHP is a software development language developers use to create products.] I wasn't the first person to come up with this idea. I had heard people talk about PHP Heroku, and PHP's a much bigger market than Ruby has ever been. [Out of the top million websites, a third of them are PHP and only 5,000 of them are Ruby, a rival software development language.]

It was probably around 10 o'clock one night, and that's usually primetime for me to have an idea and start building it. I've always been a night owl and nighttime is when I do my side projects. That night I felt lazy. I was too tired to go out and start prototyping this platform as a service and start building it, so I decided to throw up a landing page [a one-page website with a specific call to action], and I was still too tired to even program a back end, so I used one of the mailing services to collect e-mails for me. And I came up with the name PHP Fog. I registered the domain name. I put up the landing page, it was one page, and put one paragraph of text and put a link on Hacker News and fell asleep. The next morning I woke up and there were 800 people signed up for the service.

LE: What was that like when you woke up and you saw 800 people had signed up?

Carlson: It was a thrill; it was a rush. It was amazing because this was kind of the missing piece compared to my past projects. I had spent a decade trying to do startups and this was the missing piece that I never had seen before, how do you find people that want to use your thing? This was an idea that the people were ripe for the picking and they were right there and I knew how to get them because *they were me*. They were people exactly like me, trying to do things exactly like me.

LE: You know how they think. You know where they hang out, right? Clearly Hacker News is where developers, especially startup developers, hang out, right?

Carlson: I was hoping that I'd get a few comments in the Hacker News thread that would help guide me, and I got way more than a few comments. There was a huge discussion. This was clearly something that a lot of people were interested in and wanted.

LE: What was your next step after that?

Carlson: That night I said to myself, "Okay, I've got to build it now. I have 800 people." . . . I called it a private beta, so I hadn't written any code, but 800 people were expecting to be let into the beta, so that put a fire under me. That night I started building. I started building it the way that I traditionally built ideas and side projects. I thought about the coolest technology I could and started prototyping that technology and building an ivory tower. A week later, I had been working on it hours every night, pouring into the morning, and by the end of the week I was not even close to having something that was ready.

LE: You got excited and you thought, "I have 800 people waiting for me. I feel a responsibility to the community."

Carlson: Yes. I was working on it and by the end of the week I thought, "I'm not going to get anywhere this way." So I trashed all the work that I had built for the entire week and I started again from scratch. This time I said to myself, "I need something that people can at least start looking at." So I built the front end first.

LE: What happened there? What happened between you going from "Okay, I'm going to build the 'bullet-proof ivory tower'" to "Okay, I just need to get something out to my people"?

Carlson: Well, I knew that it would be months before it would be ready if I kept it at that pace. Then I would definitely be letting these people down. I decided to build the front end first and let that guide all decisions. The first thing I built was the user experience I would want to see as a customer, the minimum interaction to get started with the product. I started with the most plain static HTML you could have.

I am terrible at design, so I didn't even bother trying. I just put the basics in place.

Step 1: Pick your framework, Step 2: Give us a domain name, Step 3: There is no step 3—you should have a running application now! Then I started making those things actually work.

I have always believed in the power of great design and simple experiences. I feel like if you don't capture someone's imagination in the first 60 seconds, you have lost the game. Design projects confidence, and especially with young ideas, those early users need to have as much confidence in it as possible in order to turn into your advocates. So, I hired a designer for a few thousand dollars to make it look as good as possible.

By the time I had this ready, about four weeks had passed and I was ready to start letting people in. I now had around 4,000 people signed up on the waiting list. I knew I couldn't bring 4,000 people into the platform, but I knew that I needed to keep engaged with these people, that I had a contract with them.

I'm not sure if this was the motivation, but one of the things is that ever since that first day, with the 800 sign-ups overnight, I've just been totally addicted to traction. Traction is the blood flow of a startup, and you want to collect as much you can, as quickly as you can.

We had 4,000 people; there was no way I was ever going to invite 4,000 people in at this stage. It was a side project I was working on at night and it wasn't fully baked, but I needed to keep them engaged and I needed traction.

One of the things I thought of was a VIP thing. None of these ideas I came up with; I stole everything. I stole all the ideas; I just watched what other people did and thought about how I could apply [their ideas] to what I was doing, but the idea was to create a VIP waiting list. So what I did was send an e-mail to the 4,000 people with a link to a survey and I said, "You can get into our private beta a lot faster if you fill out this survey."

What I intended to do with the survey was make a survey that I thought would take a significant chunk of time to fill out, one that would not be easy, one that had many open-ended questions, like: Why did you sign up for PHP Fog? What did you expect from us? What's your major pain point?

LE: So you purposefully created a burdensome survey to try to weed out the passersby from the early adopters.

Carlson: Yes. So I expected a few dozen people to spend the time to tell me what they were wanting. I thought, I can handle a few dozen people. So I sent the e-mail to 4,000 people and what happened was I ended up with about 2,000 responses.

LE: Wow, 50 percent!

Carlson: That was like striking gold. The first bit of traction with the 800 sign-ups overnight was a great indication, but this was the real gold that the whole company was built on. This was the stuff that has directed the product ever since.

LE: These were not early adopters in the sense that they are tech geeks who like to hang out at Apple for the latest iPhone. These people were early adopters in what I think is a very meaningful distinction: They were early adopters for your specific product.

Carlson: Yes, and I did not expect that half of the people who signed up were those early adopters and [that they] would be so willing to open their time and their energy to tell me about their problem and their pain, which just totally reinforced how painful this was and how big of a problem I was about to tackle because, literally, these people would put paragraphs of text. They had all been thinking about this for so long and nothing on the market was there to address that pain.

LE: Was it just you digesting all this information, with 2,000 responses and open-ended text responses? Seems like this is an amazing amount of data. How did you get through that?

Carlson: I read every single one of them myself. One of my early team members analyzed all the words and found which ones came up most often. That surprised me a lot because we had some expectations about what was going to be the most interesting; Was it going to be scaling, or ease of use, or reliability? We had our ideas about what people wanted, and out of these 2,000 responses of paragraphs, looking at the frequency of words, it became very clear what their expectations were and the priority of them became very clear, too. It was astounding, what they wanted most was not what I expected at all. Just by analyzing the text we found that what I personally thought was going to be most important ended up to be the least important.

LE: And the result?

Carlson: At the beginning of 2011, I think we had around 600 applications deployed on our system. By the end of 2011, I believe it was up to around 25,000 deployed applications. So we grew from 600 apps at the beginning of 2011 to 25,000 at the end of 2011. The end of this quarter we're way past that; our sustained growth has just been huge through this whole process.

LE: Would it be safe to say that you guys are seeing exponential growth right now?

Carlson: Oh, we've seen exponential growth for over a year, yes. All of our curves look exponential right now. So revenue, apps, users, engagement, everything is exponential.

And you know, yes, part of that was listening to our customers and making sure that we were building something that addressed their pain but I don't think that's full credit. I think that part of it is the market itself. I feel like this is an idea that was a bull and I happened to grab the bull and I'm just trying to keep holding on to the bull because it's really . . . the market's driving us; we're not driving the market. The demand is a groundswell.

Work to Do

1. Use the templates that follow to create your proposed value stream.

2. Using your ideal customer profile created from the last chapter, construct the "ideal" path customers take from first becoming aware to becoming passionate about your product.

3. We recommend you work backward from "passionate."

4. Document:

    a. Specific functionality business provides or activity business conducts for each step.

    b. Why customers feel the way they do.

    c. Expected customer behavior based on how they feel.

    d. Metric to measure customer behavior.

5. Try to document only one or two business activities, or one customer action. Less is more.

Segment:			
The customer got in this state:	Because company did:	Resulting in customer doing:	As measured by posit baseline/measure:
Passionate			
Satisfied			
Hopeful			
Convinced			
Trusting			
Intrigued			
Aware			

To get this template and others, e-mail fish@leanentrepreneur.co

5

Diving In

King Sisyphus angered the Greek god Zeus with his hubris and avarice. His punishment? To roll a boulder up a steep hill, only to see it roll back down before he reached the apex and to be forced to begin again. For eternity! This is what they do with those more concerned with creating wealth than value in Greek mythology!

Albert Camus, leaving aside the nature of King Sisyphus and what got him into his predicament, believed the struggle of rolling the boulder uphill to be life affirming and believed the King, in the end, found contentment. Perhaps the King had learned his lesson and was forced to find comfort in the act of hard work, rather than merely the accumulation of materialistic rewards that one can't take to the afterlife.

> "I leave Sisyphus at the foot of the mountain! . . . Each atom of that stone, each mineral flake of that night-filled mountain, in itself forms a world. The struggle itself toward the heights is enough to fill a man's heart. One must imagine Sisyphus happy."
> —Albert Camus, *The Myth of Sisyphus*

There is, perhaps, an entrepreneur story we can pull from the Greek tale. Like the King, the job of an entrepreneur is to roll the boulder up a steep hill. Those whose sole commitment is to the riches that await are doomed to see the boulder roll back down. Those who are committed to creating value, *may* see the boulder crest and roll down the other side of the hill. Victory!

The myth of Sisyphus occurs from the observer's side, by those who witness the success of the boulder tumbling down the side of startup success. The observer believes the entrepreneur is successful overnight and momentum is easy. They see the entrepreneur as visionary and success as a reward for faithful execution.

The observer never sees the entrepreneur struggling, failing, and learning while rolling the boulder uphill!

Listen to Your Customers—or Not

In the entrepreneurial world, is there any more divisive a topic than the proper role of the customer in innovative endeavors? Other than the (near) universal acceptance that customers should either pay for product or amass in such numbers that they can be otherwise monetized, advice on how customers should influence your business decisions is all over the map. Countless books, blogs, and bloviating business gurus repeat common customer cliches: customer is king, be customer driven, the customer is always right, and so forth. Yet, it's not too difficult to find link-bait headlines claiming the exact opposite: Ignore your customer; "Mark Cuban on Why You Should Never Listen to Your Customers";[1] and Steve Jobs, who supposedly said, "We do no market research," yada, yada, yada.

The thing is, both sides are right.[2]

This brings us to an innovation axiom: The more disruptive the solution, the less you can believe what customers say they need or what they will do. *Innovation* is an overused, tired word, but let's say that innovation refers to meaningful change,

forgetting for a moment its use as buzz-wordy, marketing hype.

Clayton Christensen coined the term *sustaining technology* to refer to meaningful technology change that improves existing products for an existing market. In other words, both the problem and solution are known. The value stream is understood and

has been translated into specific processes that are being executed and, ideally, continuously improved upon. Part of the value stream includes methods of working with customers to understand what product improvements would most benefit them.

Some of these improvements are so obvious one needn't even ask the customer.

If you can boost performance, boost capacity, lower total costs of ownership, you really don't need to seek your customer's reaction first. *You can believe them, however, when you ask them if they like the idea.* You might even be able to ask the simple question, "What would you like from us?" and executing on the answer will generate revenue. Although Christensen talks primarily about technical innovation, meaningful change doesn't have to be technology driven or at least not directly so. Innovation can come from new distribution, for example, or different packaging, new features using existing technology, exceptional user design, and so on. The phrase *sustaining innovation* captures all the ways existing markets can be marginally improved.

On the other end of the spectrum is what Christensen calls *disruptive technology.* As with sustaining innovation, disruption needn't only be technological, so we talk about disruptive innovation. Disruptive innovation causes massive change. It creates whole new markets or turns existing markets completely upside down, so that suddenly (seemingly), new companies are at the top of the food chain or large chunks of a market suddenly belong to a new competitor.[3]

- The iPhone killed dozens of startup companies planning on offering mobile services across a variety of handsets in partnership with major telecoms. Entire companies were replaced by the iPhone (and then Android, too) with free or 99-cent apps. The iPhone also threw several major handset manufacturers into long, painful declines into irrelevance.
- iTunes is disrupting the music industry.
- Salesforce.com not only turned the CRM industry on its head but also was the first hugely successful software-as-a-service (SaaS) business model.
- The Prius disrupted the automobile industry.
- Amazon continues to disrupt the publishing industry.

Disruptive innovation is often stumbled upon. The nature and scale of change is a black swan, which Nassim N. Taleb defines as having three fundamental characteristics:

1. "It lies outside the realm of regular expectations" [it's rare].
2. "It carries an extreme impact."
3. "Human nature makes us concoct explanations for its occurrence *after* the fact, making it explainable and predictable" [retrospectively].[4]

Not only is the market for disruptive innovation unknown (prior to getting to market), it's *unknowable.* You *think* you know, because you have a strong "vision" of the future—but so do astrologists and fortune-tellers. You don't *know* the market until the market weighs in. If you don't know, your customers certainly don't. With disruptive innovation, you can't ask customers what they want, because they don't know what's possible outside their existing domain knowledge.

Steve Blank's new market correlates to Christensen's disruptive innovation. Steve also coined two new terms, *resegmented niche* and *resegmented low cost,* demonstrating that innovation exists as a continuum. There are many examples of applying existing disruptive innovations to new markets, something we call rippling innovation.

- Resegmented low cost targets the most price-sensitive subsegments of an existing market.
- Resegmented niche targets a subsegment that can be better served with a product tailored to their specific needs.
- Rippling innovation targets an existing market that has not yet benefited from a disruptive innovation.

The face-value believability of your customer depends on where you sit on the innovation spectrum. As mentioned earlier, if you ask your existing customers if they want increased performance, it's highly likely you can believe their response. Circa 1990, if you asked your customers if they would like increased disk capacity in their 5¼-inch drives, you'd be surprised if they said no. If you asked the same customers if they could use a 3½-inch drive, they might ask, "What for, as a paper weight?"

Instead, you must find a new market for the 3½-inch drive. You must discover the early adopter. The power of early adopters comes from their ability to recognize what it is you're up to. In other words, if you ask someone if they could use a 3½-inch drive and they say, "What are you doing, building a portable computer?" then they get it!

Believing the Customer

Here are some guidelines for when you should and when you should not believe what your customers say.

Pro tip: Believing them doesn't mean you do what they say.

- If you're talking to customers about improving a product they know and love, you can believe them.
- If you're talking about introducing new product and through interaction with them get the feeling they *get it*, you can believe some of what they say.
- If you ask existing customers if they want something radically new, their response should be treated with skepticism.
- If you ask prospective customers if they're willing to pay for your great idea, you shouldn't bank on their response—either way (yes or no).
- If your great-uncle loves your idea, that's wonderful, but not actionable advice (unless, perhaps, he's in your target segment).

Customers in your target market move from right to left on the innovation spectrum as you engage them. When you introduce a new product, early adopters are already to the left of the disruptive-innovation endpoint. This is why they are so valuable, because they provide you relevant feedback.

The moment any customer becomes somewhat satisfied with your product, that customer has moved further left of the endpoint. The more engaged they are, the more passionate they are, the further to the left they've moved.

Listen up. If you have customers who are highly engaged with your product, listen to them. Listen when they complain, listen when they ask for features, listen when they praise you and thank you. This is market pull. This is what gets you to product-market fit. Listening, however, doesn't necessarily mean doing. It's up to you to figure why the customer is asking and what the best response is. The question, then, is do you execute on what they say, and if so, what do you execute on?

The answer depends on whether you understand your market segments.

Remember that chapter?

You should execute on the things customers say when they are members of the market segment you've decided to crush. If you have segmented your market properly and are tracking engagement with your product by segment and tracking feedback by segment, you will know how to prioritize features. (By *features* we mean any characteristic of your business or any activity pertinent to delivering value to your customer.)

This could be distribution, packaging, messaging, product features, and so on.)

Listening to what your customers have to say is only one way to validate your assumptions and grow your business. There's also the ethnography of watching and measuring what your customers *do*.

Lean startups use three primary methods of testing the validity of their assumptions:

1. Customer interaction.
2. Running experiments.
3. Analyzing data.

Customer Interaction

Customer interaction is a catchphrase for the myriad ways successful entrepreneurs engage with their customers in order to learn from them. Some of these methods include:

- Steve Blank's customer development.
- Observation.
- Various user-centric design methodologies.
- Consultative sales.
- Living the life of your customer.

We are perhaps biased toward customer development as a result of having worked in high-tech startups through the frustration caused by executing unknown processes. Steve Blank offers a remedy to such unknown processes in *The Four Steps*

to the Epiphany. At the risk of restating the obvious, there are two primary objectives to all these techniques:

1. Learn. Your job is *not* to be faithful to your product, value, and market assumptions, but rather to validate or invalidate them, in order for you to be able to iterate toward reality.
2. Don't waste. The point isn't to fill out worksheets, create new deliverables, fill out your assumptions in triplicate, or increase interview efficacy by conducting the stand-on-your-head interview technique™. What do you need to learn to move the needle in your business?

In a story told in perhaps every lean book written, a Toyota chief drove through the 50 United States and the 10 provinces and three territories of Canada, mostly in a minivan, in order to experience what American and Canadian auto consumers experienced in their daily lives.[5] This is customer development done by the world's largest automobile manufacturer, so surely it can be done in your business!

Customer Development

Here are the eight basic steps we outline for practicing customer development:

1. Document your primary assumptions:
   - Who is your customer? (market segment)

- What problem are you trying to solve? (pain, passion, customer goal, job to be done)
- What's your (pie in the sky) solution idea? (not features, but value proposition)

2. Brainstorm other business-model hypotheses:
    - Partners, distribution, and so on.
    - Product platform, design, functionality.
    - Sales and marketing funnel.

3. Find prospects to talk to:
    - Use your social network (e.g., Facebook, LinkedIn, Twitter, and so on).
    - Craigslist, surveys, meetups, forums, and so on.
    - If you are unsure of who to talk to, start broad and work to narrow the field to those who understand the problem you're trying to solve (early adopters).

4. Reach out to prospects:
    - E-mail and phone-call techniques.
    - Selling before building and informational interviews.
    - Don't overplan; just get started!

5. Engage prospects:
    - Customer-problem-solution presentation.
    - Use open-ended conversation techniques.
    - Be respectful of people's time and expertise.

6. Compile-measure-test:
    - Iterate on customer, or problem, or solution assumptions.
    - Move on to minimum viable product (MVP) testing.
    - Pivot because something in your business model is fundamentally wrong.

7. Problem-solution fit/MVP:
    - Iterate on product toward market viability.
    - Quantify the value you provide the customer.
    - Investigate the sales and marketing road map.

8. MVP achieved:
    - Market viability validated, move on to validate other business-model assumptions.

- Return to earlier assumptions because something is wrong.
- Pivot because something in your solution hypothesis is fundamentally wrong.

Sounds simple, right? You can be done in a couple of months at the outside. Wrong. Startups iterate and pivot and persevere on all that, trying to find product-market fit with their no longer minimal MVP, easily spending years trying to figure it out.

These steps represent one possible approach organizations might find helpful when implementing customer development. The reality is that since all organizations are different, it's up to you to figure out what works best based on the uncertainty you face, where you are in your product development, and what resources you have available to you.

Your goal isn't to go through the steps. Your goal is to learn. The process is rarely as linear as it might seem. You can learn a ton about conversion funnels at the same time you are validating your market segment assumptions. Really! You don't have to wait until step 15 in the Cooper-Vlaskovits Paint-by-Numbers, Startup-to-IPO Blueprint before you learn how to sell B2B.

Case Study: Don't Just Get Out of the Building, Get Out of the Country

embrace

In 2008, a group of talented individuals led by Jane Chin came together to make an impact on the world. They were MBAs, lawyers, and engineers from the top universities around the world: the Indian Institute of Technology, Harvard, Stanford, and MIT. This group had very little real-world experience in terms of building a business and commercializing products. They didn't know what they didn't know, they had little fear, and they approached the world with open-mindedness. Rather than pursuing careers in Silicon Valley or Wall Street, with the help of Andy Butler at D2M, a design consultancy, the Embrace team entered the world of social entrepreneurship.

The problem they hoped to solve? Save babies being born prematurely in third-world countries. The solution? Make available an extremely affordable incubator at a price level appropriate for the third world.

Andy Butler: "To start out, they were thinking, 'Let's just take a conventional incubator paradigm and try every way to cost reduce it,' and there are a whole bunch of ways you can lower costs using off-the-shelf components rather than specialized components, and so they went down that path and made progress exploring severe cost reduction for a stationary incubator."

In the lean spirit of *genchi genbutsu*, "going to the source to see for yourself" (*The Toyota Way*, p. 40), the team not only got out of the building, but got out of the country. They went to India and spent time working in the hospitals and interviewing doctors. They found quite quickly that the primary need was not to find solutions for preemies, per se, but rather for low-birth-weight children, regardless if brought to full term or not. The bigger impact idea was a mobile solution for undernourished, underweight infants.

Out in the market they saw that though children were tragically dying due to premature birth, the bigger problem, in terms of the sheer numbers, as well as long-term sociological impact, is undernourished mothers giving birth to undernourished children. Because the infants don't have enough body fat on them, they suffer hypothermia while the mothers work. So the mother can keep the baby warm as long as she holds it next to her body, but because the mothers have to work, they can't hold the baby. There are periods of the day where they have to let the child essentially generate its own heat and, during those periods of time, they suffer hypothermia and it doesn't result in death but, rather, it results in physiological issues. Either delayed development, neurological damage, or even physiological damage, which puts a long-term burden on the society because these children grow up having severe medical issues.

Having a much deeper understanding of the problem, the team switched gears. Instead of doing some sort of sustaining innovation—making something existing perform better, faster, or cheaper—they looked toward developing a solution that didn't exist; a solution that would somehow allow the mother to keep the child close beside her and somehow keep the baby warm, while still able to perform work in the field or in the factory or her own home.

Butler: "Through their engagement with reality and away from the theoretical thinking, and in large part due to their open-mindedness—in that they weren't an incubator company; they weren't tied to a particular solution—they were open to change the paradigm."

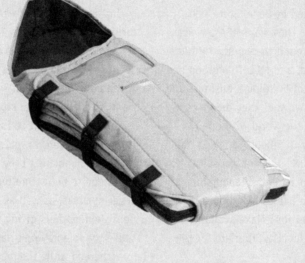

The team went into a period of heavy testing, "fail early, fail often" prototypes for all sorts of proposed solutions. They learned fast and evolved their ideas. They remained out in the field in rural villages in India. They went to the source. They talked to midwives, worked with mothers who had low-birth-weight children, worked with the local doctors who were struggling in rural hospitals where electricity was intermittent. It was through that experience that they came up with their current solution.

As is the norm when working on the disruptive side of the innovation spectrum, one can't simply ask the customer what they need. A woman with an undernourished baby would hardly say to inquisitors, "You know what? I need this really sophisticated incubator sling that I can bring with me to the fields!" Engagement and creativity on the innovators' side is required to reveal the solution if one is to be found at all.

Butler: "You can ask them what their pain is. You can ask them what they struggle with. What they worry about. What they desire. But ask them to articulate how they'd satisfy those issues, that's beyond their capability. So it's the designer and the innovator's job of taking that information and being creative in fashioning potential solutions and learning as much from the rejection of proposed solutions as the acceptance. The rejections themselves reveal a whole range of values that you may or may not have been aware of. You always find a treasure trove in rejection."

The "Aha!" moment for the Embrace team, around which the whole architecture eventually revolved, was getting to a system that was essentially passive. They had to come up with an energy storage mechanism that would work in the fields or in locations without electricity.

Butler: "It turns out you can engineer paraffin to melt at different temperatures and so when it goes from a solid to a liquid, it can absorb way more energy and when it converts back from a liquid to a solid, the energy is released gradually so you can store hours of heat energy in what looks like two or three Ziploc bags of paraffin."

So say you are a mother. You are undernourished, but have also recently given birth to an undernourished daughter. You work in the fields every day. It is necessary to bring your baby to the fields. Before you go, you melt the paraffin pouch over fire or even on a black sheet metal and put it into one sleeve of the Embrace "sleeping bag." When you get to the fields, maybe you can hold her for a little while, but reluctantly must get to work. You have to pick the grains. So when you go to put the baby down, you put her into one pouch of the Embrace "sleeping bag." In a side compartment, paraffin is solidifying and as it does, it releases energy that keeps your baby warm, so she doesn't become hypothermic.

How you interact with your customers evolves over time and depends heavily on what you are trying to learn. At the beginning, the most important objective is to simply establish what will hopefully be a long-term relationship based on empathy.

The most typical problem entrepreneurs have when first speaking to a customer is that they are unable to resist talking about their solution. No matter how they originally frame the conversation in order to get the meeting, the entrepreneur inevitably starts out with "I have this great idea!" This is pretty lame. The feedback you get is lame. It's way less painful for your customer to nod and say, "Yep, that's a swell idea!" and send you on your way than it is for them to get into an involved discussion about why your idea is lame, only to hear you say things like, "Eh, you just don't get it."

If you don't have a deep understanding of the pain or passion of your target customer,

you have no business talking about your solution. No one cares about your product. Seriously, no one cares about the features, the platform, the architecture. They care about solving their problem, and if you are truly in the business of solving the problem, you should want to know as much as you can about it from the customer's perspective.

Over time, after you understand their problem deeply, then you can start working on qualitative validation of solution specifics, and you can start working on learning how people like them want to be marketed and sold to. Also, you can start showing them early versions of the product and watch as they attempt to use it. You can learn what is required for the product to work within the customer's environment, whether it be home, vacation, social setting, work, and so on. What type of product will work within their existing life or work flow. With any hope, further down the road, you

can validate what functionality is a must-have. You can establish what will turn them into passionate advocates, rather than just satisfied customers.

Be a Zoologist

Observing your customers in their natural habitat is a powerful way to understand a day in their lives; in other words, you can begin to empathize. When TechStars entrepreneur Reece Pacheco co-founded HomeField to help college coaches manage and share game video, the effort involved supporting nontechnical people with a technological solution was surprising.

Pacheco says, "It was not until I spent time in the coach's office that I began to understand the problem we were solving. It was different when we were on his turf, than, say, bringing him in to look at what we were building; not only the pictures on the wall and the DVDs stacked on his desk, but the way he interacted with us."

Turns out supporting coaches (their target segment) was a big technical hurdle. The coaches used specific IT-mandated browsers, and didn't really understand the difference between e-mail in a desktop application versus browsing web-based e-mail.

Pacheco reports, "We had one guy who couldn't access a video because his e-mail client was Lotus Notes. Uploading videos would time out, because the computer would go to sleep before the video file was uploaded. But these things were our fault, really, not our customers'. We needed to understand their environment, provide the right, easy-to-follow instructions and make the product incredibly easy to use, if we wanted to be successful."

Scott Anthony documents a couple of great examples from Procter & Gamble. CEO A. G. Lafley observed a woman using a screwdriver or scissors to open a Tide box. This from a woman who said she liked the packaging! Watching a woman trying to clean up coffee grounds spilled on her floor inspired P&G's Swiffer quick-cleaning line. According to Anthony, the makers of Wrangler and Lee jeans, VF Corporation, revamped their jeans labeling and created new in-store displays after observing a woman shopper bringing

an armful of jeans into the dressing room. The current labels were useless regarding fit for different body shapes.[6]

Steve Jobs visited his retail stores not to ask customers what they wanted but to observe customers, supposedly even hiding in the bushes![7]

Observing customers is a matter of intuition. You are attempting to glean insights into what the needs and desires of customers are, but it's up to you to envision the solution to those problems. The customer

owns the pain, whereas the founder owns the vision.

Be a Doctor

Doctors poke, probe, and prod in order to understand not only what patients are feeling (both emotionally and physically), but *why*. Patients often are reluctant to tell the truth about such things out of fear, denial, and perhaps a lack of self-awareness. Empathy is an important component of doctor-patient relationships in order to enable better

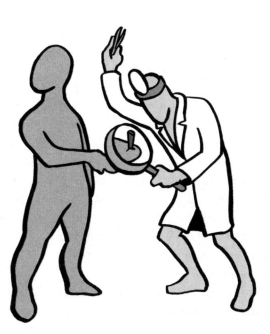

communication, but also so that the doctor can understand underlying issues that may be affecting the patient's health.Not that all doctors have a good bedside manner!

Nonetheless, entrepreneurs must aspire to the same thing. Empathy is a cornerstone of successful entrepreneurship. You simply cannot solve a problem if you do not deeply understand the problem you're solving, and you cannot design a solution if you do not deeply understand those that will use it. Further, you cannot have this understanding for huge, undifferentiated groups of people, but by understanding the needs and desires of your subsegments, you might be able to design an experience they will pay for. Additionally, perhaps, you'll learn what needs to be added or taken away, or the different ways required to market and sell to different segments.

Empathy, like most other skills, appears innately in some, but can be learned by others. *Empathy for others* means to "walk in their shoes," and that doesn't mean buying the same shoes. It doesn't mean "what you would do in their situation," but rather trying to understand from *their* perspective *why* they do what they do.

We find that the most difficult part of having these types of conversations with prospective customers comes from the inability to succinctly describe the problems you hope to solve. It's rather beyond us, however, how one hopes to solve a problem one can't articulate.

Here are example problem statements that don't get to the root of the real issue.

"We save enterprises money": It's true, businesses love a positive return on investment (ROI) when they purchase a product. But they don't purchase a product in order to solve *the problem of a lack of ROI.* They purchase a product to solve a problem (perform a job). Positive ROI comes from a product doing the job well enough to make or save more money than the cost of the product, plus any number of other hard and soft cost factors, including switchover costs, brand risk, security, and so on.

"Better way to hang out with friends": It's true, friends like to hang out with each other. You might even say they are passionate about it, but they're not looking for a cool, new wiz-bang mobile app to help them hang out more. They're really not. The problem a mobile social app developer is solving is not *the lack of a mobile app!*

"Small businesses need to have a web presence": It's true, many small businesses don't have an online presence. For many, it's too hard or at least there's a fear that it's too hard. For some, it may be too expensive, or at least there's a fear it's too expensive. Only those fooled by hype desire a web presence for the sake of having a web presence. If you are merely solving the problem of needing to have a web presence, you're not solving a real business need. *Why* do they need a web presence? Is a web presence actually the best way to solve the need?

To truly understand a problem, you *should not* initially propose a solution. Otherwise, the reaction you get will be to the solution and not whether the problem exists.

Getting Customers to Talk

Assuming for a moment that you are able to articulate your customers' problem assumptions, a conversation might begin like this:

Hello, I am [your name], and I'm researching the [your industry] market. When speaking with [target customers], I often hear they face difficulties with [problem1/problem2/problem3]. Do any of these sound familiar to you?

Example:

Hello, I am Brant Cooper, and I'm researching business startups. When I speak to startup founders, I often hear that they find it difficult to know who exactly their customers are, how to validate product ideas, and how to communicate with customers. Do these sound familiar to you?

Let's unpack this a bit. The conversation is not about you, though people will want to know who you are. Get that out of the way quickly by introducing yourself and giving a very general description of why you're talking to them. As quickly as you can, flip the conversation to be about the person with whom you're speaking. To do this, briefly describe one to three problems you think resonate with them. Then, ask them if they have experienced those problems.

What are the worst possible outcomes?

- They tell you to go away: So go away; they are either not a potential customer or not friendly.
- One or more of your problem statements are incorrect: What a great opportunity to learn!
- They understand your statements as accurate, but personally don't believe they apply to them: Great! Still an opportunity to learn. How did they overcome these obstacles? What problems are they facing?

Either you're talking to the wrong person or you stand to learn a lot. If you're talking to the wrong person, you still have an opportunity to learn. Ask if they know anyone who has faced the problems. Try to discern why you thought they would be the right person to talk to, but they actually turned out to be wrong. There is something about them that will help you tighten your market segment definition and help form a list of questions you can use to qualify future leads.

You can't learn this stuff from thinking harder or "just doing it." You have to go meet them. What's the worst that can happen to you? Someone slams a door in your face? Hangs up on you?

Of course, they could laugh at you. That would be pretty bad.

Case Study: What's the Worst That Can Happen?

SimpleEnergy is a TechStars company seeking to help homeowners reduce energy consumption and save money with the help of a wireless thermostat. Much to their credit, SimpleEnergy didn't spend a lot of time and money building out a line of wireless thermostats from the get-go, but rather created several mockups.

Founder Yoav Lurie:

> It was a simple thermostat; all it had was an up and a down button and a little screen. But the beauty of it was it was connected through Wi-Fi to your router and then you would be able to control it through your iPhone or your iPad and we'd provide the ability for any other developer to build an entire ecosystem around our products.

They built several mockups, playing with the design, how it would look in various houses, various interior designs, and so on. The idea was to have energy utility companies distribute the thermostat to their customers. After hustling to land meetings with several prominent utility executives, they got an awkward reception:

> We took this thermostat to them and they literally laughed at us. We could not understand why they laughed at us, because we really thought this was brilliant. Then they pulled out of a drawer this beautiful $500 thermostat. They said, "We have to pay a door-to-door salesman $60 per lead for every household they convince to *take one for free*."

After two similar experiences, one with an industry regulator, they knew they had a problem. "The regulator helped us get that the problem is not with the tools to help consumers, but that people don't care."

Even in the worst possible scenario, there's learning to be had. The episode didn't spell doom for the company; rather they had to look at the problem from a different angle. The founders stuck with their vision of helping consumers reduce energy use, but how?

If SimpleEnergy were to ask consumers straight up, "Would you like to save money on your electric bill?" The likely response would be a near unanimous "Yes!" Who doesn't want to save money? If they had asked, "Would you like to reduce energy consumption?" Again, most consumers would view that as a positive. We would hazard a guess that even if asked in a survey, "Would you like a new thermostat for free?" most people would say yes.

Unfortunately, this exchange would have a tenuous relationship with reality. The real question is this: "Would you significantly change your behavior in order to incrementally save money and reduce energy consumption?" When confronted by a sales representative at the door with an offer for a free thermostat, that reality comes barreling home.

"What for?" the homeowner asks.

"Well, it connects to your Wi-Fi and you can monitor your energy use with your iPhone."

"Oh, please!" [*Slam!*]

The point is that *how* you interact with potential customers is critical to learning. In this instance, one can validate the need: Consumers would like to lower energy bills, and some consumers would like to reduce energy consumption. It's difficult, however, to validate the solution proposal with any degree of confidence. Consumers are not great at predicting whether they would be willing to change behavior, nor, if they were asked to come up with their own solutions, would they likely come up with innovative ideas.

The innovation is up to the entrepreneurs. The utilities had all the tools necessary to allow consumers to track their energy consumption, but still, the consumers didn't care enough to use them.

"We went out looking for someone who would help us figure out how to get people to care," said Lurie. "So we tracked down Dan Ariely,[7] who has written two *New York Times* best-sellers on why people act irrationally and how you get them to do what you want. We pivoted from being a thermostat-building company to a social gaming company. We credit Dan for helping us design the underlying game mechanics that drive much of our application."

Validate your idea in two stages:

Things you should learn about your customers' problem through interacting with them:

- Top—one to three pains or passions within the context of your product/solution proposal.
- How people deal with pains today and why the existing workarounds/solutions fall short.
- What is the cost of the problem?
- How deeply held is the pain or passion?
- What is the primary obstacle to converting? Why would users decide not to buy?
- What is the customers' practice when buying other related (or semirelated, not necessarily competitive) products? In other words, how do customers expect to be marketed and sold to?

Things you should learn about your proposed solution after validating the problem through interacting with customers:

- Do your customers view your solution ideas as belonging to a new market? In other words, can they instantly compare it to other solutions out there? (If so, not a new market.)
- Do your customers currently have the necessary environment to successfully include your product into their existing work flow or their daily life?
- Can they envision your product existing in their life and, if so, under what conditions?
- Would they pay $1 for it? $1 million?

Case Study: A Nonprofit Lean Startup

We feel strongly that the challenges of innovation in uncertainty are felt not only by business startups, but by innovators in the nonprofit world, too. Rob Emrich, founder of multiple startups, shared with us his story about how he successfully iterated his nonprofit and how his vision evolved as he "got out of the building."

Lean Entrepreneur: What's the name of your nonprofit?

Rob Emrich: Roadoflife.org is our website; it's the name of our program. The actual nonprofit is called the Keren Emrich Foundation. We provide health-education curricula to schools and teachers.

LE: How did you get started?

Emrich: When I was a lot younger I had a sister who passed away from cancer. She had a nonpreventable type of cancer called neuroblastoma. I was a real young kid when she died but it affected me profoundly. As I was older, in my last year of college, I had a cousin who died of a brain tumor and my mom had a breast cancer scare and my aunts had breast cancer.

So when I was a senior in college I decided I wanted to do something to make a real difference in the fight against cancer and raise a lot money for that cause.

LE: What did you do first?

Emrich: The first thing we did was what would be called "getting out of the building," the equivalent of customer development in startups. We specifically made appointments with the head of the cancer division at the Ohio Department of Health, who was extremely helpful to us along the way.

What we found out really quickly—and it would have been easy to just be stubborn and go out and raise money—but we found out there's not really a problem.

LE: Classic. In what way?

Emrich: I mean, there could always be more money that goes to cancer research but even if we were tremendously successful and we raised $50 million for cancer research, that is a drop in the bucket on a year-to-year basis compared to what the federal government puts into cancer research, let alone all the other charitable foundations combined. We had no way that would have made us any better at giving away the money we raised.

LE: So you got out of the building and the feedback was, "Hey guys, we appreciate your enthusiasm," but, then, "Here's the bigger picture. Here's how the ecosystem works. Money is not really the big problem for us."

Emrich: The people at the Ohio Department of Health made it really clear the problem isn't research and you're also not in a very good position to make any significant difference in research, whether through money or ideas or better allocation of funds or whatever.

A lot of times you actually can get in the way; people who donate money get in the way because they donate to the wrong things that really don't have that much promise. They told us the really big issue out there is prevention and specifically, prevention for children. A large percentage of all cancer deaths are preventable, through really simple things like eating better, not smoking, and exercising more. There's also a massive epidemic of childhood obesity, diabetes, and other diseases of excess. We ended up latching on to that a lot more.

What we found out is that there's a really big challenge in prevention and specifically when it came to children because by the time you're an adult it's harder to change your behavior.

Our next step was to start to investigate that as much possible. We found out that there are actually quite a few curriculums that were out there—some from the American Cancer Society, some from other tobacco-prevention programs—but just look at the outcomes.

There are still a lot of obese kids and that's a near-term indicator for a long-term problem. Why isn't this working?

LE: You actively looked at outcomes and thought, "Look, current methods don't seem to be working." So you actually took a sort of skeptical approach rather than just execute a good idea?

Emrich: Right, and as soon as we realized we needed to work with kids, we wanted to find out what was happening in the

classrooms, so we actually started talking to teachers. That was like another example of us "getting out of the building."

LE: How many teachers did you talk to?

Emrich: We went to dozens of teacher conferences. I would say we probably talked to 50 teachers during the course of the initial development. What we found out is some of them had been given these curriculums, but this is a critical point: They were never actually using them.

We couldn't figure out why they weren't using them, because we knew they had them. We would go into the classroom and we'd see a curriculum from the American Heart Association sitting on the shelf.

LE: How did the American Heart Association get the curriculum to the teachers?

Emrich: Usually they got a grant that put them into the schools. There are a lot of people that can say yes or no, so usually a district will make a decision, and this is an important point about how complicated getting a product into the nonprofit sector can be. A district can say no to a curriculum, a school principal can say no, or a teacher can say no.

What we decided to do, based on knowing how many levels of no's we could get, was to just avoid going to the two levels that could've given us a no, and we went right to the teachers who could give us a yes or no answer.

LE: And this is based on your time spent with talking to teachers.

Emrich: Yes, about how curriculum gets into classrooms, how they even are allowed to teach certain things. How they choose what they teach.

What we found out is that it is very individualized. Although the district believes they have a really specific set of standards, for the most part teachers did what they wanted and they were evaluated based on the tests that students take at the end of the year. We realized, after talking with so many teachers, that the reason they weren't actually teaching the other curriculum that were out there was because they didn't have time during the day and because they had an enormous amount of pressure to teach these academic concept standards.

This is a really critical thing; other nonprofits had probably talked to teachers, but they'd come in with a preconceived notion that they had to have a peer-reviewed program that's been used in small cohort studies and demonstrated to be successful and then go in and give that to teachers. It's hard for teachers to do a 50-lesson approach, however, so all the other curriculums that had been built, it was either you do all 50 of these lessons or you don't do any.

We knew that that was completely unrealistic. So immediately we made a decision to sacrifice what's called program fidelity versus adoption.

LE: What does that mean exactly?

Emrich: Like how often a teacher actually completes a lesson or how well the program is actually followed to the letter.

LE: So you find out about the teachers' pains. How they do their jobs every day. Then you say, "Okay, we want to do something. Something is better than nothing so we'll sacrifice some fidelity in order to get adoption." Is that sort of the thought process with that?

Emrich: That was one of the thought processes and the other is: We're going to go directly to teachers to get an up or down answer from them right away. So we started to put stuff in front of them and say, "Is this enough?" What we found out was it was difficult to teach what we were putting out there because it wasn't aligned to the academic content standards. So, at the time—and this is different now—but at the time every single state had their own academic content standards. It was part of the No Child Left Behind act passed by Congress to begin the process of standardizing what's taught in schools.

So no teacher actually had time to teach any lessons during the day, because they only had to teach what was in the academic content standards and what was going to be in the test at the end of the year.

So our big insight was that we took our lessons and transformed them to align to the academic content standards for both national health education standards and math. This was like our big innovation that actually helped make our program much more successful.

This was a pivot that I think was critical. So instead of just teaching a kid about health we would talk to them about their body mass index (BMI), based on teaching them a lesson on long division. For all the things we wanted to teach we found out where it could correspond to something that students already had to learn, and then we taught health in the context of the academic content standards.

LE: Why do you think that hadn't happened before?

Emrich: I think no one actually got out of the building and talked to teachers and observed teaching in the classroom. I think the programs were designed by doctors who were much more interested in building small cohort studies that could be peer reviewed, would demonstrate that the programs work in a vacuum. When a teacher is forced to actually teach all those lessons, it works very well.

Once we had built the program, it was online and any teacher could use it, it still wasn't being used much and we didn't understand why. So we got back out of the building and they kept telling us, "Well, I like to have a book in my classroom." We're always reading about these new smart whiteboards that are in all the classrooms. It turns out teachers didn't really know how to use them yet.

LE: So there's this supposed technological innovation, these smart blackboards . . .

Emrich: And computers . . .

LE: And yet the adoption wasn't very high; people actually weren't using them. They were actually telling you, "Look, we want a physical paper book."

Emrich: Right. So they actually wanted to be able to tear the pages out of a workbook, photocopy them so they could give them to the kids, because that's what they're used to doing. They go through a lesson plan that they probably developed at home after hours or over the summer. They make photocopies on the copy machine at the school and for some of them it was, "We don't have a printer, but we do have this copy machine."

LE: So this was after you had already created all the online content?

Emrich: Right. We did that in conjunction with teachers. Then we aligned it to all the state academic content standards and changed the nature of all the lessons. Then we found out that we still were missing part of the story: Younger teachers were teaching our curriculum because they were using this technology; they had been taught how to use it and were using it.

LE: So you guys had aligned the contents to the academic standards, you guys built an online platform, and younger teachers thought, "That's pretty cool." They were using it.

Emrich: Right, but the more experienced teachers, which make up the vast majority of teachers, weren't.

LE: At that point was it actual conscious testing?

Emrich: There were two types of experiments that were running. One, about the actual changes that our curriculum produced, like what knowledge, attitudes, and behaviors had changed with the kids, and we did that with pre- and post-tests. So that was one level of testing, that to be relevant on a long-term basis, we had to demonstrate that what we were doing mattered.

The other thing was just in terms of: How do we get more teachers to do this? That was the usability testing we did. That's how we found out that older teachers were uncomfortable using a laptop in the classroom or a computer. It just didn't make sense for them. So through surveys and talking to teachers directly at conferences, they would say,

"I want it printed out," and we would say to them, "It's so easy to print out. This format automatically creates a PDF from the Wiki. We spent a lot of money using this technology; just print it yourself."

LE: Their response?

Emrich: They didn't do it. We thought they were going to do it but they didn't. We didn't see our adoption rates go up. They didn't have printers, or they didn't know how to use them, or they were just not comfortable doing it that way. We eventually listened to them and printed our own version through Lulu.

LE: You guys printed your own book through Lulu, the online self-publishing service.

Emrich: Right, and we had school districts buy it. So state governments and school districts bought our curriculum. We had teachers download the curriculum and then we asked them, "Would you be more likely to teach this if you had a physical copy?" Almost all of them, 99 percent of them had said yes. So what we would do is match them up to a funder who was willing to pay for the paper curriculum and in that way, we became completely self-sustainable. So, this is significant; our program wasn't paid by donations anymore. It was paid either from the school district or a teacher or anyone who wanted our curriculum, and they actually paid us for it. We stopped asking for donations. I mean we still got significant donations from Microsoft, from Aetna, from Dannon, from big companies, and the federal government, but we stopped asking.

LE: Being able to have the freedom to not ask for donations, how did that affect you guys?

Emrich: It allowed us to completely focus on delivering a better curriculum that would be used by more teachers, rather than creating this narrative about "all the great things our nonprofit is doing" in order to get more funding. That's normally the paradigm. Every nonprofit tells a story and they come up with things that sound like facts about what they're doing, like, "This is how many people slept in our homeless shelter during the course of the year. This is how many meals we actually fed to people."

LE: Because they have different problems and it's not just a smaller version of a big company.

Emrich: That's probably one of the biggest problems. When you're trying to make a change, there's a whole bunch of people who are just telling you what big nonprofits have to do with these already. They're not telling you don't worry about this now, when you get bigger you can worry about it. All they're saying is that you need to have the following checks and balances and you spend all your time working on administration.

LE: Why don't you give me some vanity metrics for fun, actually? How many downloads? How much curriculum has been distributed? What are the big numbers?

Emrich: For us we looked at the amount of curriculum we distributed and the University of Maryland Business School did a study for us. This is specifically so that we could create a social ROI analysis of how much each curriculum was worth to each child. So we took all of our kids and multiplied them by this number that they came up with for us and that's how we get our $70 million of curriculum distributed, and over 250,000 kids have used our program.

Work to Do

1. From Chapter 3, you hopefully have a few market segments defined, with corresponding problem statements. From Chapter 4, you have documented assumptions from the five parts of your value stream:

- Growth engine
- Minimum viable product
- Conversion
- Funnel
- Acquisition channel

Now's the time to figure out how to validate your assumptions.

You can use one template for each interviewee:

Segment: Interviewee:		
Assumption	Hypothesis	Result
Persona exists/details correct:		
Customer has problem/pain/passion:		
Customer will respond to solution (high level):		
Customer will be satisfied with specific functionality *x, y, z*:		
Customer will become passionate when:		
Customer will make final decision to buy when:		
Customer will trust the company when:		
Customer will trust the product when:		

Segment:		
Interviewee:		
Assumption	Hypothesis	Result
Customer will want to learn more when:		
Customer will become aware of the product by:		

2. All this data does not come from one interview, but, rather, it is collected over time as you form a deep relationship with your customer.

6

Viability Experiments

W inners experiment. The world is changing fast—strike that, the rate of change is increasing. You are being disrupted. The pundits screaming at you from the TV, what are they on about? They're being disrupted. It's what you do when you become obsolete. Innovate or die. You can double down on "ignorance is bliss" or you can start running experiments.

The idea of viability experiments is to test critical aspects of your business model, before you build them out. Just as a scientist runs experiments to prove a theory, so should an entrepreneur. Just as researchers and engineers use iterative processes to

discover new things, so should founders use such processes to discover what will work in the market.

> "The real measure of success is the number of experiments that can be crowded into 24 hours."
>
> —Thomas Alva Edison

As quickly as you are able to posit your market segments, you want to think of ways to validate that the segments exist as you describe them. Getting out of the building to interview prospective customers gives

you your first insights into whether you've described them and their problems correctly, and now by running experiments you work to confirm customer behavior. Experiments represent the first opportunity for your potential customers to experience at some level your value proposition.

Augment what customers say they're going to do with tests that show what they actually will do!

The basic premise of viability experiments is that the quicker you can determine a failed approach, the better. If you require an expensive custom mold to be built for your product, wouldn't it be better to understand the viability of the product prior to building the mold? If you wish to open a restaurant, shouldn't you check whether people like the type of food you plan on serving? If you must develop software for a year to finish a product, isn't there a way to test whether you're building a product people want?

Viability experiments do not only apply to product. You should test any element of your business model that has significant uncertainty. Will a retail store carry a product like yours? If so, what do you have to do to get shelf space? How many page views do you need before advertisers will pay you enough money to sustain your business? Will people buy high-end art online without experiencing the piece in person?

Eric Ries adopted the term *minimum viable product* (MVP) to describe these experiments, as long as they result in validated learning.[1] Originally the phrase described the minimum functionality necessary to be viable in the product, as evidenced by the willingness of customers to pay, because it sufficiently addresses their problem or passion.

Ries's definition includes all sorts of creative *viability experiments* that result in learning and reduced business-model risk. We believe it's valuable to separate out the first attempt at putting product in front of customers and call that an MVP, versus running purpose-built experiments to educate your product development assumptions and other risky aspects of your business model.

So for this book, *viability experiment* refers to tests you run to validate aspects of your business model. This epitomizes Ries's build-measure-learn framework. We are holding out the term MVP for the first stab at releasing product that creates value for a specified customer segment. What follows are the most familiar methods of running viability experiments.

The Infamous Landing Page

The landing page[2] test is probably the most familiar to people. The basic premise is that you put up a basic one-page website comprised of your messaging and a call to action, drive traffic to the page, and measure clicks on the call to action.

Landing Page smoke tests are at the same time the most abused and underutilized of tests. Most abused because the interpretation of the results is highly subject to experimental bias: Entrepreneurs see what they want to see. The Landing Page test has three variables in play:

1. How good is your acquisition method? If you drive traffic using Google AdWords, but nobody is searching for your solution, then you haven't really tested your value proposition but, rather, your ability to drive traffic via search marketing. Furthermore, if you don't draw the right traffic, in other words, your target segment, then you can end up with hundreds of e-mail addresses from casual passers by who have no deep interest in your product.

2. How good are your messaging, positioning, and design? People who click on

the call to action are persuaded (among other things) by their belief in whether the product is targeting them (positioning), if it might benefit them (messaging), and if the design reinforces the product appeal to the necessary degree. If you're selling bridal products, but the landing page looks like a GeoCities website circa 1999, you're going to have a hard time converting visitors *even if they would value your product.*[3]

3. How good is your value proposition? If you've driven the right people to the page, have articulated your messaging and positioning well, and your design doesn't subtract or distract, then you might, in fact, be able to test your value proposition. If people don't click on the call to action, you have a long road in front of you. If people do click on the call to action, you still have a long road in front of you, but perhaps enough reason to continue the journey.

At this point, you might reasonably ask, why run a Landing Page test? Here are some good reasons:

- As mentioned earlier, if you run a high-quality test, you can learn whether you have a fighting chance.

- Collecting e-mail addresses provides you a list of people to follow up with as you pursue the idea (including, one would hope, early adopters).

- There is the possibility, again, of truly validating an idea.

Recall that Lucas Carlson at AppFog started with a landing page test that generated 800 e-mail addresses overnight. Unlike other entrepreneurs who instantly believe that whatever number of addresses collected proves idea validity, Carlson doubled down on testing with what we call a "high hurdle" test. He wanted to only let into his beta program early adopters willing to jump through a hoop. The willingness of customers to fill out his painfully in-depth survey was great validation of the idea through indication of a deep level of pain.

How, then, is the landing page underutilized? Because it's still primarily a tool for high-tech startups, when in fact it could quite easily be deployed by startups outside of tech, as well as by big companies.

We once counseled a biotech entrepreneur who had invented a technology for folding proteins. He related to us that he was stymied because his technology appeared applicable to many, if not all, protein families with some future investment and fine-tuning. However, at the time, it only worked for a specific set of protein families. As such, he was unsure whether the protein families he could fold at the time were commercially interesting, and whether he should invest time and money into configuring his technology for another specific set.

We reframed this question through the lens of market risk and technical risk: Was the current set of proteins commercially viable? Yes or no? What was the technical risk of supporting other protein families?

Either way, what sets of protein families, irrespective of his ability to fold them, showed market pull? In other words, could he de-risk the market further before accumulating additional technical risk?

We suggested he consider a landing page viability test that allowed those working with specific proteins to opt in based on information provided. Then, we also asked him to consider running ads in a medical journal pertinent to his target market segment, which would actively test demand for various, specific protein families.

Concierge Test

The Concierge test is testing by doing. Never a week goes by that we don't hear of a new online multisided marketplace idea. These entrepreneurs have grand plans to build an online platform that brings together two or more parties who aren't readily accessible to each other.

In the instance of creating a new market, in other words bringing new buyers and sellers together, the Concierge test is conducted by manually bringing buyers and sellers together and repeating that process until you learn (1) whether taking a cut of the transaction would support a business, and (2) what part of the transaction can be automated.

This test might be useful in non-marketplace examples, too. In many instances, if you can't make a transaction happen in the real world in real time, it's not likely to work online, either. If nothing else, you will learn what it will take to get the parties to the market.

Services-based businesses are good examples of Concierge tests. If someone pays you for a service, you pretty much know a pain exists and someone is willing to pay for it. (This is beyond the point that many product startups get to!) This, of course, doesn't mean you have a scalable business. Whether a product-based startup can be built from a successfully sold service is no small matter.

Converting a services business into a (scalable) products business is always a tough proposition.

(We once worked with a successful consulting business to help establish a products division. Despite the fact that executives could never get their heads around non-billable hours, we were able to build an MVP, execute one major pivot, and land a six-figure annual license deal within eight months. Because of not meeting business-plan expectations and other internal issues, however, even this win was not enough to save the project.)

Presuming one is able to prove viability with the services version, what is the next biggest risk to offering a product-based solution instead? Two things come to mind:

1. Is the problem even solvable with a product? Believe it or not, some problems are not. Some problems are human based. Problems caused by personality, habit, emotions, or behavior may be big problems, but products might not do the trick. (Products relying on infomercials and smarmy direct-marketing techniques often rely on this fact in order to sell products to the unaware.)

2. Are customers willing to substitute human service with a product? In long-term services businesses, the trust engendered by personal relationships is often necessary to create passion in the business. This may be threatened by product. Which isn't to say that you shouldn't pursue the opportunity, but you might need to look for a different market segment.

To move toward a product-based solution, one needs to find what within their existing process can be automated, using existing passionate, service-based customers as early adopters. They will be your bellwether to see if you can provide benefits of automation beyond the value your service-product offers.

Case Study: Curating User Experience

Steven Cox's vision was to let musicians teach. Through his own experiences as well as those of friends, he knew that the toughest part about being a musician is making a living. So many musicians turn to teaching music. The toughest part about teaching is finding and retaining students. So being an Internet entrepreneur as well as a musician, he decided to combine those passions and create a lead-generation site for music teachers, called Click for Lessons. We spoke with Steven and his co-founder, Chris Waldron.

Cox experimented with several MVPs that alternatively offered unlimited leads to teachers at $30/month, tried to create a free model with advertisements, and sold leads on a per-lead basis. It was an idea—bringing music teachers and students together—in search of a business model. They grew the lead program to over 4,000 instructors in 15 major U.S. cities with revenue exceeding six figures, but growth was slow and hard-fought, and eventually stagnant.

Through failed experiments and speaking with teachers, the Click for Lessons team learned a couple of key points:

- The musicians they targeted were living paycheck to paycheck, and many didn't have credit cards.
- If they paid $6/lead, they fell $6 in the hole.

To find students, Click for Lessons simply used online marketing techniques to snare students looking for teachers, and sold their information to the handful of teachers they had recruited.

Steve Cox: "The epiphany came after talking to a bunch of our instructors. I'm telling them they can earn thousands of dollars per lead—they just have to get them to buy-in. I'm frustrated, complaining to a buddy, who says: 'The problem is you're trying to get the musicians to be like you.' And I thought, 'He's right.' I'm a business guy; I like the interaction with my customer. These musicians don't really want to run a business. At the same time, we're getting angry calls from the students, saying, 'You guys are worthless—none of the teachers called me back.'"

Cox went back to the office and pulled the plug. Several days later, they had a new MVP.

Chris Waldron: "It was January 2008, and based on what we had learned we went out and recruited 30 instructors by hand. We got them to sign agreements and commit to certain revenue or pay rate that we were willing to pay them, and then we hand matched them to actual students. For the students, we rigged together a phone system, literally like ripped open the wires and rewired it. We had some open source from a phone system, and we hacked together a call center and published an 800 number and basically for half a day took calls on the student side and the other half recruited teachers."

A classic concierge MVP!

Up to that point, Click for Lessons was just an Internet marketing play, which wasn't the type of business they wanted to build. It matched neither their values nor their vision.

Cox: "If all we could be is a company that was really good at search engine optimization, that wasn't exciting to us. Music is emotional, and by sitting in the middle of the transaction we have all the data related to the actual student experience. That was exciting for us to be able to leverage in building an actual brand that could be considered the place to go to buy services. The vision that we started to create in 2008 is to become the Amazon of services."

So they had finally identified a viable online marketplace, but the Internet is awash in failed marketplaces. Do a Google search for any local small business and you will get a dozen online business directories, each imploring owners to "claim their business," each with pedestrian five-star consumer reviews capability. To grow, Click for Lessons needed to establish its "shadow force": its core competency not readily visible to the outside world, but that drives market differentiation. They rebranded as TakeLessons and learned to bring new value to the equation.

Cox: "We continue to evolve the platform as we figure it out. We didn't know what was required, but we knew that we had to control the experience more than before."

TakeLessons learned that if they can deliver enough students to the teachers they're okay with taking a lower price as long as they're making consistent money on a weekly basis. A typical marketplace brings buyer and seller together and then leaves it up to them to conduct the transaction, but that's not the way small business works.

Waldron: "One of the biggest insights when moving to this model, which still blows my mind to this day, is there are many teachers who would rather not address the fact that their customer owes them money. They're concerned they'll lose the customer. They felt awkward in front of little Johnny saying, 'Hey, tell your mom to pay me $150 this month,' and they would teach for another month without getting paid. So we saw that if we collected the money, the teachers feel more comfortable."

Cox: "It's like we were getting back to the vision the long way about. Teachers just want to teach. They don't want to market, sell, schedule, or collect payment. As a platform, we needed to provide value so the teachers want to be on the platform."

Unlike other service-based marketplace platforms, which must bend over backwards to keep teachers from violating terms of service by going outside the system, TakeLessons was creating demand to be on the platform. The big win for the teachers, of course, is steadier work and peace of mind.

So hiring the next instructor in New York City on the same block was not as valuable as hiring someone in the next market over. TakeLessons looks at the demand in a particular area: all the leads, all the searches, and all the visits, so they're able to identify hot spots in the system.

Waldron: "What we're able to do is to understand that if this teacher application comes through and she says that she travels five miles and also has a studio, what we're able to do is to create what we call a coverage score. So this is 100 percent coverage, and then based on the subjects that she teaches and based on whether she travels, we're able to see how much of our demand she covers."

They know when they add a teacher to the system they are getting a return on marketing dollars. They can also see from a national perspective where demand is short. To make this work, of course, they needed students, too, but rather than just leads, they needed relationships. Building out the call center rather than driving bookings online allows TakeLessons to not only increase the conversion rate, but learn. Many companies are so focused on automating and reducing costs, they don't have the opportunity to talk to and glean insights from customers.

Waldron: "Our revenues would be literally a tenth of what they are if we did not have that high-touch method. I can tell you that in our student support call center we average 175 calls a day, Monday through Friday. One thing we found interesting, for example, is that one reason why a student likes going with us is they actually don't feel guilty when they cancel. They can call up TakeLessons, cancel with that teacher, get another teacher and a 30-second conversation and there's no guilt associated with quitting."

Cox: "The key insight we had was the need to protect the student's experience."

In order to protect it, TakeLessons disengages with underperforming teachers on a regular basis. If they find the instructor routinely gives a less-than-stellar student experience, TakeLessons chooses to place the student with another teacher.

The student's experience is largely dependent on the quality and dedication of the instructor. The experience is made better by curating instructors.

Waldron: "When we talk about our teachers, it's not that we scraped 30,000 profiles and called these our teachers. Our teachers have signed contracts, they've attended orientations, and they have agreed to uphold the way we treat customers."

Student complaints obviously affect teacher evaluations, but data also helps inform decisions. TakeLessons monitors student engagement by subject, billing plan, geographic area, and by instructor. They measure lessons taken per month to indicate that they are learning and progressing. They measure month on month retention by calendar and user cohorts.

Teacher engagement is measured by many factors, including how often they update their calendar.

Waldron: "We could sign up a hundred instructors this month but if none of them log in 30 days later to review and update their calendar, the teacher's never going to respond to bookings."

They measure the time to contact new students.

Waldron: "So when we send them an alert either by text message or by e-mail saying, 'We have a new student for you,' we measure the next time they view their dashboard. We can see how quick they are to reply and respond. Once they actually talk to the student they have to click a link and we measure that. We can align or measure how closely related that is to the teacher's retention and how good they are and the quality of the students' experience."

TakeLessons does webinars so teachers can learn from other teachers, and they measure attendance.

Waldron: "We have a teacher in Atlanta whose average retention is 40 lessons, which is amazing; so how does she do that? She'll put together content and we facilitate a webinar and she'll run it, and teachers from around the country follow up after with questions."

Having grown up with a relatively high customer acquisition cost (which enabled their learning), much of TakeLessons analytics focuses on reducing that cost and maximizing lifetime value. So they run experiments.

Waldron: "We often test pricing. We'll take a teacher, for example, say Jessica, she's in Houston and her average retention is 22 lessons, and we have 60 students to book. So we'll adjust her pricing maybe up $5 and down $5 and run a cohort analysis of students who are starting at the same time, with the same teacher under different pricing, and then see how that relates to their retention. The goal is to maximize the lifetime value. So if we charge $5 less but the student stays 14 lessons longer, we're making more profit on a per-student basis, and the teacher is happier as well."

It's an intricate loop whereby TakeLessons works to help teachers be better teachers, in order to protect the student's experience, in order to retain students so that teachers are more successful. This loop is TakeLessons' "shadow force."

By constantly working to improve the loop, they increase customer passion on both sides of the marketplace, grow, and differentiate themselves from the competition.

Cox: "Our next big inflection is where we figure out how we can get students to share their experiences, and the music teacher community is very connected. So how do we continue to provide more value to them? We need to continue to help instructors learn from each other how to be great music teachers."

Waldron: "So that's the point, do we have product market fit for delivering on the one thing that both teachers and students want, which is each other? I would say yes, and we do that job excellently, but in order to build the vision we need to create more passion. We talk about it, and Steven just reinforces that all the time."

Cox: "It's like there is no product-market fit. We have to get more teachers where they're needed and make them better every day. We need to improve the user experience every day. We need to continuously add more value."

Waldron: "That's why it's really hard if you want to build a brand that people trust. We could just create a local dot-com or a Yelp where it's just fine, but our vision is to be able to take this and expand it into other services that people buy for their home. If we want to be able to do that and then leverage that, we have to build a brand people trust."

Cox: "Our investor, Maynard Webb (former COO of eBay), told us the next generation of marketplaces like TakeLessons were building a marketplace for the equivalent of the eBay Powersellers—proven merchants with good track records—something the company can stand behind."

Wizard of Oz Test

Similar to the Concierge test, the Wizard of Oz test requires little or no actual product development. It could also be called the Hamster Power Generator test, similar to the cartoons in which you discover hamsters on exercise wheels are powering the car engine. Basically, you provide a front end for your product where someone can buy, yet you fulfill the product's purpose manually.

This is about as *lean* as it gets. In lean manufacturing, a production stage is started only when demanded by the downstream process. In the Wizard of Oz test, the product itself is in action only when requested by the customer through placing an order.

Zappos started out as a Wizard of Oz test. CEO Tony Hsieh tells of meeting Nick Swinmurn, founder at Zappos, in 1998:

Nick summarized his entire pitch in three sentences: "Footwear is a $40 billion industry in the United States, of which catalog sales make up $2 billion. It's likely that e-commerce will continue to grow. And it is likely that people will continue to wear shoes in the foreseeable future."

He reserved the domain name Shoesite[4] and without building out any sort of inventory system, he literally walked down the street to the local shoe store, took photographs of their shoes, and posted them on the website. Several months into the project, Nick was getting $2,000 worth of orders per week. They weren't making any money, because after an order was placed, "Nick would run to the local shoe store, buy the item, and then ship it out to the customer."[5]

In 1998, Nick Swinmurn used a classic example of a Wizard of Oz test to test market risk. So did another company from the same time period, CarsDirect.

Case Study: Idea to Wizard of Oz in under 90 Days

Day 1

Back in 1998, Idealab founder Bill Gross wanted to buy a new car. So off he went to his local Southern California dealership, where he immediately experienced the typical new-car-lot runaround: "Oh, that car's not in stock. What you're asking for is very rare. We don't have that color on the West Coast. You're better off buying what we have on the lot," and so on.

Like the entrepreneur he is, Gross said, "There's got to be a better way."

He decided to build a website where you could go online, configure the car you want, see the price right then and there, put a deposit down with your credit card and you're set for delivery. Big deal, you might say, but remember, this is 1998. Amazon.com was three years old. The idea scratched Gross's itch, but lots of people pushed back on the idea:

- "People won't use their credit cards online."
- "No one will put money down on a car, sight unseen."
- "Maybe you'd do that, but there's no way anyone else will."

Rather than sit around and debate, Gross built a test. "Let's put up a website and let's build the proposition out of what we want to offer, and then let's see if anybody wants to do it; if so we'll build the company, and if not, we won't build the company, but let's just find out."

Idealab hired a founding executive, "Bob," to help prototype the idea within 90 days.

Day 45

Bill asks Bob how it's coming along and he says: "I've been calling all the car dealerships, Ford and Honda, and I'm having a difficult time sourcing the cars."

Bill responds, "What? What are you calling them for? We're just going to put this up and see if anybody wants to buy a car. If someone buys, we're going to go down to the Honda Auto Mall and buy the car at retail and deliver it to the person on a flatbed truck and lose money on it."

Day 70

Bob has a problem building the "configurator."

"The what?" Bill asks.

"You know, the way to allow the customer to choose all the different options. It's really hard, too many packages, too many different variables to make this work cleanly."

"No, no, no. Just let them type in a blank field. We'll have a human read the thing. Don't worry about it."

Day 80

Bob has run into another issue.

"Launch the site," Bill says.

"You haven't even heard . . . "

"Turn it on!" So on a Thursday night, Bob launches the site. Friday morning, Bill meets with Bob.

"Well, what happened last night?" Bill asks.

"We sold four cars."

"Hurry up and turn the site off!" They quickly took the site down because they had just lost money on four cars, not just two, but at least they had an answer. People will order cars sight unseen on the Internet via a direct-sales model.

CarsDirect became Internet Brands in 2005 and went public in 2007.

Crowd-Funding Test

Although some entrepreneurs spend three months writing business plans for their gadgets, others make a product video and seek funding on Kickstarter. Kickstarter and other crowd-funding sites are a highly disruptive force that allow entrepreneurs to test and validate product ideas very quickly, with little product development.

As of this writing, Kickstarter has led to the successful funding of over 24,000 projects, backed by 2 million people who contributed $250 millon.

The Olloclip is one such example. The brainchild of Patrick O'Neill, the Olloclip is a pocket-sized, three-in-one lens you can quick-mount to your iPhone to dramatically improve photo quality. From the outset, O'Neill's ambition was to get the lens into Apple's retail stores, but that's no small ambition.

"There's so much you have to do: you've got to get the company set up, streamline production of your product, and be able to produce in mass quantities. Your packaging needs to be right. You have to get that developed and designed and manufactured and everything takes a long time. Everything takes longer than you would think and costs more, but you've got to do it right."

So you can bet the farm on your idea or create prototypes on a 3D printer and launch a project on Kickstarter.

Thirteen hundred backers and 1,500 units later, they were in business. "That gave us 1,300 really enthusiastic, motivated early adopters who would go out and take our product and use it and spread the word. So that just branched out to more and more people. Apple found out about us because of Kickstarter."

Case Study: Two-Sided Market Lean Startup

TaskRabbit's original logo, sourced through 99designs.

Lean Entrepreneur: So correct me if I'm wrong, but you sort of got started on a community forum, is that right? There were discussions happening on a particular forum where this marketplace sort of emerged by itself?

99designs: Absolutely. So SitePoint is this huge community of web and design technology people. In their discussion groups there was a really popular design forum and we noticed this emerging behavior where people were saying, "Hey, I'm looking for a logo. Do any of you have any ideas of what sort of things I should do?" and then seven or eight designers would chime in with concepts or ideas and at the end of the thread they'd be like, "Oh, hey, I really love that one. What's your PayPal address? Can I pay you some money for it?"

Since that started happening with some regularity we created a new forum for it to grow, and then we decided to attach a fee to keep things under control. That didn't seem to dampen people's enthusiasm at all. Soon after we had people saying to us, "Give us tools to make this easier to do," and so it was one of those really easy decisions on what to build. We built the minimum viable product for what was, at the time, called SitePoint Contests, and it was simply an extension of the discussion forum with some extra tools that helped people collect and organize designs and pick a winner and announce what their prize was going to be.

In 2008 we spun it out on its own to 99designs, and ever since then we've incrementally added—and sometimes removed—features and things that people need to run a contest well.

LE: The forum you created for these transactions was sort of an MVP itself, proving the viability before writing a line of code. Plus, since this was in an established design community, you didn't have to guess what your market segment was; they were already right there.

99designs: I think that one of the wonderful things about a big technical community is that there are little pockets of markets, and I think part of the trick is being able to find those markets and listen to what they're asking for and perhaps see a little bit beyond exactly what they're asking for and build them what they need.

LE: What were your thoughts around the pricing strategy? Did you want to weed out those people that you felt were never going to pay?

99designs: Putting a small price on it was a mechanism to ensure that people have some skin in the game; it keeps out spammers, and it protects both sides of the market, right? We were trying to protect customers from designers who might be submitting stock and we're trying to protect designers from customers who don't really have any intention of paying. Also, let's not underestimate that creating cash flow for this was an important thing because SitePoint had always been self-funded.

LE: It's funny that some entrepreneurs want to overcomplicate their business models and worry about money later. So I love the fact that you're just, from the get-go going to say, "Well we've got to test to see if there is a revenue model here."

99designs: Absolutely. It's not a business if no one's going to pay for it.

LE: What about determining what features to build?

99designs: One of the things Mark [co-founder Mark Harbottle] is a genius at is listening to what people are asking for and then figuring out what's the simplest thing that will satisfy the most people.

We've always been extremely close to our customers and our designers, watching in great detail what they do, how they do it, how they're responding to us, and what their needs are. One of the very first things we built was a rich dashboard that gave us insight into the marketplace dynamics, and it's always a balancing act between the two sides. We've always tracked metrics on both sides and used them to make decisions about what features make sense to build.

LE: How do you know when not to listen to some requests?

99designs: There are definitely some kinds of mechanisms for sanity checking the feedback that you're getting from customers. You always need to be thinking about why they're asking for something, not what they're asking for. So are they asking for a feature that's actually a symptom of a greater problem and if that's the case what's the simplest way that you can fix the greater problem so that they don't have that requirement anymore?

A lot of our feedback comes through our designer-support team and our customer-support team, and we're constantly sanity checking volume as well because, you know, typically it's very much a noisy minority. When a problem arises, it's problematic and it's difficult for you as a customer-support rep to deal with, so that's why it sticks in your mind and you think that we need to address it. But when we look at it in the greater stats context, we can either live with this problem occurring or we can address it at some point or look at the bigger problem and address it over time.

LE: I'm curious whether you see the product being pulled in different directions, and how you monitor whether you're maintaining the value prop for your existing customers as you're adding new stuff or changing stuff. How do you deal with that?

99designs: We follow the metrics closely. We look at things like Net Promoter Score on a regular basis and we have another score internally we call a Design Quality Index and so we're looking to see the number of referral visits we're getting a month. We actually encourage people to leave testimonials for us, and also from our designers, we are able to measure how many of those we are getting.

We have a very closely built-in feedback mechanism that allows us to see if we are delivering a quality product and if people who are getting that quality product are happier. So if we saw anything where we were moving away from our core and people weren't getting what they were wanting, then we would start to see changes in those. But it is difficult—it's hard to please everyone, and then certainly, some of your early adopters can also be your noisiest detractors, because they're the ones who don't actually like change and liked the ways things were when you were small and kind of exclusive almost to them and so, you know, you kind of almost have to take it.

LE: Any advice for entrepreneurs who believe they're facing this chicken-and-egg, two-sided marketplace dilemma?

99designs: Yep. I mean I think it's pretty clear which one you need to focus on; it's a supply/demand problem. So if you create demand, then supply will follow. Our strategy in the first year or two was to just try to be the marketplace that had the most projects on offer. So we focused a lot on the customer side of the business, and I think in the early stages of the marketplace business that that's kind of the right thing to do. If you're providing the right opportunities for your suppliers then it basically stabilizes itself early on.

LE: Did you ever face the dilemma where there is an incentive for people to leave the marketplace? Like say they found a designer that they really liked and so then they don't really need the marketplace any more, or has that really been sort of a nonissue?

99designs: Absolutely. Our vision has always been to provide ways for freelance designers to monetize their work. Contests were the first piece of that puzzle. We think of contests as similar to a dating service. It's a great way for customers that don't know what their design requirements are to meet a great designer. I'm sure you've been through the design process and no matter how great a designer is that you meet, often they're not the right person. So the contest format really helps people match up with someone who gets them and is going to meet their needs and then they're going to reconnect with that person for ongoing work. It's an interesting challenge for us in that we've captured the first piece of the puzzle and now we've just got to iterate and provide a compelling experience for the ongoing design work.

We also understood pretty early on that this was part of the value proposition for designers. Designers are, in our contest model, by its very nature, speculating their time. They're submitting concepts with a chance to win the project, but when they win, they have a high chance of getting follow-on work from the customer. So we actually go out of our way to promote that, even if it goes off-platform, as ironic as that sounds. That's actually true to our vision and true to the value proposition, which is creating opportunities for designers. So we're obviously constantly looking at how we can build new tools and create a great way for that ongoing relationship to be fostered, but we get a lot of benefit from the designers' participation in the first place in making that contest experience super rich and super valuable for the customer.

LE: So it's staying core to your original vision, your original value, but then, also, over time, figuring out new ways to add value that just continues that relationship with the designers.

99designs: Yes, absolutely.

Prototyping

Prototypes have long been used in manufacturing, design, computer programming, and electronics to de-risk product development. A prototype might be a simulation of the end product or an early version that is progressing down the actual development process.

A prototype allows both builders and potential customers to evaluate whether the product is being developed correctly, such that it will solve the problem it intends to solve. Depending on the purpose of the product and stage of the prototype, it can help answer questions like:

- Will it fit; are the dimensions correct?
- Will it fit aesthetically; does it look good?
- Is the design usable?

- Does the core technology work?
- How close to solving the problem is it?

Hardware entrepreneurs, especially, rely on prototypes. Just as with batch-and-queue processing, the further down the path mistakes are discovered, the more expensive the resolution. If you are queuing product components between production stages and find a component problem far down the line, you have a stack of unusable parts, often already integrated with other parts.

Similarly, if you wait too long to test your product in a real environment, the harder it will be to uncover the problem, and development done down the line from the problem

will have to be redone, perhaps completely re-engineered.

Today, engineers use computer modeling to predict problems and employ 3D printers to produce prototypes very rapidly, within days or hours, that can be tested in the field with small sets of customers to validate fit, features, and design.

In the end, there are an infinite number of viability tests. It's up to your creativity to design an experiment that removes a risk from your business model. People have used mockups, wireframes, mini-apps designed to test specific user behavior or eliminate technical risk. Pop-up stores, food carts, and 3D models cost less than building out product and may inform you of the market opportunity.

To determine what you should test, draw your business-model ecosystem, identify all the participants you believe you need to be successful, and posit the value proposition necessary to involve each of them. Determine which components are mission critical and which you can eliminate while in the near term. Prioritize the entities, and you can get a picture of where your biggest risks are. Design experiments to overcome the risks.

With virtually all products these days, the number-one risk is: Does anyone care? Your best experiment is one that informs you with a solid yes or no.

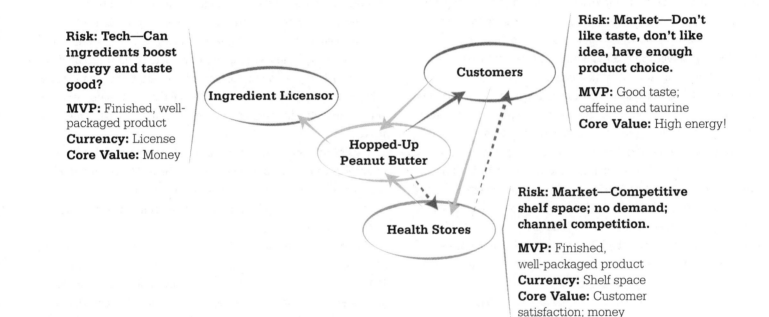

Risk: Tech—Can ingredients boost energy and taste good?

MVP: Finished, well-packaged product
Currency: License
Core Value: Money

Risk: Market—Don't like taste, don't like idea, have enough product choice.

MVP: Good taste; caffeine and taurine
Core Value: High energy!

Risk: Market—Competitive shelf space; no demand; channel competition.

MVP: Finished, well-packaged product
Currency: Shelf space
Core Value: Customer satisfaction; money

Ingredient Licensor

Customers

Hopped-Up Peanut Butter

Health Stores

Case Study: MVP: Motor Vehicle Prototype

Kickstarter is a great way to sell before building visual or less expensive products—products for which the customer can easily grasp the value proposition or those for which the downside to failure is relatively inexpensive. What if your vision is to build a radically new vehicle, however? Such an undertaking takes an incredibly large investment, typically several million dollars.

Lit Motors faced that dilemma. Two years ago Lit Motors was in a position to raise $1.5 million for their first investment round, from venture capitalists who were impressed with their idea.

Lit Motors is a transportation startup, focusing on electric two-wheeled vehicles for personal transportation. Their C-1 brings together the safety and convenience of a car with the efficiency and agility of a motorcycle. The main difference between the C-1 and every other two-wheeled vehicle on the road is their gyro stabilization system, which gives it the stability and safety of a four-wheeled car. This represents the first real safety innovation in two-wheeled vehicles in 80 years.

"So that's the engineering side of the business," says founder Daniel Kim. "We've got great technology, it's really cool and it works. But on the other side we heard, 'It seems to make a lot of sense, but do you have anyone who will buy it?' That was something none of the engineers could answer."

The company management had a conversation with the entire team about whether to take the money with the lower valuation and build out the technology, or take less money, attempt to de-risk the market, and raise another round later at a higher valuation.

They chose to go the latter route. "Basically we decided to create our own qualitative marketing research clinic. We knew what the technology risk is and we're going to be able to de-risk that. It's just a bunch of ones and zeros and a lot of electrons, and that's established. But trying to figure out the market bit is hard, especially with technology like ours and in a market that has had a pretty rocky road."

Lit Motors decided to provide as much as possible of the customer experience of buying a radical new vehicle. "We wanted to create the most realistic scenario of an actual showroom experience that we could." So they hand-built a showroom and a full-scale prototype of the vehicle inside the laboratory.

"We built a bike you could sit in, that had the real experience of sitting inside the enclosed motorcycle. The same experience that you'd have if you walked into a showroom at a place like Toyota and you got to sit in the car. The door felt real, the experience was basically real, the only difference was you couldn't drive it off the lot."

They put together a short 1.5-minute day-in-the-life video depicting what a morning commute might look like. It was a cost-effective way to give a showroom experience for a vehicle that didn't really exist yet.

Lit Motors opened the showroom up to the public and took pre-orders on the spot. They also looked for why people didn't buy, and what would get them over the top to purchase.

- They ended up getting nearly 100 people who put money down on the spot—a real transaction for a preorder.
- The people who bought on the spot were those who basically had this sort of idea for a while. They wanted some kind of small, fuel-efficient vehicle. Maybe they had the two-wheeled concept in mind, maybe they didn't, but as soon as they saw the C-1 they said, "Sold, all in, let's do this."
- They learned that a key point was spousal approval and so designed the bike to appeal to both masculine and feminine aesthetics.

Lit Motors hand-built the prototype in a similar manner to actual production

techniques, to learn about what scaling the process might require. The sheet metal stamping tooling that typical car companies use would have cost millions of dollars and wouldn't have allowed for changes on the fly. Instead, they hand-shaped the sheet metal themselves.

"This gave us a similar result, allowed for quick design changes, and taught us quite a bit about how the actual production process will go. This de-risked the technical aspects of production."

Perhaps what is most notable about how Lit Motors approached the inherent uncertainty in the market is what they didn't do. Most simply, they didn't scale up or optimize for production or selling the C-1. They optimized their processes for learning.

A common mistake of startups of all types is to scale production too early in a vain attempt to compete with and imitate large, established businesses. Large, established businesses aren't fatal to disruptive startups, but lack of traction or market indifference usually is.

Lit Motors' learn-and-validate-first approach to de-risking the market helps them navigate the treacherous, far-right side of the innovation spectrum, rocky and stormy waters in which many a disruptive startup has foundered.

Work to Do

Use the template below to track experiments you run to validate specific assumptions.

Segment:		
Assumption Viability Test	Hypothesis	Result
Persona exists/details correct:		
Customer has problem/pain/passion:		
Customer will respond to solution (high level):		
Customer will be satisfied with specific functionality *x, y, z*:		
Customer will become passionate when:		
Customer will make final decision to buy when:		
Customer will trust the company when:		
Customer will trust the product when:		
Customer will want to learn more when:		

7

Data's Double-Edged Sword

Data is the weapon of modern businesses. Like a sword, it is only as useful as the person who wields it.

Although data can't make decisions for you, if you're tracking the right data, it provides you with information that must inform your decisions. To an entrepreneur, finding patterns in the data is nirvana. Market signal is embedded in the data: that which informs where you should direct your efforts, where not to, when to double down, and when to pivot.

But like a double-edged sword, data should not be brandished thoughtlessly, as careless use is potentially as risky to the entrepreneur as it is useful.

Most modern businesses, including startups, are inundated with data. This causes a couple of fundamental problems. First, many are reluctant to properly instrument their value stream—in other words, measure the effectiveness of business activities—for (a very legitimate) fear of merely increasing the speed at which they drown in data. This concern is not without foundation, since the

> Baseball scout Grady: "Now there are intangibles that only baseball people understand. You're discounting what scouts have done for 150 years."
>
> Billy Beane: "Adapt or die. [. . .] You don't have a crystal ball. You can't look at a kid and predict his future any more than I can. I've sat at those tables with you and listened to you tell those parents 'I know, I know. When it comes to your son, I know.' And you don't. You don't."
>
> —Steven Zaillian & Aaron Sorkin, *Moneyball* (Columbia Pictures, 2011)

second most prominent problem is successfully extracting useful knowledge from the data.

The trick is in figuring out which metrics to track. Tracking the right stuff actually solves both problems. As a startup, you are already juggling resources in order to get done what you need to get done, but how are you figuring out what needs to get done?

Several things to keep in mind:

- Focus on what moves the needle of your business.
- Actionable knowledge pulled from data makes your resources *more* efficient.

- Not all metrics need to be technically produced and analyzed.

Actionable data means just what it says: Data from which you will take action. Tracking the cumulative number of mobile application downloads is a rather worthless metric if no one's using your mobile application. Once you know people are using your application (based on data), the same

measure of downloads may become important as you track marketing activity efficacy.

The number of people liking your restaurant's Facebook page is meaningless if no one is actually going to your restaurant. The number of page views on your web page tells you little if no one's buying your product. Eric Ries call these "*vanity metrics*."

vanity metric: A vanity metric is one that is inaccessible, not actionable, and not auditable. It's not actionable because it doesn't map to a clear, meaningful effect on your business.

Vanity metrics are great for bragging rights and perhaps useful to raise money from impressionable venture capitalists, but they can be potentially destructive if used to manage the business, as they allow uninformed entrepreneurs to slice their own

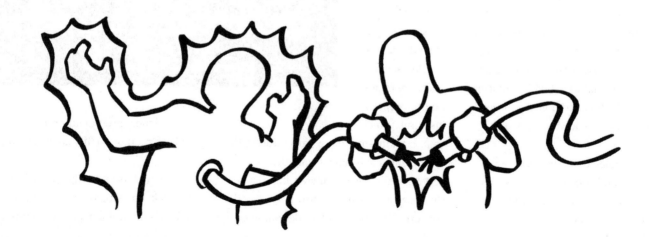

feet off, instead of slicing through the competition.

We once worked with a company that raised money on the number of active users and a viral coefficient that wasn't calculated correctly. In effect, they were vanity metrics. Leaving aside the fact that media and venture capitalists love vanity metrics, there's real danger in trying to scale your company based on believing your vanity metrics.

Actionable metrics are always contextual, hence will vary by company type and stage. If you have already nailed product engagement (in other words people love your product) then your engagement metrics are no longer the ones that will move the needle of your business. Although they should still be tracked to ensure you don't lose engagement, your focus might shift to acquiring more users to engage. Similarly, tracking data that tells you what color your "buy now" button should be isn't very compelling as you focus on building out a field sales team.

From your value stream, you can determine how to measure what moves the needle.

The key to determining which metrics to measure and when is to optimize from the inside out:

Entrepreneurs want to focus on buzz. They figure their lack of traction comes from a lack of eyeballs. What they're really saying is, of course, the right segment hasn't yet discovered the solution they built. In other words, the company is having trouble finding anyone who cares. Building positive buzz isn't marketing's job; it's the product's. Marketing can increase awareness of the product, but if the product sucks, that's what the buzz will be. Marketing is for leveraging buzz that already exists.

Engagement and passion are critical. You don't have a business if you don't nail engagement and passion.

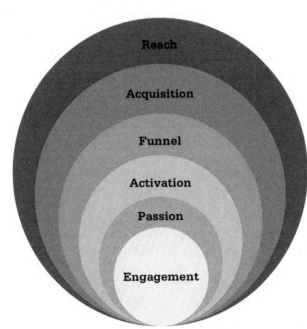

Engagement + passion + reach
= product-market fit

You waste reach without engagement and passion.

So what you must nail first is engagement with your product.[1]

Engagement means that a customer uses the product in such a way as to satisfy the need for the product. In other words, the product has performed the job it was hired for. Customers have reached their goal. Their problem has been solved. So how do you measure it?

Going back to the value stream, what is the specific functionality or interaction with your product that drives the value proposition promised? How often should a user interact with that functionality to realize the promise. Measure that for engagement. If you don't reach the expected level of usage, you must either iterate on the functionality or you must change your usage expectation.

Although presented here as three separate components of lean startup—customer interaction, viability testing, and actionable data—in fact, these must work in tandem. For instance, data tells you what part of the business model needs improvement; customer interaction and iterative testing help determine what works. It's critical that these components are not nestled in big company silos that only serve to delay figuring things out. You don't want business-intelligence specialists spending weeks generating custom reports that show engagement dipping, while product managers create 10-page feature lists, the design team schedules their six months of deliverables, and software engineers work on issues pulled from the bug database.

Whether in a big company or small, high-tech or low-tech, cross-functional teams should be organized around solving a problem that *moves the needle* of the business.

Case Study:
Disrupting the Undisruptable

By now you have likely realized that the fast-moving and iterative lean startup processes don't apply just to Internet companies, but just to hammer it home, we spoke with Tom Fishburne, founder and CEO of Marketoon Studios. Tom ran marketing at Method Products, a company that designs and manufactures nontoxic, biodegradable cleaning supplies.

Lean Entrepreneur: As a marketer, how did you become interested in iterative forms of product development?

Tom Fishburne: It occurred to me that where we were in consumer packaged goods [CPG] seemed very similar to the early days of web development. We had these lengthy waterfall-style product development cycles that severely restricted how we could go to market. Once you get down the path of the development process, there comes a point where you can't change requirements, even when you have new information.

✓ CONCEPT TESTS
✓ FOCUS GROUPS
✓ INTERNET PANELS
✓ STORE INTERCEPTS
✓ IN-HOME TESTS
✓ MORE FOCUS GROUPS
✓ BASES I TEST
✓ BASES II TEST

WE FINALLY GOT THROUGH ALL THE MARKET RESEARCH REQUIRED TO LAUNCH OUR NEW PRODUCT.

BUT WE'RE RETIRED NOW.

z z z

TOM FISH BURNE

© Marketoonist

And because it's such a massive effort to launch new consumer products, you end up with a philosophy where you do a lot of product testing, and then you have a big launch. But all too often, the testing doesn't map to real-world conditions and you end up with a big launch followed by a big failure.

The response to the failure is simply to increase the amount of testing, which makes it even harder to get ideas to market.

This mindset also creates a sense of risk aversion.

The crazier ideas never see the light of day, because they can't survive the testing methodology to get to market. Even though they may be great ideas, you never get the product into the consumers' hands. The only ideas that launch are those that are similar to what was already out there. This is problematic because, by definition, launching things that are similar to what is on the market means there's not much innovation.

LE: So how do you apply lean startup–like thinking to a consumer packaged good?

Fishburne: The traditional school of CPG says that it won't work because you have to scale up to massive production lines. What I learned in my experience at Method Products, a scrappy startup CPG company, was that, in fact, you could place small bets and do things on a small scale and then learn in the market rather than artificial pseudo-learning from focus groups and huge launches.

We were trying to create innovations in a very stodgy category of household cleaning. So we had to take a radical approach to have points of differentiation.

To de-risk the market, we did a lot of rapid prototyping in-house, including a 3D printer that let us print new bottle designs. I had worked in an environment at General Mills where when we launched a new product, there would be a structural design stage when you do some exploratory work coming up with a new bottle design, but then it was pretty much done. There was maybe time for one revision, but because it would take such a long time to get a physical sample, it would eat up a lot of your development time.

At Method, we tried to flip that around and by having a 3D printer in the building. We could have a discussion, turn that into a sketch, then into a CAD drawing, and then we'd have a physical bottle in our hands. In launching one new bottle design for a concentrated laundry detergent, we had upwards of 45 different design iterations from beginning to end, over a short period of time. It was fundamentally agile software development programming, and every week we'd have a new bottle and then we'd continue to refine it.

LE: Why is it important to get feedback from the market fast?

Fishburne: The danger of any kind of innovation is that you breathe your own exhaust and just listen to what's in the room. We tried to listen to our insights and instincts but we also had to remain open to information coming from the outside. We had varying degrees of success at that. When I started at Method and we were very small, we had no customer input; it was just listening to ourselves. A couple of in-market failures were reminders that sometimes we miss the mark and it was important to have the customer voice in the room.

LE: Where did your fundamental insights about how to innovate in cleaning supplies stem from?

Fishburne: A lot of marketers in these categories had come to the point where they assumed this was "a low interest category." People don't care about design in cleaning because they always have their bottles under their sink, forgetting the fact that people have those bottles hidden under their sink because they're designed in such an ugly way.

I think sometimes this happens in a lot of categories where the category knowledge hasn't been questioned for a while, and people create products that fit into the set of established rules, forgetting that there could be a different way of looking at it.

Method opened up some people's eyes to the fact that there were different ways of looking at even these old categories. It resulted in a re-evaluation of the overall category, and we saw competitors looking at what Method was doing and trying to copy it. That raised the ante for Method to continue to innovate and stay ahead, because the bigger companies and bigger brands were seeing Method on a shelf at Target and quickly trying to come up with their own versions.

LE: What do you find inhibits innovation in product development for CPG?

Fishburne: I often think about how large a launch needs to be. Big companies may start with a crazy idea and think, "We're going to do a small-scale trial," but very quickly they have to answer the question, "That's great, but how do we scale it so that it goes into 3,000 stores?" It's tough, because businesses are trained to look at the big launch. They have two launch windows a year, and they gun for those.

Many big CPG companies are struggling with that because they want to be more innovative and entrepreneurial, yet they have to meet that 3,000-store hurdle.

LE: How do you use the market to inform your vision?

Fishburne: I'm inspired by businesses that can look at smaller-scale in-market trials. Method tried to do this. We realized for the price of a billboard ad in Union Square we could build a working pop-up store instead. Sometimes we sold products that weren't available anywhere else in order to get real market learning. Effectively, it was a free trial because we were making money in the store and making simple bench samples to see what people thought about them. So I think there are a lot of opportunities for businesses to do that.

A lot of brands do pop-up stores for marketing purposes but it actually can be a powerful way to get in-market learning on new ideas too. Other markets can take the pop-up store approach, too, because it forces you to think about your brand in an entirely different way when you have to outfit a whole store as opposed to just outfitting a shelf.

If you're just looking at a competitive shelf in a Safeway, you're looking to the left and you're looking to the right and you think to yourself, "How do I break out of the clutter with these other products to the left and the right?"

That inherently puts the blinders on because you're shaped by what the category looks like today. Whereas if you have to create your own store you have to have your own vision for what you want to be as a brand and that's pretty powerful.

New Products

Problem-Solution Fit

Whether you're a startup or an existing business, when you're building new products, what moves the needle is learning whether the product is aligned with the right customers and is solving a real problem. Much of the early data is qualitative.

Set a goal for interviews: "We will talk to 10 customers and validate that they have problem *x*."

Identify key learning objectives, for example:

- Customer belongs to the previously defined market segment *x*.
- Customer feels deeply about the problem hypothesis. They experience the problem you think they do.
- Customer is actively seeking a solution or currently uses an unsatisfactory workaround.

You are looking for a pattern: If two people feel deeply about the problem hypothesis, five respond, "Meh," and three have no idea what you're talking about, you need to iterate.

Ask yourself:

- How do I find more people like the first two?
- What differentiates the two from the other eight?
- Can I refine my problem statement?

Go out and observe your segment and interview them again. Iterate until you find a pattern. Hopefully you can see why there's not much use for developing a product prior to finding such a pattern.

As you uncover the segment that is defined around a shared problem or passion, follow up with solution interviews. Use the same steps.

"We will interview the customers we have identified as early adopters to validate that our solution idea interests them and will work in their environment." By looking for feedback, you are inviting them to participate in its design versus simply trying to validate your existing thoughts. Frankly, if they have no input of their own, you haven't found early adopters.

Pro tip: If your product leans toward the disruptive side of the innovation spectrum, asking customers straight out if they will use the product or pay for it is next to worthless.

That noted, many first-time entrepreneurs still waffle about asking potential customers to pay for a product still in development. Noah Kagan of AppSumo suggests that entrepreneurs try his "velocity to dollar" hack: Ask for money sooner rather than later, while still in development. The sooner you get an actual dollar from a customer, the more likely it is you are solving a real problem.

Flip the value equation such that you are doing them a favor by making the product available.

This is a simple form of test-selling, which most certainly has its place in any entrepreneur's toolkit, but don't forget that test-selling can close off other interesting customer development possibilities. Could you have learned about other customer problems?

If responses are once again all over the map, you need to tighten your segmentation or solution statement. You want to discern, for example, between those who might prefer a mobile application versus a web app, a family pizzeria versus a hole-in-the-wall for hipsters, a product sold via the Internet versus a brick and mortar.

Remember, what product you end up offering is totally up to you. You are not doing what your customers say they want, but rather gathering data that instruct you regarding how deeply the problem is felt, the likelihood of adoption of different solutions based on current behavior, and whether customers are early adopters for your type of product. If none of your early adopters use smart phones, a mobile app might not be the best place to start.

Viability

Once you've validated that a customer segment exists that feels deeply about the pain or passion you're addressing, you might start running experiments to test (1) customer believability; (2) product fit; (3) business-model viability.

The data you collect depends on the test you run. Using ideas from the previous chapter or those that you dream up, run multiple experiments that expose problems with your segmentation, product ideas, or business-model assumptions. Continue to interact personally with customers in order to calibrate the quantitative data you're collecting from the experiments.

Each time your pattern breaks, you've likely identified a different subsegment. You want to track your data by subsegment, by bucket. This is how you learn to scale. Assuming that your customers are fungible and homogenous, results in problems down the road.

Recall our segment matrix:

	Depth of Pain A	Budget B	Ease of Reach C	Ease of MVP D	Size of Market E	Values F
Segment 1						
Segment 2						
Segment 3						
Segment 4						

To get this template and others, e-mail fish@leanentrepreneur.co.

As you build product or create a viability test—for example, a Wizard of Oz test in which you pretend the product is done, but you actually fulfill it manually—you might find that some customers you thought were in Segment 1, actually don't feel the pain deeply enough to sign up for your product. Should you put them in a different bucket? Do they fit in Segment 2?

Customer interaction and experiments are conducted to uncover and mitigate business-model risks, including most fundamentally, is the problem you are addressing worth solving from both your and your customer's point of view, and is it solvable?

Surveys can help corroborate segment assumptions on a larger scale, but should not be relied on solely.

When the data indicates that yes, the problem is worth solving, you've reached the point of building product. Now's not the time, however, to go back inside the building until the product is done. All through the product development cycle, you should continue to interact with customers.

Product-Market Fit

Imagine you have a group of customers you have been interacting with on a regular basis, and you have a deep understanding of them. You continue to interact with them on two levels:

1. You validate how you can acquire more of the same.
2. You validate that the product you are building addresses their needs.

For the first, you begin to run tests on acquisition channels and sales funnels[2] to ensure that you understand where this particular market segment hangs out, who influences their decision making, and what you need to provide so that they move through the emotional states of the buying process.

To measure, again start with a hypothesis: "Posting my beta invitation to Hacker News will result in 1,000 visits and 100 sign-ups." If you don't receive 1,000 visits, was there something wrong with your post? Was it down-voted because it was deemed inappropriate? If you didn't receive 100 sign-ups, was your messaging wrong on the landing page? Was Hacker News the wrong site? The results likely give you data you can act on.

PRODUCT MATCH PERSONA

EASY

YOU FAIL

8 BILLION PIECES

For the second, you might perform usability testing and measure customer interaction with your product. You don't want to (and likely can't) measure everything. Initially measure that which you define as engagement and activation.

Activation is important to measure, since it exposes the gap between when customers first sign up or buy and when they first try to realize the promise made to them. Many problems can inhibit activation during a critical time in the customer-vendor relationship, including password problems, activation e-mails going to spam, shipping problems, poorly understood instructions, misfit, "*blank-slate*" *effect*, and so on.

blank-slate effect: The blank-slate effect is the problem of a customer not understanding what to do with a product. In web design, for instance, a user logs in to an application for the first time and it is unclear what to do next to start effectively using the application.

There are many ways to counter these issues, but you don't want to work around all of them if they all don't affect you. On the other hand, you can't afford to miss them if they are occurring! Minimizing the time it takes to get customers going is critical to moving your business forward.

To measure engagement in an early product, you want to measure the specific functionality (features) the customer must use regularly over time to achieve the value proposition. Is there a metric that might establish when the customer is done; in other words, at what point should she have experienced the product's benefits?

In other words, what indicates product satisfaction?

You iterate on product development, messaging and positioning, and market segments until you see organic growth within a defined market segment. This is what the passion metric is for. The passion metric is your own algorithm based on some combination of product engagement data, proclivity to share product, and customer demand for more functionality.

It's not always possible to directly measure these, but you should substitute non-automated measures where instrumentation is not possible and offline measures where online measures are not available.

Online Engagement

We've discussed engagement for online products quite a bit; that's measuring the specific functionality people actually use consistently over time. Satisfaction with other aspects of your business model include interviews, managing channel programs, customer support, and so on.

Offline Engagement

Don't let the offline nature of your business dissuade you from using online tools. You are limited only by your creativity in using the Internet to measure offline satisfaction, engagement, and passion.

There are a variety of ways people track engagement of offline products, including loyalty programs, satisfaction surveys, website tools (e.g., support), toll-free product-support numbers, retail-store interactions and observations, third-party reviews, traditional market research, and social media.

Sharing Product

As we've stated before, all marketing is based on word-of-mouth. Back in the 1970s, Breck shampoo actively encouraged viral word-of-mouth activity by its customers.[2] The commercial says: ". . . and then you'll tell two friends, and they'll tell two friends, and so on, and so on," as the screen doubles the number of customer portraits repeating the same words, and doubles again, and again.

Funny how Internet marketers "discovered" viral marketing!

It's far easier to measure word-of-mouth marketing (including virality) online. Network-effects products are those in which the value of the product increases the more the network of users grown. Theoretically, the value of you using Facebook increases the more your family and friends are on Facebook. (It's actually not as straightforward as it sounds, since the more people, the higher potential for noise, the less valued the connections, and hence a decreased product value. The quest to improve the experience never ends.)

To measure network-effected word-of-mouth, you measure the number of invites a customer sends out and the number of those invitations that result in new active customers. This is the viral coefficient and must be greater than 1.0 for network-effects businesses that depend on scale to succeed. In other words, for every one person who signs up and uses the product, more than one of their network will also use the product.

If your business model does not depend on scaling to millions of active users (in order to monetize that scale, typically via advertising), your word-of-mouth coefficient *does not* have to be viral; it does not have to be greater than one! That doesn't mean, however, you can't try to achieve that. The higher the viral coefficient, the more organic growth you win.

To induce and measure word-of-mouth marketing for products that are not network-effects businesses, you can do a few of things:

1. Run a campaign that encourages users to invite other users. This can be a temporary friends-get-in-free or a long-term agreement like getting one month free for every new paying customer you bring on board.
2. Use social media tools like Facebook, plus coupon codes to track conversions.
3. Build a method into the product for users to invite friends, and track that as you would the viral coefficient.

Proclivity to share can also be measured through survey-based approximations. Net Promoter Score and MustHaveScore are two examples.

It's important to understand that product usability is the key to getting users to invite others whether or not you have a network-effects business. People don't share bad products, they ignore them.

Customer Pull

Urgency for your product can be measured in several ways. Demand for product improvements such as feature requests and even problem reports often indicate a strong need. There's a possibility for false positives from people trying to be helpful, but for the most part, people who don't need your product won't complain about it.

People reporting specific integration requirements, for example, are indicating they are traveling down the purchasing path. Others may voice a desire for different channels, more stores carrying your product, for instance, or specific resellers. These need to be measured not as undifferentiated requests, but rather by market segment. You must be able to discern the difference between demands generating from valuable market segments and those from opportunistic segments, some of whom may take your product or business in the wrong direction.

There are clues in feedback indicating what your "whole product" looks like. The features, channels, environment, and partners your ideal customer segments require to fully realize the value you are delivering is how you expand beyond the minimum viable product.

It bears repeating that building features just because you can is a recipe for missing out on what might make you wildly successful. Also, you don't necessarily build what is asked for, but rather you first must understand why they're asking.

Existing Products

All of the preceding applies to existing products, too, but the processes are more complex. You likely already have customers, though it is also likely that you haven't done the work to divide them into useful buckets. Surveys are a good way to help segment existing customers. Key items to learn:

- What is the core problem they are trying to solve?
- What do they love about the product?
- What would they like to see improved?
- What benefits have they seen from using the product?
- How likely are they to share the product with friends and colleagues? (Net Promoter)

- How do they describe the product to friends and colleagues?
- How disappointed would they be if product were no longer available? (MustHaveScore)
- Where do they "hang out"?
- Who influences their decision making?

Use interviews and engagement data to corroborate survey results. If there are discrepancies, you likely have a problem with survey-question wording.

For complex products and those that have been out in the marketplace for a while, measuring product engagement is more difficult. More functionality means more things to track.

To get beyond this, you must be able to visualize customer product usage similar to the pre-purchase marketing funnel or pipeline: There are a number of actions that a customer typically goes through before purchasing the product, and then there is this magic moment when prospects convert to customers by pulling out their credit cards.

Similarly, there are a number of actions a customer must go through in order to realize your value proposition. Create an engagement map that maps out the core actions a customer *must* perform when experiencing your product in order to realize value. To each action, there may be a number of sub-steps, a number of features that the customer might interact with in order to accomplish that step.

Continue to break down the product to the level at which you can establish the specific product functionality where, if you increase its use, you increase engagement.

This is an example of how one figures out what moves the needle of the business, assuming that increased engagement means increased user satisfaction that might lead to product passion.

For a marketing analytics example, engagement for the chief marketing officer (CMO) might be viewing reports a certain number of times/week. There may be other features, such as communication tools between the CMO and her marketing manager to request new campaigns or reports.

Activation for the marketing manager is creating reports and setting up the tool to track social media, conversion funnels, and marketing campaigns. Engagement might include viewing the dashboards on a daily basis.

The old-school way to improve the product is for internal silos to debate over what features to add:

- Sales wants new features that overcome current objections.
- Marketing wants new features to better position the company against competition.
- Product management wants new features based on customer feedback.
- Engineering wants new features based on new capabilities.
- Support wants specific bugs fixed.

Debate and compromise lead to requirements documents, engineering specification, and a six-month plan for the next version.

This method is too slow in today's world and doesn't help in determining what the customers actually *need*.

The high-performing, agile lean startup method means forming a cross-functional team to investigate why one module isn't performing as expected and then experimenting with ways to improve that specific functionality. The new functionality is tested on a subset of users before being released to all.

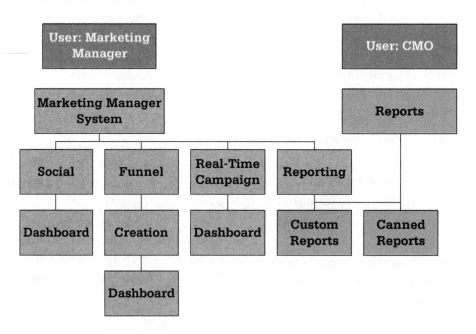

Case Study:
Instrumenting Growth

Meetup's story takes place not long after the rise and fall of the Internet, version 1. Only a few years prior, business valuations, Wall Street, home prices, and naïve optimism were soaring. While some were championing the end of business down cycles, others were bemoaning the end of physical books and in-person socialization. The dot-com crash and 9/11 changed all that.

Meetup started in early 2002 in New York in response to 9/11, as a way to bring the community together in the real world, offline.

It was an experiment: Would strangers meet offline after meeting online?

"Remember, there wasn't social media at the time," says Andres Glusman, vice president of customer development. "Even the idea of online dating was extremely weird. Would strangers meet online?"

A few months and fifty thousand users later, the experiment looked like a success and the experimental culture that founded the company became a persistent feature.

Meetup started as a free, crowd-sourced, voting-driven mechanism for bringing people together. Only if there were enough RSVPs would the meetup actually happen. Through that system they grew from zero to about a million users. After having discovered a market need, they searched for a revenue model.

They were getting pull from different customer segments.

Andres explains: "The Howard Dean campaign was using it, all of the political campaigns and other large organizations were using it, and they were throwing money at us to build enterprise-driven tools. But that wasn't really our vision. We were watching how people used the service and saw that individuals were creating their own groups, rather than voting on others."

So with the million users and money being thrown at them, they made a big bet toward locally driven groups. They re-architected and re-launched the entire service, driven by watching how people were using it. The next year, they risked alienating tens of thousands of customers by shifting from an entirely free platform to one in which organizers paid group dues.

"It was an extremely hard decision," says Andres. "It was a very difficult thing to go through, but it was another big experiment we made in search of the right business model."

Meetup lost a great deal of groups, but the activity didn't go down much. What they were left with was a smaller but much more engaged audience.

As they grew and became more sophisticated, they didn't move away from experiments, but rather became more efficient at their experimentation. So instead of looking at the data and making big bets, they used the data to "send up trial balloons."

"It sounds obvious in retrospect," Andres admits. "There are ways of testing in small ways, prior to redesigning an entire experience, to ensure we're on the right path. So instead of investing all the time and resources into a big change and then having to support our users, why not invest the time and resources into helping our users learn and evolve as we do."

All change has a cost associated with it. Not only the engineering time and money, but the implementation and the costs associated with supporting users who must navigate the change.

Meetup has evolved their approach toward launching a bunch of small experiments that inform a big experiment. Once they have insight into something new that is actually working, then they double down and move as deep and as broad as they can, knowing they have a high likelihood of success.

"We've put together a usability lab that will run 400–500 usability sessions this year," says Andres. "Our objective is to shorten the time in between someone in the company thinking, 'How would a user respond to this?' and actually watching the user respond to it. Right now, that means never having to wait more than two days to see how a user will respond to something."

Having achieved impressive user numbers, figured out a revenue model, and implemented fast, agile product experimentation, the key question becomes, what to test? What *moves the needle* of the business?

Meetup knows the data. They've experimented with marketing outreach, corporate users, and advertising, but in the end, it's all about the meetups. Meetup attendees eventually form their own meetups and then start paying monthly dues.

"The number of people who are interested in attending meetups is provided by RSVP data. You have to join Meetup to RSVP. Fifty percent of all meetup organizers started as meetup attendees. Their product experience is central to them creating new groups inside the platform."

The product experience requires a delicate balance. Growth can adversely affect value realized by existing customers. This is why feature-mongering is potentially dangerous to a product's long-term success. Meetup is actually a network of groups. It's not just about being able to participate in one meetup, but about the ability to serve multiple interests by being a part of lots of different meetups.

"One of the things that we experimented with is to share more about who else is going to the meetups, how you are connected to them, and what other groups they belong to. This very simple test had a huge impact on individuals joining other groups. It proved the concept that we should be optimizing the experience to help people understand more about who else is going to be there."

To tackle this scope of experimenting, Meetup organizes into five to six cross-functional teams that are focused on what they call an "I-statement." The teams address a part of the user experience from a user's point of view. They are trying to solve a problem or enable something really interesting for the user to experience. One of the teams, for example, is an analytics-driven team that focuses on creating smart meetup recommendations. Since enaged users join multiple meetups and engaged users become organizers, it's important that users get relevant recommendations.

A team is typically comprised of a product manager, a user-interface developer, a back-end developer, a community specialist, and an analyst doing qualitative analysis. Their charge is to design a series of experiments that are meant to make progress toward solving for their core I-statement. They manage a portfolio of different-sized experiments. They are not just satisfied with small experiments that might eke out mild percentage increases in engagement, but insist on going after big changes, too.

Not that the process is perfect.

"When we were running experiments around improving meetup recommendations to users, we ended up changing both how we labeled what we were recommending and the algorithm for producing recommendations," says Andres. "Problem is, we launched them both at the same time. We saw massive improvement, 40 percent improvement from the change in the algorithm and the change in the header. So at the point we were like, 'There is something really fascinating that just happened here,' but we couldn't point to what exactly and we went back and then systematically undid the experiment we did.

"So we said, 'Okay, let's roll back half that. Let's run a version with just the title changes. Let's run a version with just the algorithm.' We ran every permutation we could so that we teased out exactly what caused the jump. We were able to glean this insight into the essence of the algorithm and how people respond to it. We said, 'Okay, we struck gold here, how else can we use that nugget of insight now in other parts of the experience and propagate it throughout the site?"

What has the impact been on Meetup?

Improving recommendations have led to higher meetup RSVPs, more conversions to paying organizers, and a dramatic increase in growth. But the big impact comes with learning how to ask the right questions.

"One of the reasons we're experiencing success right now is that we've shifted our focus away from thinking about ourselves as groups and shifted to be more about what's the individual member's experience inside the context of being part of a group or many groups.

"It's a subtle difference, but when you come to understand that Meetup creates value as a result of helping you find and engage with the people you want to meet and who are doing the things you want to do, it suddenly is asking the question in a slightly different way. How do we help people find the right people who are doing the things they want to do? Asking that question opened our eyes to all of these different experiments we could run. In running those experiments we saw that there was an impact, that we could make significant impact.

"So what we've done over the past year is have an evolution of understanding how we create value for people. We fundamentally believe that great companies do three things really well: (1) ask the right questions, (2) execute many rapid experiments in pursuit of the truth, (3) double down on what they learn from experiments."

Work to Do

1. Build your actionable data plan.

Segment:			
Assumption	Metric	Hypothesis	Result
Customer will be satisfied with specific functionality x, y, z:			
Customer will become passionate when:			
Customer will make final decision to buy when:			
Customer will trust the company when:			
Customer will trust the product when:			
Customer will want to learn more when:			
Customer will become aware of the product by:			

2. Build an engagement map.

8

The Valley of Death

The Valley of Death is where startups go to die.

You have a minimum viable product (MVP) and a little customer interest. Or you have an MVP you've been iterating for months and have customers, but no serious traction. Or you have a solid product some customers are passionate about but little organic growth. Or you have a pretty impressive number of paying customers, but can't figure out how to find more. Or you're growing and feel poised for a breakout, but your margins are virtually nonexistent and you are skating on the edge of insolvency.

Your viral coefficient is 0.42. You are officially a Minimum Viable Business (MVB).

If you're on the disruptive side of the innovation spectrum, your death will be lonely, one of indifference as you wander aimlessly, unknown to your competition and customers. On the other hand, if your idea hews closer to the sustaining side of the innovation spectrum, your death will be instigated (and celebrated!) by your competition and perhaps even unknowingly facilitated by your anti-segments.

Nearly all startups can build product. This isn't a problem. Founders fail to create enough value for customers; or they create value, but not for enough people; or they fail to truly understand the core value they provide and who might *most* benefit from it.

They don't understand their must-have use case. Or they don't understand how to translate the winning use case for one group of customers to use cases for other segments.

They have customers, but little passion. They have customers with passion, but they don't know anything about those customers, so they don't understand how to get more.

The typical entrepreneur's response to all this? Build features or hire a PR agency. Neither is likely to work.

Getting out of the startup "Valley of Death," as Eric Ries describes it, requires using the same principles we've already outlined—customer interaction, experimentation, and data—but how you use these must evolve.

You're likely no longer validating initial assumptions. You need new assumptions, new experiments.

To escape the Valley of Death you need to move beyond your minimum viable product, and you need an optimized conversion funnel and a customer acquisition strategy that's ready to scale. The end of the MVB phase is product-market fit.

Way back in the day, we worked with an enterprise software company deploying their product for a leading U.S. financial-services company in a consumer-facing application. It took 50 seconds for customers to log in. The lifeblood of the software company was its professional services team, which had to customize and integrate complicated, buggy product into the huge, complex systems of early Fortune 500 customers, the revenue from which could not be recognized until customer sign-off.

The professional services team jumped in to solve the log-in problem, through a straightforward, analytical, and iterative process of eliminating bottlenecks. They didn't search for the biggest bottleneck but rather for the first one between the user and the desired result. They didn't perform workarounds; they fixed problems. When the core engineering team was required to fix APIs, they were forced to despite their complaining. Accumulated workarounds were likely the cause of the problem in the first place.

The team knocked off a five-second issue here, a three-second issue there, until discovering a full table scan that took 25 seconds on a large table! Issue resolved.

This is how to think of your startup endeavor, as well. What's the next bottleneck? How do we remove it?

Minimum Viable Product

At a recent Agile Conference in Scandinavia, presenter Dr. Venkat Subramaniam said, "programmers should have the courage not to write code." This applies to all startup product developers no matter what the product. Please. Stop.

You should be building out product features *only* if the following applies to you:

You *know*.

If you are still learning, you should not be building features; you should be building experiments (which may contain features). It's an important distinction.

Think of your product as having an intrinsic feature threshold. This threshold maps to the pain or passion of your market segment; once that threshold is met and the pain is resolved, adding more features will not resolve more pain. This bears repeating:

Economists call this declining marginal utility—we go as far as to suggest that if you build features into your product, release them to the world, and do not measure whether they are used or desired, you are inflicting harm to your existing value

proposition; that is to say, the marginal utility of too many features is negative.

Increasing *stuff* that doesn't add value dilutes existing value. Period.

It's also extremely wasteful. Your testing team is wasting time testing it. Your

sales team is wasting time and money selling new unwanted features. Your marketing team is wasting time marketing it. Your support team is wasting time supporting it.

To *know* means the customer demand is *pulling the features* out of you. How do you know? By understanding the customers within your target segment *deeply*. You have knowledge and signal:

- Your customers have been segmented into buckets grouped by pain or passion.
- You can prioritize which segments are "high value;" key to growth.
- You understand which customers are passionate about your product.
- Feature requests, support needs, feedback, and engagement from these specific customers or channel partners is increasing and urgent.
- The direction in which you're being pulled (what and who) is congruent with your vision.[1]

What should engineers be doing if not building features? Plenty:

- Fixing bugs and refactoring existing product.
- "Going to the source"—in other words, going to the customer and learning about customer needs.
- Serving on cross-functional teams charged with improving company operational processes.
- Automating quality-assurance tests.
- Designing and implementing new experiments related to existing products.
- Experimenting with new, disruptive ideas.
- Improving your *shadow force*.

These are not rhetorical suggestions. Leading organizations must adapt. The elimination of old-school silos—not through touchy-feely, new age, kumbaya, can't-we-all-just-get-along idealism, but through building cross-functional teams charged with finding and eliminating business model bottlenecks—is the key to success in the value-creation economy.

Your First MVP

The minimum viable product (MVP) is your first attempt to deliver value to your customer. If you have made the effort to interact with potential customers and have run experiments testing your customer, problem, and solution assumptions, your first MVP will be the first effort to deliver *validated* value to a *known* customer.

In this context, an MVP is not a landing page or a mockup of your application. It's

not a model or nonfunctioning prototype. Your minimum viable product is comprised of the least amount of functionality necessary to solve a problem sufficiently such that your customer will engage with your product and even pay you for it, if that's your revenue model.

It will take more than one try. You're not going to nail it the first time out. In fact, you're never done. In today's value-creation economy, there's no such thing as done, which is why you might as well get your product in the hands of a few customers as soon as possible. You won't learn what you're missing or getting wrong until you let someone try and use it. Hence the *minimum* in MVP.

Your product may or may not require an artful design, 42 features, beautiful packaging, a kickstand, and blue buttons to be *viable* to your chosen market profile. A viable product, at the very least, delivers just enough of its value proposition that customers will use it. The trick is admitting you don't *know* all that's required to be viable.

Releasing early to early adopters is the most efficient way to learn what's required. Too much product hides the specific functionality that provides viability. The core functionality that provides value such that customers are satisfied because the product fulfills its promise forms the foundation of your future business.

It doesn't guarantee high growth or even success, but you can't achieve those without it.

Most failed startups fail in the MVP phase. Iteration through features can quickly become flailing, to the point where founders are no longer able to recall the vision or the original value proposition. Or perhaps the value proposition was vague from the outset!

Reid Hoffman, founder of LinkedIn, famously said "If you are not embarrassed by the first version of your product, you've launched too late." The idea causes massive cognitive dissonance in the startup world. Entrepreneurs are scared that:

- A buggy product will kill the brand.
- Customers will leave behind an unfinished product and never return.
- Their idea will be stolen.

Buggy Product

Although perhaps reasonable at first glance, these fears are largely unfounded. The suggestion to release a product earlier rather than later doesn't mean you should release an unusable product.

Unfinished Product

Investor Paul Graham says: "[launch] when there is at least some set of users who would be excited to hear about it, because they can now do something they couldn't do before."[2] You don't truly *know* when your users will be excited until you *try* to excite them. Launch doesn't mean release it to the world and make hay about it. It means get it in front of early users to understand whether you have uncovered the quantum of utility or whether you are at least on the right path.

Entrepreneurs often swing from one extreme to another. If they focus on *minimal* they forget *viable* and if they focus on *viable*, they don't know when to stop building.[3]

If you have a controlled, early release that turns out to not be viable, it's easier to retool compared to building until you think it's done, whatever that means.

This is the point of iteration. You make a reasonable stab, otherwise known as a hypothesis, also known as an educated guess. It's not exactly right. Some customers seem to be kicking the tires but in a rather lackluster fashion. Make changes and try again. If, on the other hand, you keep building features, delaying your release—and then the product isn't exactly right—not only did you lose time finding that out, but it's harder to know what you got right and what you didn't!

You want to understand what product functionality produces your must-have use case, as this provides the foundation of your product moving forward. The must-have use case is the one you must not destroy as you continue to build out the product and bring on additional market segments.

Once you are able to provide the utility that excites the user, you will find that the early adopters are willing to put up with glitches. This is the classic definition of the early adopter. As thought leaders in their space, or as social leaders that others look to for new products, they tend to forgive product issues as long as the core benefit addresses their pain or passion.

The great irony to the idea that customers will never return to a faulty product is that the entrepreneurs who espouse this philosophy stake their entire business on their *personal belief* that their fully fleshed out product isn't somehow faulty. But there's always one more bug to fix, one more design element to clean up, one more feature to add. You know this because you don't fire your engineers and designers after release. You need them to fix bugs, clean up faults, add features.

But I thought you said the product is done!

Entrepreneurs often say you can't launch early, because the product isn't *done*, but once it has been declared *done*, they then think the only thing left to do is to tell the world as quickly as possible. Done only really means the date they chose months ago has arrived. Because the day arrives, it must mean it's time to launch to full fanfare, pray to the media gods that TechCrunch highlights the product on its front page; that the

Wall Street Journal declares you a visionary. *We must release because it was in the plan!*

After all, these founders believe, the only thing missing is product buzz.

What about beta programs, you ask? Most beta programs are part of a prescheduled launch process, primarily used to fix major bugs.

Beta used to represent a feature-complete product. The term has evolved over time to the point that in some organizations, the beta release is in essence the final release,

because the developers recognize that it will continue to evolve over time. This really is the essence of most software these days, so beta ceases to have real meaning. Google's Gmail was in beta for five years, way beyond product-market fit.

If you are not going to release early, how do you know when the product is *done*? What if you're wrong? Building a big product does not make success more likely. Remember the feature threshold; the winner isn't the one with the most features.

Stolen Product

The idea that people troll the Internet to steal ideas is amusing. It's characteristic of either over-believing in your idea or not having enough of an idea. Consider this:

- After releasing a product, the hardest thing to do is to get people to care. Contrast that to the fear that trolls will not only find your product, but launch a company to compete with it!
- Have you heard of any stories in which an idea was stolen because it was released too early?
- Face it, there are very few *truly* new ideas. It's highly likely someone is already considering, if not building (or has built), your idea.

- You're going to launch someday anyway, right? All the time you're not releasing, you're not getting early customers. Customers are what create the business!

It's actually hard to build someone else's idea.

Case Study: The Minimum Viable Audience

Whether you call them your customers, your market segments, or your audience, they provide the necessary context paramount in effective product development of any sort. We spoke with Brian Clark of Copyblogger, considered one of the founding fathers of content marketing, about his concept of the Minimum Viable Audience.

Lean Entrepreneur: How was Copyblogger born and how does it relate to the Minimum Viable Audience?

Brian Clark: Initially, the idea was that if you create high-quality content, people will share it if you can draw enough attention to it in the first place. As a one-person blog, I wrote a couple of articles a week. I didn't publish everyday because I wanted everything that came out to be good. But my fundamental idea was: If you build an audience, you can build a business.

I had no idea what I was going to sell. No idea. I had no products, no services. I really didn't want to be in a service business. I looked at companies like 37signals and I thought, "Oh, I'm so envious. I wish I could start a software company."

It's funny because seven years later, we're a software company with a hundred thousand customers. But it was all because I had built the audience and all of the opportunities that subsequently came to me, again, because I had built the audience. And as such, we're intimately familiar with what the market that we'd created wanted. That's invaluable to the lean concept for startups—really, for any business.

LE: This relates back to the beginning of blogging.

Clark: The idea starts with the blogging subculture getting started in late 1999, early 2000. By 2005, it was starting to get to that point where people were thinking, "Okay, there's got to be a commercial angle to blogging." At that point, many people were still arguing whether it was okay to put ads on blogs.

I started talking about it, and said, "You know what you really ought to do? You ought to build an audience and sell them things." And everyone just freaked out, but because that was radical compared to the conversation that was happening at that time.

And I can tell you for the first three months of Copyblogger, it was awfully lonely. I had no contacts, I had no friends. Every day I had to create great stuff and somehow draw attention to it.

The initial three months, I tried things, a lot of them failed. Some worked. I learned from that. You can't build it and hope they come. That doesn't work. But if you put something up there and you work to get attention to it in some fashion, you're either going to get indifference or you're going to get a positive response. During that period of time, I was going through this process of doing more of what worked and doing less of what didn't work.

In the process I got to the point where I had enough of an audience where they started telling me, they started promoting the content themselves and that grew the audience organically. But most importantly, I think from this discussion standpoint, I started to get an insight into what was lacking in the market.

Your audience is never going to tell you "I need XYZ." They're going to tell you, "I have this problem. I have this desire. And it is unfulfilled." That, to me, is entrepreneurial gold. I always had faith in that process and that's how the whole company was built.

LE: How did you know that build-it-and-they-will-come won't work?

Clark: I think I had a vision but vision has got to be flexible. You have a general viewpoint of what you want to share with people.

You've got to stick with what you know but, when it comes down to the brass tacks, the audience is going to say, "Yes, I want to know more about that," and "No, I don't want that."

If you just relentlessly push forward what you think that other people need to know, we call this "feeding people broccoli ice cream." Yes, it's good for them, but they're not interested in it. You're basically lost out in the cold. You're not having any kind of resonance.

What are you going to do about it? I think from the social or ideological standpoint, maybe you carry forward. As an entrepreneur, I think you go with what the audience or the prospective market actually wants.

LE: How do audiences drive pivots?

Clark: I was thrilled and I even wrote a *Forbes*[4] article about this when I saw that you two were mentioned in a *Fast Company*[6] article using an example of the Beastie Boys, who started out as a punk band in New York back in the 1980s, when hip-hop was emerging.

These were very progressive guys from Brooklyn and Manhattan in a punk band, then they eventually started including rap songs in their act, and they saw the audience reaction.

It was a much stronger reaction compared to anything that they have been until then. This is a brilliant example because how do you pivot without feedback? And how do you get feedback without an audience?

That was the story of Beastie Boys. That is how they became a Rock and Roll Hall of Fame rap group that started as three Jewish guys as a punk band. That's an amazing story but it's the same story I think you're seeing play out with startups who start out with an audience online because like you two have said before, it's simple, but it's not easy.

But it's so well worth it because in addition to starting a successful company, which is hard enough, you're building a media asset, right, with the website that builds the audience. That's worth the money in itself, and I don't think you can discount that.

I've been offered a couple million bucks for Copy blogger.com, not the businesses that generate the revenue. That's pretty amazing when you think about it.

LE: How do you counsel entrepreneurs afraid to take the first step?

Clark: I tell you what, I admit to small-business people and entrepreneurs all the time that I'm a freak. I was a writer who started a software company. That doesn't happen often. I was geared to make content, to create stuff, to put it out there.

I was driven to do that even at the expense of my former career. In that sense, I'm strange. But the whole concept behind *Entreproducer* is you don't have to be the content creator. You're the entrepreneur. And that is an aspect to modern business that we're seeing emerge that has to do with content, how one company markets better than the other. How one company provides a sales experience that is superior to another company's. Why does this person choose that company in often undifferentiated marketing?

But you have to think like a producer. You don't have to be the writer. You have to be the guy who makes it all come together.

Isn't that what an entrepreneur is, the person, the man or woman that brings it all together?

And at the end of the day, I'm just saying, why not also add the audience in?

There are instances in which the lean startup mantra "release early, release often" needs to be more carefully managed.

- In the B2B world, some customers don't want early-release products. Their own internal processes demand that products must be fully vetted before they are released into their particular environments. In other words, these customers are not early adopters.

- Large, well-known businesses need to protect their brands. Releasing products that are minimally viable to some, but buggy and poorly designed to others, could potentially have a negative effect on their reputation. Even with releases to a controlled audience, there's a chance of having negative results bleed over to unintended audiences. Startups don't typically have this risk.

Even in these cases, it's worth considering that not releasing doesn't really resolve the primary issue. If you wait to release, you are still assuming you *know* what the final version looks like. Waiting to release a finished product is going to gain you a lot more negative attention if the product isn't right versus letting out a controlled release.

There are options:

- Be careful which customers you choose to release early product to.

- You could, of course, release under a different brand. In other words: Create a new entity solely for the purpose of testing your ideas.

- You could manage the press. The media wants exclusives. So give an interview, talk about problems in the industry, your vision, and when you hope to get the product out to the masses, while testing an early release with an exclusive set of customers. It's really more likely to be harder to land the interview than having to face a mob of angry customers who will never forgive you for releasing such a horrible product.

- Build and release separate "mini" products that test risky aspects of your main product.

Beginning of the End or End of the Beginning?

Once you've learned what it takes to deliver your value proposition, there's no longer a need be *minimal*. Once you've validated the value you are creating and for whom, it's time to expand your product somehow.

We've heard startups dramatically declare, "We're not doing lean startup. We have lots of momentum and our users will leave us if we do an MVP." Exactly!

Or rather, exactly, you should not be *minimally viable* after achieving product-market fit. Build out the product, but continue to test and release quickly:

- Build within the *demands* of your target market segment.
- Build to experiment with adjacent segments.
- Build to block competition, if necessary.
- Build to create passion.
- Don't inhibit the core value proposition!

The idea of the whole product is that there may be more to your value proposition than you first thought or first built into your

MVP. You might have to provide additional products, features, or services; support different platforms; or make the product available through other channels.

The gap between the initial product and the potential product is made up over time or might be fixed in the near term with partnerships. In the end, the customer's experience with the whole product may represent the difference between a satisfied customer and a passionate one, or what moves you from early adopter customers to early mainstream. There are many aspects of the whole product that you cannot know until (1) you have validated your customer and (2) you have validated what solution will work. It's ludicrous to plan, let alone implement, a whole product if you have not validated your core value proposition, your must-have use case. There are too many unknowns:

- How does the customer expect to use the product?
- How does the customer expect to buy?
- Will other ecosystem entities be necessary to my business model?
- Is there anything beyond the early adopter?

Case Study: Social Impact Lean Startup

ROOZT

Roozt is a marketplace that connects cause-oriented retail brands with online shoppers who want to buy fashion-forward products that "give back." Rather than build out the platform in 2009 when he first envisioned it, founder and CEO Brent Freeman sought to prove that such a market existed first. Like most consumer-facing businesses, their primary risk was, "Do people care?"

Brent Freeman: Almost everyone says they want to support socially conscious, causes-related, responsible brands, but we wanted to prove that people actually would shop that way.

Their first MVP was just an e-commerce website released under a different brand. "We knew the name sucked but we just launched it anyways," Brent says.

They barely knew where to start, building a simple website that leveraged Amazon in a way such that they could pick out the cause-oriented products they wanted to sell, embed them into the site, and create the shopping experience they envisioned. When people went to purchase a product it simply linked out to Amazon.

"We were a glorified affiliate portal, but for products we wanted to support."

They started their marketing efforts in learning mode as well, reaching out to family and friends, running small-scale Google AdWords and Facebook ad campaigns; enough to measure market response and see if their hypothesis would actually be supported by customer dollars.

Freeman: We knew the product wasn't perfect. We knew our concept wasn't perfect. But we also knew that if we threw enough stuff against the wall and talked with our customers, we'd see what really sticks. Most importantly, we knew that progress was better than perfection, and that if we tried to come up with the perfect idea before we launched, that we would sit there for a long time.

Iterating constantly based on learning, they eventually built out a product that acted as a virtual marketing machine for cause-related brands, which today boasts over 100,000 users, 200 brands, and 5,000 SKUs.

The key to success has been providing easy-to-use tools that teach and enable brands to engage with the customers Roozt brings to the marketplace, primarily through highly engaging e-mail newsletters. Their learning is now concentrated on testing other customer-engagement vehicles, like apps, and seeing how they can reduce the conversion funnel to a one-click experience.

An MVP Takes Guts

What's the biggest risk to your business?

Countless times we've asked entrepreneurs this seemingly simple question and countless times we hear the same response:

- Generating buzz.
- Customer adoption.
- I need users.
- Growth.
- Scale.

If you have anything at all of interest, getting coverage in today's crazed, page views–ruled media culture isn't that difficult. What's hard is finding anyone who cares.

Okay, so many of you read the first sentence and ignored the second. "Really?" you're saying to yourself. "I can get media coverage?"

Sure. Have you actually tried sending an e-mail to an editor at your favorite online rag? They are begging for stories. Yes, you still need an angle, but it's a link-bait life and your story doesn't even have to be real.[5] But if you have not proven the viability of your product, please, please don't.

A startup we spoke with in New York City serves urban pet owners. It's the sort of idea the media loves. It's cute. They received tons of attention, all of which they felt was worth bragging about. Here's what their adoption looked like after all the TV coverage:

Page views	Sign-ups	Engagement
10,000/day	2,500/month	5/week

What does scaling acquisition do for this company?

Regardless of what you might think, the biggest obstacle to your idea is that no one cares. The hardest thing for you to admit is that though your friends and family tell you that you have a great idea, it's actually worthless. Your baby's ugly. You have too many features. You have too many ideas packed into one product.

When you pull a product off the shelf of a retail store, how many problems does it solve?

Guess what? That you solve a problem that you yourself endure is great and all, but it doesn't make a business. When you got out of the building and went around and said to your potential customers, "Wouldn't it be cool if . . . ," or "I got this great idea . . . ," or "What do you think of . . . ," or "Would you pay for . . . ," you didn't really get any market validation.

We once worked with a team at a Lean Startup Machine workshop whose leader insisted that people are motivated to overcome personal obstacles through public urging by their closest friends. There's no doubt that for some this is so, but feedback among mentors and other workshop participants was resoundingly negative. Feedback outside the building conducted by team members was overwhelmingly negative. Yet the feedback the leader himself found was unanimously positive. What's wrong with this picture?

It's very easy to find evidence to bolster the views you already have, especially those that you are emotionally attached to. Very few minds are changed in political or religious arguments or in great-idea discussions.

It's difficult to let go of ideas, to face the facts, as it were. It's difficult to go through a process that seeks to *invalidate* your idea. By the time you are building your MVP—again, as opposed to a viability experiment—you should be well beyond emotional evidence being the rope you're hanging your hopes on, to mix a metaphor.

Whereas your viability tests were your best attempts at "all right, if this doesn't work, my ideas and assumptions are seriously wrong," the MVP is your first attempt at "all right, if this doesn't work, my implementation is wrong."

Thinking Through Viability

Fundamentally, your MVP should be the *validated* core functionality of your value stream. It's the discrete functionality that fulfills the promise you're making to the customer. Nothing more, nothing less.

AppFog built their product from the outside in. What is the minimum—from the customer point of view—required to achieve the value promised; the minimum to satisfy the need?

To shoot long is to waste; to shoot short is to learn what's deficient.

Minimum doesn't mean sucky, but sucky might be sufficient; viable is the crux; minimally value-creating.

Perhaps for your particular segment, viability means:

- The look had better rock; it must be aesthetically pleasing.
- It must fit seamlessly within the customer's existing workflow.
- It must require no more than three clicks.
- It's so easy anyone can do it.
- Customer must be able to easily open package, but it also must be tamper proof.
- It's disposable.
- It's green.

- It must integrate with system x.
- It must complete tasks x and y, and report back z.

Or looking at what it might not need *at the outset*:

- A terminal command line is sufficient.
- Packaging is superfluous.
- Usable more than a handful of times.
- It's hard to use, but works.
- Looks kludgy, but does what it's supposed to.
- Does x, but not yet y.
- Reporting not automated.
- Requires manual intervention.

Case Study: **But My Marinara Is to Die For!**

Up until the 2008 financial crisis, Dan Palacios was a real-estate developer. Ouch! During the meltdown, Dan lost most of what he had spent years building. A list of remaining assets included not much other than a killer marinara sauce, according to Dan's supportive but rather nonmonetizable fiancée and friends.

Normally, during a recession one doesn't look to open a restaurant, let alone a Chicago-style, gourmet pizza restaurant using fresh, organic ingredients and selling them at $25 per pie, in downtown San Diego. Things don't look up when sporting a credit report featuring recent foreclosures.

The old-school method of opening a restaurant seemed unlikely. The chance of finding the investment necessary to lease restaurant space, build out a kitchen, hire staff, and so forth was, as they say, less than zero. How might one go about learning whether one could create a viable restaurant business in a lean startup fashion?

One possible scenario would be:

- Figure out who your ideal market profile is and where they live.
- Iterate on an MVP, until the product is validated.
- Measure customer passion.

Dan set out to do exactly that. He knew who his customers were, or more accurately, he knew who they weren't. They weren't people who bought from the national pizza franchises. They weren't people who couldn't care less about fresh ingredients. They weren't people who lived outside his delivery radius. They weren't college kids, because they had to be able to afford gourmet pizza.

Most importantly, where do customers in the right market profile hang out or live in or near downtown San Diego? Palacios figured his ideal customers were visitors of the local farmers' market: Although not necessarily wealthy, patrons tend to be willing to pay more for high-quality goods. They were passionate about food and fresh, high-quality, organic ingredients.

They were part of a community: young, technology adept, vocal, and social. After visiting the farmers' market, he learned that in order to serve food there he had to have a catering license. To get a license, you must have a commercial kitchen. But to have a commercial kitchen, you need a restaurant, right?

Dan was cleverer than that. To create his first MVP, he rented space in a commercial catering kitchen. Evenings, Dan tried to build a downtown delivery pizza service, and every Saturday, he brought pizza pies to the farmers' market and handed out samples, guerilla-marketing style. Although revenue is the ultimate measure of success, Dan knew he was onto something when he suddenly appeared in Yelp, with five-star reviews almost across the board. Berkeley Pizza consistently scored in the top five on Yelp's best San Diego restaurants list. The reviews came from the farmers'-market crowd.

"Suddenly," Dan says, "customers wanted to invest in my restaurant." He quickly got interest from local restaurant groups, as well. Within a year, Dan was out of the catering kitchen and into his own restaurant space.

"The plan was always to open a restaurant, but I wasn't going to get investment for $25 pizzas, not with my credit score. I had to prove my market. The Yelp reviews not only drove business, but demonstrated I had a market that loved my product."

MVP Testing

Testing evolves as you release your MVP and start the trek across the valley of death.

As you first posited and then validated you should have metrics that define customer satisfaction and passion. If you have customers in multiple subsegments, you must determine whether these metrics differ between the groups.

You state as an objective the value for those metrics you must achieve to be ready to scale your startup endeavor.

You run experiments on the product, messaging, and positioning, and acquire (relatively) small tranches of customers to test against and measure the results.

You interact with customers to learn where you are still off on the product, messaging, and acquisition.

For product, measure satisfaction and passion by segment:

Web App Example

Segment	Minimum Functionality	Satisfaction	Passion
First-time startup founder needing the ability to read market signal for their product	Assumption wizard, survey tool, dashboard	Uses online wizard: 1/week, Sends survey: 1/month, Views dashboard: daily	Resubscribes, acts as reference, Net Promoter
Experienced startup founder wanting clarity on quality of business-model assumptions	Assumption wizard, survey tool, dashboard, team tool	Uses wizard: 1/week, Sends survey: 1/week, Views dashboard: 1/week, Shares w/ team	Resubscribes, acts as reference, Net Promoter

Pizza Restaurant Example

Segment	Minimum Functionality	Satisfaction	Passion
Gourmet diners: love fresh ingredients, local independent restaurants	3 types of pies, delivery	Buys pie for delivery once every 2 weeks	4- or 5-star Yelp review
Young urban professionals: like independent restaurants, microbrew; tired of chain pizza	3 types of pies, small eating area, beer/wine license	Visits restaurant weekly	Shares coupon code on Facebook

You put your MVP into the marketplace and reach out to the early adopters you've identified. You measure your satisfaction and passion metrics. If necessary, you run specific campaigns in order to measure these metrics, for example, coupons on Facebook, to measure sharing for the pizza restaurant.

Remember that the objective of "satisfied" is to measure whether you have the right functionality for the right customer profile. The objective of "passion" is that new customers will be put into the top of your funnel with minimal effort on your part, or they'll pay a high margin, or resubscribe.

Passionate users must be satisfied first and they must take some action to spread the word about your product. If this is not happening, you're not ready to blow up your customer acquisition. You must first close the word-of-mouth loop. This is a major bottleneck of growth.

At this point you have three primary variables you are playing with:

1. Do I have the right customer?
2. Do I have the right functionality to satisfy the customer?
3. Do I have the right stuff to evoke passion?

If possible, you want to measure in cohorts. What this means is that you are grouping customers based on a shared characteristic—for example, when they first became a customer—and comparing the groups' metrics relative to that date.

For example, the data looks like this:

Segment A: Passion Data

Sign-up Month	June 2012	July 2012	August 2012
June 2012	10% very disappointed	15% very disappointed	15% very disappointed
July 2012	NA	11% very disappointed	17% very disappointed
Aug. 2012	NA	NA	15% very disappointed

As a cohort, the data looks like:

Segment A: Passion Cohort

Sign-up Month	Month 1	Month 2	Month 3
June 2012	10% very disappointed	15% very disappointed	16% very disappointed
July 2012	11% very disappointed	17% very disappointed	NA
Aug. 2012	15% very disappointed	NA	NA

Assuming you made changes to your MVP monthly, you're able to track the impact of your changes. Note that you also want to compare segments:

Segment-Passion Cohort

Date	Segment A	Segment B	Segment C
June 2012	10% very disappointed	15% very disappointed	16% very disappointed
July 2012	11% very disappointed	17% very disappointed	17% very disappointed
Aug. 2012	15% very disappointed	13% very disappointed	12% disappointed

It's important that you're not measuring everything under the sun. Too much data is not an excuse for not analyzing the appropriate data!

To test, you need customers, though you're not ready to blow up your acquisition channels. It's a good time to start testing your acquisition assumptions, though.

In addition to product, you also want to experiment on your messaging and positioning. You're not in optimization mode here, but rather still learning. The reason this is critical is that messaging and positioning form the promise you are making to the customer. Satisfaction is the measure of fulfilling the promise. Passion is measuring satisfaction plus some other factor that propels users into acquiring more users for you.

Segment	Positioning	Benefit	Passion Assumption
First-time startup founder needing the ability to read market signal for their product	World's only market signal receiver	Ability to measure and visualize market response to product	Founder's customer retention improves by 25%
Experienced startup founder wanting clarity on quality of business-model assumptions	World's only market signal receiver	Ability to organize team around improving market performance	Over-the-top user experience Startup's customer retention improves by 10%

In Chapter 3 you hypothesized where your customers hang out, and in viability testing, you worked to invalidate, iterate, and then validate where, in fact, you could locate them. During this process, you actually accumulated people you could go back to and test your MVP with. Although you should continue to work with those people, it's also a good idea to test with new people based on what you've learned.

Segment	Influences	Online Hangout	Offline Hangout
First-time startup founder needing the ability to read market signal for his or her product	Eric Ries, Fred Wilson, Mark Suster	TechCrunch Hacker News Facebook	Lean Startup Circle Startup Weekend Coworking facility
Experienced startup founder wanting clarity on quality of business-model assumptions	Steve Blank, Mike Maples	*Wall Street Journal* Business Insider LinkedIn	TV Networking meetup

Using standard methods of low-energy acquisition—reaching out to influencers, running a small AdWords or Facebook ad campaign, using your network, posting on specific forums, tweeting, direct mail—you not only bring in more customers to test, but are testing various acquisition channels.

Once you have customers to test, there are various methods for learning more about your customers. Simple surveys, split-testing (running two or more landing pages and splitting users between them), and online marketing services are all effective depending on what stage of learning you're in. Such methods really should be augmented through in-person interviews and usability testing, however. Interviews tell you why. Looking at the data tells you what your customer did, but you don't know why they did what they did until you ask them. Usability testing allows you to watch the customer interact with your product without your influence or the influence of other customers like in traditional focus groups.

As you do when looking for patterns in data, you look for patterns in the customers that you speak to. Can you draw better buckets to group them in? Do they have similar problems using your product? Do they give similar responses to your emotion-evoking, open-ended questions?

Case Study: O2, Telecom at the Speed of the Internet

Lots of organizations say they are customer-centric but what does that mean? Companies have disrupted industries around the idea of customer service itself, so how those companies understand *customer-centric* must be different from how Google or Apple or Facebook describe it.

Zappos, for example, sells shoes online. "Well, so what," you might say, "a lot of companies sell shoes online." Zappo's shadow force is customer service. From Tony Hsieh's *Delivering Happiness*:

> "We had a customer e-mail us the other day," I said. "He had ordered a pair of shoes that we had in our warehouse and we surprised him with a shipping upgrade so that he got his order in two days instead of our original promise of a week. He said he loved our customer service and would tell his friends and family about us. He even said we should one day start a Zappos Airlines."

Apple, however, offers little to no customer service, yet is arguably more committed to the customer experience than any other high-tech company in the world.

Stephen Devereux was on a team called Futures Innovation at O2, the United Kingdom telecommunications provider. "We were challenging the business, at that time, to really think differently about how we delivered products and services to our customers. We deliberately branded ourselves differently from the traditional sort of strategy name to be more forward thinking, and deliberately use the word 'innovation'."

As a telecom company in an industry not known for being either customer-centric or innovative, O2 had performed well, not only moving its way to the number-one telecom provider in the U.K., but also building a brand recognized and admired around the world. At the same time, they could see the signpost ahead: being the plumbers of the Internet had run its course. Of course, many telecoms around the world have realized this at some point or another. U.S. companies seek government legislation to thwart innovation and protect their existing oligopolies, while squeezing every last penny out of intermediate technologies like ISDN and DSL. They spend hundreds of millions on high-priced consultants trying to figure out ways to carve out new revenue opportunities, such as applications or GPS services.

Yet disrupted they are.

O2 had a key insight, however. Devereux says: "We were in a very mature market, and we saw that our new set of competitors were not the telecommunications companies of the world, but the Internet players of the world: Apple, Google, Facebook. We had to move at Internet-speed, Twitter-speed."

These companies are constantly releasing new product. They are in beta for years. Updates come weekly, if not daily. They are constantly running experiments, optimizing product delivery. "We were lucky to deliver something quarterly. We were challenging the business to start working in a completely different way to try to take these guys on and compete with them."

The thing is, being customer-centric in this way is completely different than the customer-centricity that elevated O2 to number one in their market. "We have to think of the customer" becomes a proxy for brand protection, rather than innovation. The organization's size and complexity—people responsible for customer service, retail, PR, brand, all various voices of the customer—created obstacles to new products. "To start off any new product in our business, you have a cast of hundreds of people, because everybody has their bit of say. We were actually creating a catch-22 situation for ourselves in which we became full of inertia, unable to serve customers with new products, because we were so worried about the customers' experience," Devereux says.

The key to change was to move our more innovative endeavors to a sub-brand, where a team had direct access to experimenting with customers. In the case of O2, the sub-brand was a philanthropic initiative called Think Big, started by CEO Ronan Dunne, who believes that being part of a large organization means having the corporate responsibility to have a positive impact on society, to protect the environment, and to help the youth of today. Releasing products under this sub-brand, far away from the traditional telecom services, had a number of positive implications:

- Initiatives would not be subject to the same financial measurements as regular products.
- Customer expectations would be different. It allowed the company to experiment with internal changes.

The first product released was O2 Learn. The vision for O2 Learn was to provide a place online for students to find a video about a school lesson—like to get a bit of history on Lord Nelson, for example. A small cross-functional team consisting of a product manager, a designer, and a few engineers worked to release a version quickly. Devereux explains: "The user experience and the interface were prominently designed around students needs. Secondary to that was what teachers needed. We thought quite hard about how teachers could easily upload videos, but the rest was around the students.

"What we found very early on was that teachers were using the site as much as students. What we found was that teachers wanted to find out what good lessons look like so we immediately worked to improve the site for teachers. If that had happened in a traditional way then project managers and designers would say, 'Oh gosh, that's a change in the requirements. You have to go back to the beginning.' You know the process."

The power of the O2 brand meant that after releasing to a small group of users and ironing out the kinks, it was quickly in front of thousands.

"We had a quick time slot in order to learn, but then there was this chap, a famous celebrity chef in the U.K. named Jamie Oliver who was teaching school dinner ladies how to cook better foods for kids within their budget constraints and we ran an ad for O2 Learn on the show. So it was a really nice alignment there. As a result we saw massive spikes and it just started to grow from there. We started actively promoting last year and started doing these challenges every quarter where we'd give money to the best lessons."

Although not particularly disruptive technologically, O2 Learn made a difference to tens of thousands of kids and was clearly disruptive inside O2. "It got massive airtime within O2. This one and a couple of other projects were instrumental in proving the case that actually there is a different way of doing things. We were able create a lab and we got headcount of nearly 30 people."

It's a big win for O2, as well. O2, already known as a leading telecom, and a world-renowned brand, is recognized for assisting teachers and students. These are the sort of initiatives that, for large companies, move customers from satisfied to passionate.

Work to Do

In the MVP phase, the key metrics are user satisfaction and user passion. That's it. If you know your customers well, you should be able to report these two metrics by product functionality, by customer profile.

Segment	Specific Functionality	Hopeful	User Satisfaction	User Passion

9

Real Visionaries Have Funnel Vision

All you need to know about business today is that the Internet changed everything, right? When it comes to distribution, sales, marketing, the Internet changed everything!

Didn't it?

If you say yes, you're likely viewing the world from a seller's perspective. The activities and tactics you employ to make people aware of the value you hope to provide them, convince them you're capable of providing it, and make them trust you with the ability to get it done change over time. But that you have to go through those specific steps doesn't.

What motivates individuals to proceed along the path from awareness to trusting to passionate varies by many factors, including market segment, product, and emotional pull. This is true whether you're selling multifunctional printers to businesses or social apps to consumers. In a similar vein to "if you're committed to solving a specific problem, you should be solution agnostic," once you have targeted a specific market segment, you should be agnostic toward the sales, marketing, and distribution tactics required to serve that segment.

Beware the business "canvass" you're filling out. The more disruptive your startup endeavor, the less you know about your marketing and sales funnels, despite what you think. Just as with product development, a lean startup must learn how to market and sell.

Entrepreneurs without funnel vision conflate the two sides of a transaction: how the buyer desires to buy and how the seller desires to sell. What results is likely a horrible mismatch. The business executes a process they are familiar with, rather than the one that their buyer implicitly demands

SUSTAINING ——————|————|————|—————— DISRUPTIVE

Sales and marketing	Sales and marketing
Roadmap known	Roadmap unknown
Turnkey sales people	"Renaissance" sales person
Sales is marketing driven	Marketing is sales-driven
Marketing "Best Practices"	Experimental marketing practices

for a particular product. The buyer will not engage with a sales process that doesn't fit with what feels right to them. You can have an incredible product capable of delivering real value that never sees the light of day because of the wrong sales and marketing practices.[1]

Founders often view salespeople as experts in convincing potential customers to buy. They view marketers as people who run campaigns and build brand, and generate buzz, in order to fill the top of the sales funnel; to find potential customers to sell to. This view is fraught with problems, not the least of which is that sales and marketing are viewed merely as activities that need to be executed. If the execution fails, you need to execute the executors. If nothing else, this is a recipe for high staff turnover, departmental goals that diverge from company objectives, and sales to anti-segments.

No one truly wishes to be convinced to buy or to be sold to. If an individual is at all inclined to purchase a product, they wish to be reassured that the product will provide them the value they expect. The buyer's process is to learn as much as they can about the product, test the value proposition if possible, evaluate the company, weigh the potential value versus cost plus other factors, and then make a decision.

The Internet has changed none of that.

The selling process should, therefore, be comprised of the activities necessary to provide the buyers what they desire in order to move them through *their* buying process. Activities might include building a web landing page, crafting messaging, creating a brochure, attending a tradeshow, making a phone call, and so forth, depending on your product and segment. There are an infinite number of activities, which is why it's absurd to think that you know what the best activities are for your particular product and your particular customer profile. Yep, the Internet changed everything.

We once asked the winner of a Southern California university business-plan competition what he planned on doing with his $25,000 award, and he said, "I don't know—build a website, get some business cards . . . ." Really?

For some reason, an incubator we know was working with a graphics design company and a few marketing professionals to create a super-high-level marketing plan template for startups. Unsurprisingly, when it came time to develop the plan's list of first things to do, the list included design a logo, develop a website, print letterhead and business cards, buy pens with the logo on it, and so on.

Really?

Come on. *You're not truly in business until you've got a business card that says so. And a website. The Internet did change everything!*

Entrepreneurs are quick to either:

- Adopt the hippest marketing trends of the day. (How many articles entitled

"Why You Must Have a Social Media Strategy or Fail!" must we endure?)

- Immediately hire an agency because the founders know nothing about marketing. (What's the quickest way to burn your cash? Hire a PR agency to manage your must-have social media strategy.)

Take a deep breath.

Step back from the Twitter. Strike that. Step all the way back from the Internet.

If you operate in a highly uncertain environment—in other words, are toward the disruption end of the innovation spectrum—reject best practices. Best practices are for standardizing and optimizing the execution of processes known to work. Best practices are antithetical to disruptive startups. Experts apply best practices based on accumulated knowledge that may or may not apply to your product and your target market. These experts are unlikely to be experts in the domain that matters most to your business.

Innovate the Funnel

A startup's job is to learn, not execute. As you learn your market, new best practices reveal themselves, and they may or may not jibe with what the experts say.

One way to think this through at the beginning of your startup endeavor is to forget marketing completely. Think only of learning how to sell.

Recall the Concierge method of viability testing. Practitioners deliver their value proposition by hand, before building any product, in order to see if anyone cares. They then automate the parts of delivering that value that can be automated, continuously testing that the product delivers necessary value.

Use the Concierge method to learn how to sell, too.

Again, forget about the Internet for the moment. Sell your product in person. When Eric Ries and the IMVU team brought users in to test an early version of their product, they learned much more than that their product was all wrong. When a teenage girl refused to share IMVU with friends, because in her words "What if this isn't cool?" they learned a powerful marketing message. Growth through referrals was going to be impossible if the product wasn't cool. *Cool*, as ambiguous as that may seem, was critical to closing the deal.[2]

Selling in person instructs you about what is needed to close a deal, what objections must be overcome. What you do and say evokes a response that provides you indications about whether you're on the right track and what *emotional state you need to evoke* next.

The parts of the selling process you can automate become marketing.

As we discussed previously, customers go through a series of stages when acquiring any product. They must become:

- Aware—Almost always, people are aware of the product they are purchasing. (It's often said that in the case of free products, the *purchaser* is actually the product and is blissfully unaware of the fact. For this discussion, however, Facebook [a free

Internet application] is the product and not the user whose activity is sold to advertisers.)

- Intrigued—The person who becomes a customer must become intrigued with the product before moving down the funnel. Again, we're sure you can find exceptions, but the vast majority of products must appeal to the customer in some way. Customers are intrigued when they think—beyond being superficially aware—the product might be the right thing for them.
- Trusting—Fulfilling a need is often insufficient, however, unless the customer feels they can trust the product and the company delivering the product.
- Convinced—The final step that convinces the customer to buy; the promised value exceeds the price + risk, where risk might be risk of change, risk of being wrong, risk of being uncool, and so on.

After the customer prospect is convinced the product is right vis-à-vis the price and the company is trustworthy, the customer buys, right? Well, not exactly. There's a secret substep we can zoom in on where the "Magic Happens."

Magic Happens is the moment when rationality exits the equation and emotion takes over. Or vice versa. It's this ineffable something that gets the customer to pull the credit card from the wallet or put the signature on the purchase order.

We contemplated calling that step "Euphoria," which is a condition in which a person experiences intense feelings of well-being, elation, happiness, ecstasy, excitement, and joy, but that isn't exactly right.

We were thinking more accurately, perhaps, the moment should be called "Delusional," but that isn't exactly right either. Customers might feel a range of emotions from excitement to resignation, the latter arising from a leap of faith that they made the right purchase or the realization that they are exposing their private lives to the Internet.

(Creating an account on an Internet site is as much a leap of faith as a purchase order is to others.)

This isn't a trivial matter, because the next thing the customer will do is try out the product. How they feel about the product before using it will affect their feeling about the product after using it. This post-purchase stage might be called PPTS,

post-purchase trauma syndrome, but we'll handle this outside the conversion funnel. (See the section titled "Hopeful," later in this chapter.)

The titles and descriptions of these phases are not set in stone. Come up with your own, if you'd like, but they serve well as a stab at describing what motivates people to become customers. There are many instances, for example, where one might use a product regularly and feel loyalty, but are not necessarily passionate. Passion is just a label. What's important perhaps is "loyalty." Exceptions like these abound, and, frankly, you might have a leg up on your competition if you can figure out the exception to the rule and act on it.

The point of the exercise is that as a business, you must *do stuff* to help people become customers. The stuff you do varies by product, market segment, and business model. What you do is limited only by your creativity and, of course, your values.

Perhaps an activity you perform induces the customer to skip a state, as with impulse buys near the cash register. Activities sometimes manipulate people through the various stages in ways that are ethically dubious. The line is thinly drawn. A business that thrives on one transaction per customer might resort to any means necessary to convince a person to buy, uncaring whether they ever buy again. That negative experiences move at the speed of the Internet makes such tactics more dangerous, but appealing to fears and emotions is a proven sales method. They are age-old tactics.

Our purpose here is to not stand in judgment, but for the sake of our discussion and with the hope that *providing value* is not a cyclical trend but, rather, a movement forward, we write with the belief that the purpose of marketing and sales is in delivering a *known* value to a *known* customer. All activities, then, are for the purpose of making customers aware of, demonstrating the existence of, and building operations in support of this value. There is a laundry list of activities that might work at each emotional stage. For new businesses with

no customers, your job is to *learn* which activities work best for your product and target market segment. For businesses with existing customers, your job is to align the best activities with specific market segments. For big businesses seeking to disruptively innovate, your job is to create a group to act like a new business with no customers.

Just as developing a product requires a cross-functional team to ensure you are building features people need, experimenting and executing on your marketing funnel might benefit from a cross-functional team to eliminate conversion bottlenecks. As more sales and marketing functions happen online, a team that includes design, product marketing, engineering, sales, and perhaps other resources in order to create experiments, interact with customers, and measure the results is a fast, efficient way of discovering what works.

How can you learn what the best activities are? Dive into your proposed funnel, create hypotheses, and test them.

Staring into the wide mouth that is the top of your funnel is like staring into the abyss. There are an infinite number of activities to make people aware of your product, for instance. But you can't test infinity. Having numerous activities to contemplate makes it difficult to *learn* the best and most profitable activities.

By flipping the funnel, you are forced to think through one buying cycle completely for one market segment. Related activities for each step become rather self-evident and act to flesh out your marketing and sales plan and provide additional aspects to test. As we did with the value-stream mapping exercise in Chapter 4, we imagine the path that one persona—one market segment—uses to traverse through the stages.

E-Commerce Example

Funnel State	How do you know?	Customer now wants to:	So, what do you do now?
Customer	Input credit-card number and clicked "complete purchase."	Realize value proposition	Get them into product experience ASAP! [go outside funnel]
Magic	Sitting in shopping cart page	Wants to buy, but is a bit reluctant	Free shipping! Message from the CEO!
Convinced	Clicks on "check out now"	Wants to buy	Stellar shopping cart experience Five-star seller rating
Trusting	Adds item to shopping cart	To know purchase is risk-free	Money-back guarantee, secure shopping, seal of approval
Intrigued	Reads description, plays with product images, changes colors	To know product is right	Provide customer reviews, magazine seal of approval, endorsement from Oprah

On an e-commerce shopping site, you can easily measure what state the customer is in using off-the-shelf analytical tools. At each customer state, the customer *needs* something, in order to move to the next state. You, the site owner, have a myriad of things you can do to provide the *need*. It's pretty easy to imagine, for instance, the different tactics one might use to invoke trust or to up-sell. As a matter of fact, for most e-commerce sites, where both the customer and the product are known, e-commerce best practices can probably be used to optimize sales. (Best practices, of course, includes usability testing and split-testing.)

If you're doing anything radically different, the amount and depth of experimentation required increases. It's important to not allow best practices to interfere with creativity.

Consider the state of social shopping. Although still in its nascent stage, the extent to which social media can be used to enhance online shopping and increase conversions is a giant lab right now. You can't predict exactly how new things might result in big conversion improvements.

Consider also social entrepreneurship. How you acquire and measure trust is a different beast compared to selling standard products. The customer must believe not only that a green product will bring value to their lives, but also that the product is truly green.

B2B Software-as-a-Service (SaaS) Example

Funnel State	How do you know?	Customer now wants to:	So, what do you do now?
Customer	Input credit-card number and clicked "complete purchase"	Realize value proposition	Get them into product experience ASAP! [go outside funnel]
Magic	Demo was successful, pricing page studied, competitive analysis studied	Buy, but is a bit reluctant	"Buy now" discount
Convinced	Clicks on "check out now"	Buy; needs boss approval	E-mail sales for references; provide competitive analysis
Trusting	Signs up for 30-day trial	Test product	Thank customer, send "getting started" package, offer personalized customer support
Intrigued	Reads product description, benefits, requirements; testimonials; media reviews	Equate price with value	Online return on investment calculator
Aware	Comes to landing page from tweet	Learn more about the product	Messaging and positioning; special offer

Enterprise Software (or Hardware) Example

Funnel State	How do you know?	Customer now wants to:	So, what do you do now?
Customer	Purchase order received	Realize value proposition	Implement product [go outside conversion funnel]
Magic	Verbal commitment	Wants to buy, but is a bit reluctant	Make a deal: discount in exchange for reference if customer satisfied
Convinced	Champion tells sales person references check out well. Solution passes internal audit process.	Pricing and contract	Timely delivery of pricing and contract. Look for signs of reluctance or other problems.
Trusting	Proof-of-concept successful	How to overcome risks of startup	Meeting with the CEO; assurance from board member
Intrigued	Reads description, reads trade industry review, learns about others using product	To know product works and will fit into existing environment	Run proof of concept

Selling to Businesses

In 2003, Mark Leslie, founding chairman and CEO of Fortune 1000 company Veritas Software, coined the term *renaissance sales rep* to describe the individual "able to develop [her] own sales model and collateral materials as needed." In other words, without marketing's help, this rep is able to *learn* how to sell a new product. In contrast, the coin-operated sales rep is to be hired only once the sales process is *known*; "when the formula for success has been developed (a repeatable sales model) and all of the support requirements for sales reps are in place."[3]

Steve Blank describes what happens to startups that do it wrong—scaling marketing and coin-operated sales reps before the sales process is known, before the market is known—as the startup death spiral: Sales starts missing its numbers. The board gets concerned. The VP of sales comes to a board meeting, still optimistic, and provides a set of reasonable explanations. The board raises a collective eyebrow. The VP goes back to the field and exhorts the troops to work harder.[4]

What follows is increased opportunistic sales, reps going off the reservation. You see sales staff turnover, lots of finger-pointing at marketing and product developers. A quarter or two later, the vice president of sales is gone, followed by the VP of marketing, and, finally, the CEO. Often the board brings in a more experienced CEO, but their experience is with running a large organization. Still no *learning* is accomplished, only more failed execution. Renaissance sales reps operate differently. They can sell product without brochures, even without demos. They do consultative sales, meaning that, from the customer's perspective, they provide *value*. They are trusted. They understand the needs of the customer and work to address the need, rather than simply sell product.

Paul O'Dea calls this rep a "sales specialist." A sales specialist has the following traits:

- Deep domain expertise in customer's industry.
- Integrity; ability to gain trusted advisor status.
- A complete communicator, able to listen, question, and listen again.
- Engaged in continuous self-improvement and education.[5]

In many early-stage startups, the CEO is the sales specialist or renaissance sales rep. The founder should be developing these relationships, building an empathic understanding of the customer, not the least of which is understanding what their needs are.

Like their SaaS and even consumer-oriented business counterparts, founders often concentrate too quickly on demand creation and filling the pipeline, without first understanding the two fundamental principles necessary to scale the business:

1. Are you addressing a real and deeply felt need?
2. Do you know how to sell this product to this buyer?

The only way to find out is to engage the market. Yes, lean startup is about developing product iteratively, releasing quickly and often in order to gauge market acceptance, but it is also about learning *how to sell* and thereby *how to market*.

The larger or older the enterprise, the more complex and sophisticated will be their purchasing process. There will likely be numerous players:

- The end user of the product
- The head of the department where the end user works
- The IT department
- Compliance
- Security
- Finance
- Purchasing

Even in smaller companies, you will have to find an internal product champion to help you navigate the process, including overcoming politics and executives opposed to the project. Some companies will only purchase from preferred vendors. Others require working with specific resellers or systems integrators. You might face requests for proposals (RFPs) heavily influenced by your competition!

Yes, you may even have to wine and dine your potential customers.

As a salesperson, when interacting with customers, your objective is twofold:

1. What is the buying process *according to the buyer*?
2. What activities will move the buyer into and through the funnel?

You are seeking out objections. Some are predictable; some are not. The best way to learn is to do it.

As Chris Guillebeau says: "You won't always get it right at first—sometimes you'll discover additional objections as you go through the initial sales process with real-time customers."[6]

You step through your educated-guess process—a process that should be somewhat vetted through early customer development—until you encounter an objection and learn what must be done to overcome the objection. You do this through each stage of the funnel. The next time through, you hope to find a similar pattern, only this time you are prepared for the objection.

After several iterations, you might include a Frequently Asked Questions (FAQ) section on your website or in the sales representative's toolkit, which proactively addresses the objections up front.

> Pro tip: Marketing activities are designed to overcome implicit and explicit sales objections.

The objections might be simple to understand but hard to overcome: Are you FIPS 140-2 compliant? Are you on our preferred vendors list?

This process is valid whether selling online or offline. It's hard to discover online objectives. Go through the process offline first in order to learn what objections you must overcome.

In the B2B world, regardless of whether an online product or offline, regardless of whether using the Internet to market or sell, customers care about increasing their revenue, market share, and customer loyalty, while decreasing costs and business risk. But remember that decisions are made by human beings, so all the less obvious and subconscious decision influences must be considered, as well: the desire for career advancement, job security, peer assessment, budget protection, and personal risk.

While interacting with multiple people inside an organization, you will want to consider:

- Who is the buyer versus the decision maker versus the financial approver?
- Where does the budget for purchase come from?
- Who else influences the decision?
- What compliance regulations come into play?
- What is the purchasing process?
- Is a pilot or proof-of-concept required?
- What is the length of the purchase process?
- Are there specific channel requirements?
- Who is the internal champion?
- Who might be motivated to obstruct the deal?

In the business-to-consumer (B2C) world, regardless of whether an online product or offline, regardless of whether using the Internet to market or sell, customers care about money, time, health, the elimination of specific problems, the fulfillment or exercise of particular passions, and personal values.

These are predominately conscious needs that, given the right circumstances, people are willing to talk about.

There are also things people care about that are more difficult to articulate and are even subconscious. These include the full range of human emotion, fear, social status, sunken costs, self-perception, and instinct.

While interacting with customers you want to learn[7]:

- Who has the pain or passion?
- Who decides on the purchase?
- Who are they trying to impress?
- Who influences the decision maker?
- What are adjacent pains or passions?
- Do they hire products currently that address the need to some degree?
- What makes them feel secure?
- What makes them feel sexy?
- What do they think is cool?
- What do they dream about?
- What keeps them up at night?
- What characteristics do they share with others that have need?
- Where do they hang out offline and online?
- How do they become trustful when purchasing?

- How do they decide a product is a good fit?

Marketing

There are three marketing stages:

1. Activities to evolve satisfied customers into passionate ones.
2. Activities to automate moving customers through the conversion funnel.
3. Activities geared to get people into the top of your funnel.

You want to learn, optimize, and relentlessly execute the tactics in the preceding order.

When Steve Blank took over marketing at a floundering SuperMac, he discovered "10,000 unprocessed, unlooked at, and untouched [product] registration cards."[8]

His staff of marketing professionals had no clue who their customers were. They came to the office every day, worked on *stuff* 40+ hours per week. Likely they had periodic job-performance reviews, which measured productivity in some way, but they had no clue how to align their activities with what would push the company forward.

Blank: "It dawned on me that we had a department full of people who were confusing their titles with what contribution they were supposed to be making to the company."

Titles are not the same thing as your job. Marketing people must relentlessly pursue tactics to create passion and value, move customers through the conversion funnel, and then, when the company is ready, fill the top of the funnel.

Passionate

As we've discussed, achieving customer satisfaction is not enough. Businesses cannot achieve significant growth rates on product satisfaction alone. In truly disruptive endeavors, the fact the product exists is, in itself, so radically new, so radically pleasure-inducing or problem-solving, so radically valuable that users are passionate just because of the MVP. This is rare.

In most endeavors, whether in an existing company seeking to regain passion or a startup needing to induce passion for the first time, something extraordinary, above and beyond—often outside the product—needs to occur.

To measure this, you need to create your own custom passion metric, which might be some combination of the following:

- Net Promoter Score measures passion by asking customers their likelihood of

referring the products to others. Generally, customers will only share products with others if they're passionate about them. Otherwise, they risk their own reputation. The MustHaveScore provocatively asks your customers, "If the product were no longer available, how disappointed will you be?" Informal evidence suggests that if 40 to 50 percent of your customers would be very disappointed, you have a passionate customer base.

- High scores on third-party review sites like Yelp might indicate user passion. Sometimes reviewers just want to show off, but there's currency involved when a user takes the time to tell the world they love your product. Again, their reputation is at stake.

Other indications your users are passionate include:

- A pattern that emerges around adamant feature requests or urgent bug-fix requests emanating from a particular segment around specific functionality. Customers don't complain about a product they don't care about. They ignore it. They complain when they feel ripped off—in other words

there's a real problem to solve, but you didn't even get close to resolving it. Or they complain if you're oh so close to making something truly valuable. "If only you would . . . !"

- When you call to speak with them, they are excited to talk to you. As Dave McClure says, you want them to love you or hate you. Either way, they're probably willing to say so. Love and hate come from the same place: expectations. If you promise A and deliver A above and beyond the call of duty, customers expecting A love you. If you promise A and deliver B above and beyond the call of duty, customers expecting A hate you.

- When customers are willing to go public with testimonials, press releases, or case studies. This is typically a significant currency and may require extra concessions.

- When customers invite their friends. If users forward your e-mail newsletters to colleagues or use product functionality to upload all their contacts to your site, or share coupons, and so forth, these are pretty good indications that you've gone beyond merely satisfying customers.

- Benefits are realized. This is difficult to measure and often difficult to achieve via any specific activity.

- Brand loyalty, such as repeat transactions or cross-selling at high margin.

- Effusive praise and sharing on social media.

It's the marketer's job to not only understand these, but to come up with activities that motivate customers to act on their passion. E-mail campaigns, product features, personal outreach, and developing deep relationships help customers understand and appreciate the benefits and allow you to tell success stories.

You have to ask for references and case studies. You give rewards to those who refer others. You create philanthropy projects because your customers care. You create community, or a tribe, or a cult. The key is to make your customers your best marketers.

Creating passion is where your brand comes into play. Everything about your customer's experience with business and its products affects customer perception of the brand. People can be merely satisfied with the product yet passionate about the brand. Customers will often not self-identify as passionate, yet behave as if they are.

Satisfied

Satisfaction comes from product experience matching customer expectations. It doesn't really matter to the business if the needs have been overly met unless that will invoke passion or expand the market segments attracted to the product. Be careful! More features do not necessarily mean more satisfaction, let alone passion.

We've discussed at length the functionality required to minimally provide satisfaction. What specific mouse clicks, reports, results? What shape, color, visual layout? Does satisfaction depend on someone else's use of the product? What customer experience represents a successful encounter or use of the product? In software and mobile products, you can actually instrument your product to know exactly how your customer interacts with the product. Their usage should match your expectations for how the product helps them solve their problem or addresses their passion.

A satisfied experience at a restaurant might mean a rating of four stars or above on Yelp. It might result in a large tip. It might mean that a specific customer returns once a month or once a week.

It's often the marketer's role to measure the satisfaction. Where possible, nontech businesses should think of ways to automate

their measure of satisfaction. Registration cards are an attempt at measuring satisfaction. If you want the warranty that comes with a product, it likely means you're satisfied. If you sell a product once that requires ongoing accessories, measure the purchase of the accessories over time.

The most obvious tactic is to measure satisfaction through surveys. Providing an incentive to fill out a survey will get you a higher response rate, but you *will* get higher reviews when the customer is so motivated. Better yet, incentivize people to share the product in a way you can measure. Attach free consumables to the product that only have value if the product itself is used.

Talk to customers. Call them up on the phone. Bring them into the business. Conduct usability testing whereby you watch customers use your product with influence by you.

> *Pro tip: Conduct usability testing using your competitor's products.*

This is still the best way to learn how your customers truly feel. Beware of focus groups in which individual personalities affect how others think.

Satisfaction will also be affected by business partners, channels, packaging, customer support, shipping—anything else that

is part of the value stream. You must control the entire experience.

How you message and position the product affects satisfaction. The story you tell about the product forms the promise you are making to your customer. You must tell them the product is *for* them, it addresses *their* specific desire. If your product strays from the promise, your customer will not be satisfied. Sell benefits, not just features.

Tell a story. What's their life like after experiencing your product? How has it changed for the better? Experiment with different stories. Different segments require different stories. Learn from your customers how they describe your product to friends and colleagues.

Hopeful

Customers are hopeful your product will fulfill its pledge. They find out by using the product, in other words, "activating." Again, in the mobile and Internet worlds, it's not difficult to measure when a product is first used. The lure of vanity metrics might trick you into caring about the number of downloads and how many Facebook likes you have, but those aren't nearly as important as knowing if your product has been used properly or even used at all.

The time difference between when the customer buys, downloads, or signs up for a trial and when it is used is critical. The longer the delay, the less likely they'll ever use the product—even if it is purchased! You forget to buy batteries for the toy you purchased your kid and they play with the box. (Ergo, "batteries included.")

It's not hard to imagine a day when a company will know when you've opened a package. Your car purchase is activated when you drive off the lot. Your restaurant experience is activated when you take the first bite. Your retail electronics experience is activated when you plug the product in and turn it on. If you can't automate the measurement, go out and observe your product being activated. Or bring users in-house and watch them use the product without you saying a thing.

Activities different businesses might employ to move customers through the hopeful stage include:

Hopeful:	"Getting Started" document or e-mail, e-mail marketing drip campaign, "batteries included," free support call, follow-up sales call, free accessory

Convinced

How do you know your customers are convinced that your product is worth buying? We don't mean convinced that the product was the right one to have chosen, but how are they convinced to consider it the first time? For free products, they may be convinced when they've decided to create an account. Customers become convinced when a relationship is established, either implicitly or explicitly. Good marketers market as if it's always explicit.

Possible activities to move customers through convinced (including where "Magic Happens"):

Convinced:	White paper, vertical messaging, segment case study, demonstration, download, proof-of-concept, pilot program, prototype
Magic Happens	Free shipping, coupon, special deal, discount, for sale, limited-time offer, download now, limited number, first 10 purchasers, packaging, sales meeting, sales call

Trusting

What makes a customer trust you is complicated, yet businesses have figured it out as long as selling has existed. First impressions mean the world. It's like when you meet a stranger: Through their words and actions they send a signal indicating whether they're trustworthy. Same with a business. Is the transaction secure? Is it guaranteed? Will you be there if something goes wrong? Again, think about it from the buyer's perspective.

Trust activities:

Trust	Influencer endorsement, reference, guarantee, certification, government backing, no haggle, testimonial, badges, magazine review, analyst endorsement

Intrigued

You know a customer is intrigued when they request more information, whether online or offline. They might sign up for a newsletter, request a sales call, or activate an online chat window.

You make them intrigued through messaging and positioning. The primary role of messaging is to share the benefits your product will have on your customers' lives. Positioning describes where you fit in the customers' view of the market. In other words, how do you compare with other products? What's the compelling reason to buy you, your primary differentiation?

Intrigued activities:

Intrigued:	Web copy, brochures, video, webinars, inside sales calls, presentation, in-person sales calls, model, TechCrunch, interview. (Many awareness tactics work here, too.)

Aware

Awareness is indicated by first visits to your website, new Twitter followers, Facebook likes, and inbound e-mails or phone calls.

There's literally no limitation to the methods used to attract attention. The key is to match tactics to market segment and where you are on the adoption lifecycle. Although creating awareness is the first thing an entrepreneur wants, it's the last thing they should attract. Awareness activities can break the bank. They will attract people you *do not* want as customers, who you're *not* ready for. Instead of buzz, you get noise.

Advertising and PR work, but if you pay a PR agency $15,000 per month, they will likely attract tens of thousands of visitors to your site. How many will you sign up? Among those who sign up, how many will buy? Of those who buy, how many will use the product? Of those who use, how many will become passionate?

Of those who love your product, how many will help populate the top of your funnel?

If you don't know the answer to the last question, then you don't know what the lifetime value of your customer is and, therefore, you cannot know if the $15,000 per month for that PR agency is the right choice!

Aware:	PR, social media, blogger outreach, SEO, advertising, podcasts, video, blogging, magazine articles, news stories, billboards, sign twirlers, promo teams, tradeshows, direct mail, cold calls, surveys, megaphones, TV commercials, radio commercials, etc.

Growth Waves

Growth isn't magic. Growth is determined by customer passion + cash-flow-positive customer acquisition. Yes, you can buy customers, but that's only sustainable in very high-margin businesses. Think dot-com fiasco of the 1990s. That was a lot of buying customers and little of customers buying.

First Wave

Customer passion indicates that you've nailed the value proposition per customer subsegment. Your first wave of growth comes from learning and then executing on marketing and selling to that subsegment.

Danger lurks in acquiring customers from multiple segments at this point.

We once worked with a company whose CEO came to us all excited about their growth. "We've hired this great vice president of sales, he's totally kicking butt. We've closed half a dozen deals in the last month and things are really taking off!"

Several months later, we heard from him again: "We had to let the sales guy go. Turns out he sold 10 deals to 10 different segments. They all wanted different things. We couldn't find any commonality. It was a nightmare!"

Thing is, that sales guy was doing what he was supposed to do, but he was the *wrong* salesperson for the company stage.

For online products, it's difficult to *not* acquire multiple segments. This is okay as long as you rigorously create buckets to store them in and monitor sales, marketing, and support costs. Here are some potential differences between subsegments:

- Varying depths of pain felt will result in different engagement, different requirements to achieve passion. Hanging out in different places requires different marketing tactics.
- Different funnel conversion steps require different marketing and sales activities.
- Related but slightly different value propositions result in different product requirements, different messaging and positioning, and different paths to passionate.

When acquiring early adopters or early mainstream customers opportunistically, these differences may not materialize; they will only rear up when you attempt to scale.

Have we mentioned to start small yet? As we've discussed, look at your target market segment. Go back to your personas you created in Chapter 3. Where does he or she hang out? Presuming you add value for the person, how are you going to get their dollar? Experiment and then optimize reaching out to them.

Keeping in mind that your goal is to achieve cash-flow-positive customer acquisition, the lowest-cost option is to look online.

In the United States, it's very likely your customer is online.[9] That doesn't mean, however, that Internet users are created equal, especially when it comes to different products. People act differently online depending on what they're trying to accomplish.

- Do they search for solutions to problems?
- Do they click on sponsored results? Ads?
- What do they use for their home page?

So is search engine optimization an important tactic? Is search engine marketing? How much content should you be creating?

Like the Internet, e-mail is now clearly in the late majority in the technology lifecycle adoption curve, which means most customers are reachable that way, but there are rules to abide by. What offers can you make?

How can you induce your readers to share the content and increase subscribers?

- Do your users subscribe to e-mail lists?
- Do your users click on e-mail links?
- Do your users share e-mail with others?

What other ways do your users interact with the Internet?

- Do they read their influencers' blogs?
- Do they blog themselves?
- Do they comment on blogs?
- Do they click on ads?
- Do they follow links recommended by bloggers?

Should you be reaching out to your customers' influencers online? What kind of offers can you make for the blogger and her readers? What's in it for the influencers?

Are your users part of online communities?

- Do they participate in online forums based on hobbies, interests, or shopping?
- Do they post to Facebook? Tweet?
- What hashtags do they follow? Which influencers?
- Do they interact and comment on music, movies, restaurants, products, services, stores?

What offers can you make to communities and community influencers?

Reaching these influencers is key to early marketing efforts. Think about it. If you've created value with a group of people—a segment—and someone else wishes to capitalize on your relationship with that segment as an influencer, you will weigh the request carefully.

As an influencer, you balance the value being provided to your segment, the value bring created for you personally, the future potential value, and any costs to your relationship with people in your segment.

Imagine you run a meetup group for lean startup believers. Someone reaches out to you and says, "Hey, you've got a great group. I teach people how to write business plans. I'd appreciate it if you could tell your members about my upcoming workshop."

What's in it for you? Your members don't believe in writing business plans. You don't know the guy reaching out to you, so it's hard to imagine any future benefit to you. So your equation looks like:

No value brought to members + no value personally + no future value – personal credibility

Doesn't look too good. Now say the guy is a pretty well-known author, who has a huge following. Now your equation might look like:

No value brought to members + no value personally + large potential future value – personal credibility

Potential access to the author's network might have a huge upside for you at some point, but how does that weigh against the blow to your credibility for having recommended the workshop that goes against the group's values?

After declining again, this self-help author, life coach, and business-plan guru offers you $10,000. Hmm.

No value brought to members + $10,000 + large potential future value – personal credibility (2× if word gets out about the $10,000)

This time when you decline the offer, the business-savvy author says, "Look, I'll tailor the discussion so it's not about writing a business plan but, rather, how to think through the standard aspects of a traditional plan. Even if you don't write a plan, trying to understand your business is a good thing. The workshop is free and I'll buy beer."

Value brought to members (if content is bad, there's still beer) + value personally if content is good + large potential future value + no hit to personal credibility

The point is that when you reach out to influencers, you need to understand the value they create for their constituency and how you can add value to the influencer.

Watch what other marketers are doing and what is working. Marketing tactics come and go cyclically. What's hot works until it doesn't. Think about how you are being marketed to. If you watch TV, listen to the radio, read web ads, or click on Facebook ads or Google AdWords, think about what worked. Think about how they found you.

As you succeed in reaching more users, it's more critical than ever to define buckets for your users and keep track of their shared and unique characteristics. More than this, you must correlate your value proposition *for each* bucket. You must track engagement, passion, feature requests *for each* bucket.

Second Wave

Your second wave of growth comes from nailing the rigorous process of adopting multiple subsegments.

The difficulty in tracking and managing multiple segments varies by product and customer. In the B2B world, not surprisingly, the larger the business you're selling to and the more complex the product, the more focused you must be on one segment. In the classic crossing-the-chasm sense, the bigger the fish you capture, the more you want to concentrate on dominating that one segment before moving on to the next.

As businesses transition toward Internet-based products, marketing, and selling, you can adopt multiple segments faster. You still face the same multiple-segment issues discussed earlier, but on a smaller scale. The second wave looks an awful lot like the first wave, only you need more resources to do it.

You use build-measure-learn (BML) to interact with customers to learn how you can get them from "meh" to satisfied and from satisfied to passionate. You use BML to run experiments to validate what you've learned. You use BML to test marketing and sales tactics. You run BML against individual subsegments. You say no to customers that end up being outside your vision and core value proposition (unless you decide to pivot to that segment and leave the others behind).

This is a painstaking, rigorous process. It does not come quickly. If you already have 1,000 customers and you don't know how to get to the next level, pick up the phone. Literally. Pick up the phone and start calling each customer until you pick up a pattern. Who are these people? What are they trying to accomplish?

They are not, by the way, trying to accomplish installing your software. Their problem is not trying to make more money. They are not hiring your product in order to view your dashboard.

Use root-cause analysis to figure out why they are installing the software, how they're trying to make money and what *their* business-model bottlenecks are, what they're trying to use the dashboard for. Ask why—five times, if necessary—to get to the urgent need your customer has.

Third Wave

The third wave of growth comes from that same need to generate buzz entrepreneurs clamor for since first conceiving of their product idea. When do you know you're ready to help generate buzz?

When buzz is being created by your execution, not PR.

Buzz happens when you dominate a market segment or are doing well in several subsegments. You can't keep a lid on it, because your customers are already passionate, remember? This is truly product-market fit. Buzz at this point is easy. Media are clamoring for such stories.

Product-market fit isn't what one has discovered through customer interviews or viability tests. Product-market fit comes from the market validating your product. It occurs after iterating through market segment definitions, product functionality, and even messaging and positioning. When all three values line up as with a slot machine, and you close the word-of-mouth loop, you can declare you have found product-market fit.

The only reason why you find it hard to create buzz now is because you're not ready. You get there by adding subsegments until it happens by itself. PR is used to scale existing buzz.

As you reach for the mainstream, your marketing must appeal to multiple subsegments. This allows you to drive larger, more expensive marketing campaigns that bring more people into your fold.

This is where traditional marketing comes to the fore. Radio, TV, print ads, and PR bring thousands of new visitors to your doorstep. The messaging and positioning is broad enough to allude to the core value proposition for broader, more traditionally drawn market segments. This only occurs after you've developed the affinity from the ground up. It only comes from understanding your customers deeply.

PR is changing and requires less agency work than in the past. You can create your own relationship with online media editors. They are looking for your contributions. Start small here, too. Ryan Holiday says, "Starting small is your beachhead into the news cycle. Blogs have enormous influence over other blogs—making it possible to turn a post on a small site into posts on large-traffic sites, as the bigger often 'scout' the smaller sites. Blogs compete to get to stories first, newspapers compete to 'popularize' it, and then everyone else competes to talk about it."[10] In the B2B world, influencing data analysts like Gartner work. It may not be fair, but that's the game. You also may have to wine and dine your customers.

There's no magic bullet for customer acquisition. Starting small allows you to more easily track your cost of acquisition relative to purchase, lifetime value of the customer (how much the customer will spend over the duration of being a customer), and velocity (time to cover the cost).

Your customer's perceived relationship with you will depend on how they view your attempted acquisition.

- Subscribers don't want to continue to be marketed to; they want a respectful relationship. How can you improve upon the value you are creating for them? How can you create new value? How do you reward their loyalty?
- Repeat-transaction customers often appreciate reminders, like upgrades, accessories, deals, and such. They want special treatment to bring them around again. High-cost single-transaction customers expect service follow-up, and they also may appreciate relevant up-selling, maintenance contracts, and premier support options.
- Network-effects relationships respond to ways to increase their network, status effects, and gamification.

Marketing will continue to evolve. White papers and case studies are transparent efforts to influence decision makers, but presumably they still work. Often they're used to demonstrate due diligence to higher-ups, even if never read.

Remember, even if B2B sales requires Kabuki theater, people are paid to perform their jobs, and so they will go through the machinations and you must allow them to if you want to close the deal.

You must determine what scaling means to your particular business and what levers you have available to manage the growth. Scale depends on many factors, including values, capital on hand, customer segment, and revenue model.

"Values" simply refers to the point that if you don't want to go big, you don't have to. Scaling might mean modest year-over-year growth, or even no growth at all. For most businesses, scaling requires money beyond revenue. Limiting growth funds to cash on hand is fine, but one needs to be aware. Customer segment determines ability to pay. If you're tackling different segments, you will likely see a different growth trajectory for each. The revenue model—how you are paid—determines what metrics to track.

Fundamentally, growth takes money. You always pay out in order to get paid. Typically, you must pay for sales and marketing, plus other business operations, in order to realize revenues. Sales and marketing are usually measured versus revenues because they increase relative to sales. In other words, over time and generally speaking, operational costs are constant and so decline per customer. Sales and marketing, however, increase over time, but hopefully at a slower rate than revenue growth.

Since you pay out sales and marketing before revenue, you must have cash on hand. Cash can come from last month's profits, bank loans, credit cards, venture capital, and so on. Measuring the lifetime value of a customer (LTV) versus the cost to acquire a customer (COA) tells you if you can acquire customers profitably. For every dollar you put into a customer acquisition channel, you know you are returning 1x, where x is the LTV.

But while the LTV may be greater than the COA, each purchase does not cover your sales and marketing. You can't wait to realize the lifetime value of a customer before acquiring the next one! The closer the average deal size or the average revenue per customer (ARPU) is to the COA, the further each dollar you have today goes. By driving up ARPU or driving down COA, you increase the number of customers you can acquire per dollar over a given time period.

Tracking the cost of acquiring (COA) one customer and the average revenue you make per customer (ARPU), allows you to manage how quickly you can grow.

Assuming ARPU > COA, if you reduce the cost to acquire a customer by half, you can double the numbers of customers per dollar spent. The length of the sales cycle is important too, since you are essentially financing the cost of acquiring a user prior to the sale. How many sales does it take to pay for lengthy sales cycle in the B2B world?

Word-of-mouth is the real money maker, which is why we've spent so much time discussing product passion. Word-of-mouth only happens when a customer is passionate or loyal about a product and when you leverage the passion through specific business activities.

Experimenting with more expensive customer acquisition channels only makes sense when you understand your growth levers. Startups tend to start with labor-intensive, but low-cost, acquisitions in order to work toward expensive acquisition channels only when the core value proposition is well understood across multiple mainstream market segments, organic growth is occurring due to product passion, and the business is moving toward larger customers with higher margins.

The trajectory might look like:

- Search engine optimization, including content creation via blog, social media, video, e-books, etc.
- Search engine marketing, including Google AdWords, Facebook, and the like.
- Affiliate marketing, blogger outreach, bundling, and influencer and segment hangout targeting.

- Online advertising targeting Internet properties specific to market segments "hangouts."

- Traditional media, including trade magazines, radio, market analysts, PR, and television.

For all outreach, whether online or offline, you should consider including an online, measurable call to action.

Business Model	Transaction	Satisfied	Dissatisfied	Business Drivers
E-commerce	one time	regular repeat	return	average order value, frequency of purchase; cost of acquisition
SaaS subscription	monthly	resubscribe	chum	monthly recurring revenue, chum, lifetime value; cost of acquisition
Enterprise	one time + % recurring	maintenance, support	cancel; legal action	average length of sales cycle; average order value; monthly recurring revenue; average up-sell/cross-sell value; cost of acquisition
Manufacturing	periodic	regular repeat	no repeat	average order value; frequency of purchase; cost of acquisition
Consumer (Free)	signup + monetization at scale	regular usage	periodic to no use	average revenue per daily active user; cost of acquisition
Consumer (Free)	signup + micropayments	regular purchase	periodic to no use	average revenue per daily active user; frequency of purchase; cost of acquisition
Freemium	free to monthly upgrade	regular usage	periodic to no use	conversion to paid; monthly recurring revenue; cost of acquisition/account level
Mobile	one time or periodic or free	updates	periodic to no use	average revenue per daily active user; cost of acquisition
Retail	one time	regular repeat	return	average order value; frequency of purchase; cost of acquisition

Case Study: Ten Lean Startup Buzzword Questions with Rob Fan

Lean Entrepreneur: Let's get the formalities out of the way. What's Sharethrough?

Rob Fan: Sharethrough is a native video advertising platform. By native, we mean we integrate advertising content naturally and openly into websites. We work with brands and agencies to distribute high-quality video content they've created through their network of publishers. We report back what was successful and what wasn't. The primary pain point that we solve is getting an audience to the content they've spent hundreds of thousands producing, that they have no way to drive an audience to.

LE: Okay, on to our real questions. Question 1: What was your MVP?

Fan: When we started out, my partner, Dan Greenberg, and I had a couple of different products going. In 2008, we had a Facebook application company. We built a huge network of Facebook apps and at one point were the third biggest Facebook app company by daily active users. At the same time, Dan was doing viral video consulting, helping brands make viral videos. We saw that we had tons of content inventory, tons of publishers, so we thought, let's try to take some of these videos and let's put them into these social applications and see what happens and see if it's valuable to the customer.

LE: Like chocolate and peanut butter. You guys were the Reese's Peanut Butter Cup of Facebook!

Fan: Ha ha, yeah, sort of.

LE: Sorry. So Question 2: What was your first pivot?

Fan: Yeah. So what's funny is we actually never did a pivot . . .

LE: How refreshing.

Fan: Yeah, but we did go through a kind of refocus of the company. Along the way, we hit a point where we had to make a choice. We started building out this ad business within the company, and building out brand relationships and building out technology that we needed, while also maintaining our Facebook applications network. Along the way, we realized that trying to focus on both was just not something we could do as a nimble startup. So we ended up spinning off the Facebook apps and focusing on the ad business.

LE: Question 3: What's a warning for entrepreneurs about lean startup thinking?

Fan: Because we were so early, I think we fell into a bit of a trap when the second MVP we built, which wasn't much more sophisticated than the first, took off and was enough to scale the business for quite a while with only minor iterations.

I think because we were so far ahead in terms of where we believed the market was going, our MVP was solving enough pain that we didn't need to worry about product, and so when you fast forward, three years later, we paid the price for that. It's your classic startup story. We know that there is competition around us. The marketplace is changing. People are becoming more aware of the market. We can't just keep on doing what we're doing and expect it to be enough. So we realized we need to refocus on product. What's interesting is that for two or three years, there was only myself and three other engineers. We never expanded the engineering team because things were going fine and we had revenue, but it also meant that when you're operating a full-on business with very demanding customers, you're also not innovating product, because the entire engineering team is focused on keeping the engine running.

Source: World Gone Sour (The Lost Kids)—view the video at http://youtube/tw7uhVtpI5I.

LE: Question 4: What's the most dangerous vanity metric?

Fan: Cash. We're fortunate to be in a cash-rich business; there's lots of money going in and out. But, one thing I've learned through the years is that cash can be misleading: If it's a big number it sounds great, but it doesn't mean you're setting yourself up to succeed. The best learning is not cash.

LE: We should be in your line of work.

Fan: Cash is essentially like the user metric for us because every time we close a deal it's just like users signing up. But more important is if the brand comes back to us and uses us again. What's more important is that we continue to grow out the number of publishers we work with and expand the network so it's more attractive for the advertisers. Those metrics, which aren't nearly as sexy, are actually the ones that determine whether we are viable as a long-term business.

I'll be the first to say cash is what kept us afloat. It's what allows you to make mistakes, right? If we weren't the type of business which brings in a lot of cash, we couldn't have made the mistakes we made along the way. But still, it definitely doesn't guarantee you a fast track to success.

LE: Question 5: What is product-market fit?

Fan: I think of product-market fit in terms of the technology-adoption lifecycle. Early on you have your evangelists, and those are the guys who, no matter what, you show them any shiny new object, they'll jump on it and start using it and they'll be passionate about it and they'll speak to it and report bugs. They'll tell you what to do, what not to do, but that's not product-market fit.

Product-market fit is when you reach the mainstream customer and of course it varies by business and you have to define who your mainstream customer is. But when you have the mainstream acting the same way as an early evangelist, that's product-market fit. Are they get excited when you come in to talk about your product? Do they have opinions about it? Do they have feature requests for it?

It really comes down to identifying who is that person with those requests. If it's someone who you have seen to be mainstream in that industry, then I think you've definitely got product-market fit at that point. Then it's like, "Oh, we need to keep on building on top of that."

LE: Question 6: Best customer development learning?

Fan: What's funny is that both myself and my co-founder have no experience in the ad industry and the media world and it is probably one of the most convoluted, confusing industries to understand. So, I think, taking a very deliberate path that customer development talks about and mapping out customer archetypes and putting them up on the board: Who are the archetypes? Who makes the final decision? Who is the actual executor of the contract? What are they motivated by? Doing a lot of that stuff helps solidify, who are the people

that we're talking to and what do they want? What do they care about? How can they help us build the right product for them? I feel like we knew that there was a big budget in the media world but we had no idea how to tap into it.

The biggest thing, however—this is probably the biggest learning: Madison Avenue does not think in a very rational way or in a very logical way. I feel like a lot of startup companies go, "Wow look, I built an amazing product and now I just need a brand to buy into it and obviously they're going to buy into it."

What they don't understand is that there is an entire method to buying into it and that concept is absolutely foreign to them. So the biggest learning that we had, I think, was recognizing that one, the primary customer in the media space is actually 21-, 22-year-old new college grads who control millions of dollars in advertising budget. They're the ones who, in the end, say yea or nay to working with your company. Oddly, or not surprisingly, they aren't exactly motivated by what's best for their brands, what's best for their agency. They're sometimes motivated by who gives the best drinks, who throws the best parties, who is the most fun to talk to and hang out with. It's one of those things that, for me, especially being an engineer and from Silicon Valley, I was completely thrown back and I soon realized how relationship driven this world is.

LE: Question 7: How do you lean startup B2B sales?

Fan: Steve Blank wrote his book primarily from a B2B perspective because it was out of his Epiphany success, but I think the lean startup movement moved toward consumer-based startups and web-based startups. So you get a lot of different information out there focused on consumer startups versus enterprise startups. But the business-to-business model is actually the angle where customer development works the best.

I think the confusing part, when you're doing B2B with a field sales team, is filtering the noise from the signal, because you have people whose main job is to be out of the building, but their incentives might not be aligned with what's right for the company. You then have to really understand what you need to build that will help you learn versus what you need to build just to close a deal.

Our first salesperson was my co-founder; he's an amazing salesperson. So he was doing everything on his own. He was able to build a lot of really great initial relationships, but it was not a scalable way to grow and we were very cautious—everyone has horrible stories about hiring the wrong vice president of sales and then having to start sales over and over and over.

So we were very aware of that and we thought maybe we're just out winning in the market because my co-founder is just an amazing salesperson, right? If you have amazing salespeople and your founders are just so charismatic and able to sell that they could sell anything, sales is maybe not a good indicator that your product is ready for the market.

So what we did was bring in an outside rep firm to sell our product. The idea was that if these professional guys cannot sell, our product is not ready to go.

So we said, "Let's give it a shot," and almost immediately, like two or three months later, we were hitting channel conflict.

We put together the collateral. We had to present the decks. We had to give them one sheet. We had to print all this stuff for them. So there was a lot of stuff that we had to put together for this but, again, part of, in the lean way, you essentially are iterating through . . . having a rep firm there helps you iterate through it and just having a professional salesperson already say, "That does not look like one sheet. Do it again," is valuable input before you would go to the client.

It was catching on very quickly and we said, "Okay, this is obvious, we need to hire a vice president of sales right now."

We're constantly iterating our decks and iterating our pitches and what we've had to do now is, now that we're a much bigger sales team, is figure out how to do it in a, I guess, tempered way that doesn't make the sales team go crazy but we've constantly been iterating the way or honing down the way we communicate, the way we position stuff, the way we present stuff. That's something that we're constantly doing. So I like going out on sales calls every now and then, even though I'm the CTO, and my co-founder is out all the time and that's one of the things that we're doing when we're out there. We're just testing different concepts, different ways that people are thinking of stuff and bringing it back and incorporating into kind of how we're talking about it.

The way we've been able to do it right is by staying on top of all the things that are coming in, and so I think part of the great advantage we have is that my co-founder is still going out and regularly being on these sales calls and we have some pretty savvy salespeople who are able to cut through the crap and really understand what they're talking about; what they are saying, so they can bring back actual good feedback and we can figure out a way to position ourselves around it or put ourselves in front of the potential competitor or the issue that's happening so that we're never in a reactive way. It's hard for me to recall the moment when we've had to be super-reactive to something out in the field.

LE: Question 8: Do you practice continuous deployment?

Fan: No. We could be and I think we've thought about trying to get there but we just never got to that point, and I think the reason is that, in our business, we automatically have tons of scale. So, from the start, there never was this opportunity to start slowly building the tooling around it to allow us to get to the point where we could use continuous deployment.

I actually think of everything as inventory and unused inventory. There are moments when it's like, "Ah," because if we were only doing lean continuous deployment it would help but I think of one of the learnings I had, actually really early on, about just the entire agile thing. I had no idea what agile development was and I had to learn my way into it and I remember being extremely daunted by hearing Ries describe how his engineering team operates and how they would build software and I kept on thinking how my engineering team is so inferior. I don't know how the hell I'm

ever going to get to that point, and I was thinking, "You can't take a team from zero to a hundred."

You can read about the hundred and you can try and get to a hundred, you could dream about it, but it's not going to happen overnight and, for the most part, if you get up to even 20, from 0 to 20 is a win.

The entire thing behind agile is that there are many different flavors of agile and you can pick and choose what pieces of agile you wanted to do, as long as there are some core things that you continue to do. I think that's what people miss about agile, which kind of gets left out of the entire lean startup conversation, is a real conversation about what to pick and choose out of agile and what are the right parts of agile that really help? I think getting to the point where you start thinking of things essentially as backed up inventory or unused inventory. They're good mental models to help you kind of understand how to operate in that world.

LE: Question 9: Any thoughts on technical debt?

Fan: The path we took is a story of not keeping an eye on technical debt and letting the business totally run and control the product itself. This is kind of going back to our MVP being too successful, when we just kept on building on top of the MVP without really thinking about the long-term needs of the business, but essentially operationalizing the product without building out the foundation of the product so we could continue to build on and innovate on top of it. So we definitely hit a point when we were forced to . . . and this was actually, for me, it was like on Thanksgiving and I had to stay up all night and figure out how to scale up machines and how to keep the cache machines up for the next few days as best as possible, knowing full well that it was going to start crashing again very quickly. I was like, "All right, you've taken on so much that there's no way to even scale it in the right way that we'd probably have to . . . have to start from scratch" and that was, I think, one of the things that was a big setback for the company at the time.

The other realization that I had along the way was the business is around core product. There are many pieces of our product. The ones at the core of the business is an ad server and that's essentially what is the lifeblood of the company. The decision we made at first was because it's core, we've got to own it, we have to build it. So we spent a good two years building this custom ad server for our business needs. The problem was that it couldn't scale and it created just a huge operational burden on the engineering team at the time. At the same time, I would just log into all these other ad servers out there, which were already built and done. And it's like, "Great, it does exactly what we need and it's done."

So when I realized we needed to scale, I thought, "Right, why do I even have to worry about this stuff because, one, it's not helping me learn. It's not accelerating the business at all and, aside from just being a cool engineering challenge, it's not benefiting at all." So that was when I made the decision, "All right, let's use a third-party ad server." It may be core but it's, you know, not the most efficient use of our time.

Having an ad server that doesn't work, doesn't help the business learn or move forward at all, even if it is core.

I think the fear that I had was that this is such a core piece of our technology. We should be building it. We should be owning it and I think there is the right time to do that but when you're into the learning phase, use as many third-party technologies as you can, even if that third-party technology is going to be a core part of what you're doing because what you're trying to prove is whether the overall product offering you've built is attractive to the customer base and whether customers are willing to pay.

LE: So how do you know? Bonus question, I guess.

Fan: I think the main thing is really being disciplined about the metrics that you're watching and then having specific scaling metrics in place to be like, "All right, so we achieved *x*, *y*, and *z*, with our MVP, so now we need to spend the time building these specific chunks of a product out because we've hit some type of product-market fit here and this feels like this is probably going to stay, versus some other stuff."

When you're so early, who knows if any thing's going to stay? Once you can start seeing the permanent blocks start to form, that's when you should probably go back in and put reinforcement in there.

You need to, from the start, be very deliberate about how you're communicating debt and also what is the end of an MVP cycle, right? I think putting those metrics in early and that's one of the things I got from a lot of the lean UX stuff that's happening now is putting a lot of this information up and center, in front of everyone, really helps everyone understand where the company is, and, therefore, if you put your scaling metric up on top of, on the board or it's announced on a regular basis and you kind of talk about how we're about to hit the capacity of it and when you need to now spend time working on it, no one is shocked about that.

LE: Question 10: So what about the company culture?

Fan: From early on you have to start instilling this concept of failing fast, and I think we try to be very deliberate with our culture and to find ways to essentially scale it. So we have a weekly meeting with the entire company as a way to kind of bring everyone back together and talk about things. We've had some conversation with people where we kind of have to say we don't really know where we're going or where we need to go with this product or we don't have that strong of a foothold in this marketplace. To some employees, this shocks them, I think, to an extent, but I think they get used to it.

We also do a quarterly meeting where we bring everyone in, which is also really important because we have remote offices now. That brings them all in and get everyone synced up onto the same page and reinvigorate the company. I think all those activities, although they may just feel like they just create little bonding things, those are the types of things that form culture, and if you do the right activities and you talk about the right things in those meetings and in those instances, that's how culture is formed and that's how people start thinking in the way that the founders think.

We've done all the paperwork on values, and such, but nothing comes out of it until you actually start essentially living the values and people start learning from what you are doing and I think that's the biggest thing. You're struggling to create an environment in which people are not afraid of failing. As leaders, you should probably let them all know how you failed and then how you're learning from it and that's a great way to get everyone to then understand, "Oh, it's okay to fail," and so kind of talk about things: "Oh I tried this out. It didn't work," and to constantly talk about that type of philosophy and thinking, that is what will get everyone in a culture where everyone wants to fail fast.

LE: To wrap up, where are you now as a company?

Fan: So we are about 60 people now. We've got three offices. We've got a sales office in New York, a sales office in Chicago, we're headquartered up in San Francisco. We're at a point now where we've got an existing product that we've operationalized and that we're kind of growing and scaling out. At the same time, now, we're also at a point where we need to be innovating and building new products, whether it's on top of the existing one or things that are kind of parallel to what our existing product is, and so we're at that point now where we need to do that if we want to keep on moving and moving up essentially.

Yeah. So we took a seed round from Mike Maples at Floodgate, and then we raised an A round from North Bridge.

LE: Great!

Work to Do

Recall that in Chapter 3 you posited the functionality required to induce customer satisfaction. We hope you have tested whether what you posited bears any semblance to reality.

Funnel State: Aware	Activity	Customer Action	Metric
Aware Activity Example	Make affiliate offer; product discount to influential blogger	Visits website	Unique visitor by cohort
Activity 1			
Activity 2			
Activity 3			
Activity 4			

Funnel State: Intrigued	Activity	Customer Action	Metric
Intrigued Activity Example	Website video	Watches video	Video clicks
Activity 1			
Activity 2			
Activity 3			
Activity 4			

Funnel State: Trusting	Activity	Customer Action	Metric
Trusting Activity Example	Positive demo experience	Creates Account	Registrations by cohort
Activity 1			
Activity 2			
Activity 3			
Activity 4			

Funnel State: Convinced	Activity	Customer Action	Metric
Convinced Activity Example	Pricing page	Buys	Purchase
Activity 1			
Activity 2			
Activity 3			
Activity 4			

Funnel State: Hopeful	Activity	Customer Action	Metric
Hopeful Activity Example	Follow-up thank you, "getting started" guide, free customer support, e-mail drip campaign	Customer tries these specific things:	Activation by cohort, by segment
Activity 1			
Activity 2			
Activity 3			
Activity 4			

Funnel State: Satisfied	Activity	Customer Action	Metric
Satisfied Activity Example	Feature x Feature y Feature z	Customer uses feature x, y, z 4x/week	Engagement by cohort/by segment
Activity 1			
Activity 2			
Activity 3			
Activity 4			

Funnel State: Passionate	Activity	Customer Action	Metric
Passionate Activity Example	1 month free for every friend who signs up 10% revenue to charity	Shares with x friends Agrees to testimonial	Out of x friends invited, y sign up.
Activity 1			
Activity 2			
Activity 3			
Activity 4			

10

The Final Word

Talk to entrepreneurs tackling a consumer problem and they'll tell you how much easier *lean* is in business-to-business. Talk to business-to-business (B2B) and you'll hear the opposite. Talk to business-to-business-to-consumer (B2B2C) and you witness virtual self-immolation.

Lean startup doesn't work with consumers, because you can't believe what people say. Lean startup doesn't work for businesses, because too many people are involved in the decision-making process.

The most pervasive reasons we hear for not acting as a lean startup are mutually exclusive:

- "It's unproven; show me a lean startup big win."
- "Whatever, there's nothing new here; entrepreneurs have been doing this for ages."

There are lots of excuses for not doing lean startup, but the remedy boils down to the same idea: "Launch product based on what's between our ears."

The real reason entrepreneurs don't want to do lean startup is that it's hard. Don't talk to customers; it's hard. Don't involve customers in design; it's hard. Don't analyze data for actionable metrics; I'll have to hire a business intelligence team. Don't run experiments; it will take away engineering resources.

The reason the Myth of the Visionary persists is that if we can't hope to end up as visionaries, we'll feel lost and clueless about how to build a scalable startup. The real *visionaries*, however, are not those who predicted the future or foresaw products that plopped from their skulls in fully realized form.

The real visionaries are internally driven to make big change. They are committed to disruption. They have an idea, but it is secondary to change. They make mistakes, are wrong—fail—but relentlessly pursue their ambition. They actually take the vision out of the equation. The vision is added later, after they win. Lean startup is a method for being both disruptive and navigating change.

There is no blueprint for true, black-swan, radical, big disruption. Too many variables are involved. Previous economic, technological, and societal transformations create platform layers like Earth ecosystems that drive new innovation and make possible big wins. In our opinion, the best one can do is position oneself for such an occurrence through unrelenting persistence and non-stop experimentation.

Despite what you might think, a graveyard of equally visionary individuals surrounds the well-known entrepreneurial icons of our day.

The time is ripe. Transformation layers are once again aligning for an increasing number of black-swan events. Despite the cries of a lack of innovation, major industries are being disrupted at an increasing rate. Regardless of whether you are seeking to be ex post facto anointed a visionary, lean startup is a methodology that helps you—as an entrepreneur, intrapreneur, or a linchpin—to not only find a place in this new world, but to thrive. Lean startup is a process for identifying and eliminating business-model bottlenecks.

Like an engineer who must locate and eliminate bugs and other inefficiencies on the path toward delivering a high-performing product, entrepreneurs can view their startup endeavor as a series of bottlenecks inhibiting growth.

The question is, how do you align your organization and establish the culture and processes necessary to actively, relentlessly seek out and eliminate your bottlenecks? The lure of acting for acting's sake is strong. "Just do it" is a clarion call to be busy. *It* is where the money is.

Broadly speaking, the major choke points are at the idea stage, releasing the minimum viable product (MVP), finding product-market fit, establishing revenue-positive customer acquisition, and finally making the transition from learning to executing. In other words, after you figure it out, you need a group executing and continuing to learn or you will be left behind.

At the idea stage, through interacting with customers and running experiments, you validate that you have the right customer profiles and understand the problems they face.

At the MVP stage, you iterate on the product, run experiments on functionality, perform usability testing, and try to nail the core value proposition for the market segment. You continue to interact with customers to test that you are building the right product, learning more about their problems and learning how you will market, sell, and deliver your value to them.

Product-market fit is a continuation of experimenting and growing the product to find early mainstream passion and to establish the correct positioning and messaging.

In the customer acquisition stage, you're validating the conversion funnel, testing acquisition channels, and measuring return to ensure you have a functioning business model.

The final stage to scale is learning how to get out of the way. To scale, organizations must adapt. They must learn how to execute efficiently, while continuously learning and continuously improving.

But, of course, the devil is in the details.

The details are organized by build-measure-learn. Build an experiment, measure the action, analyze the results, and determine learning. Rinse, repeat. Rinse, repeat.

The value-creation economy is the result of technological and cultural transformations. Technology has finally been pushed to the edge for this particular wave. When past waves reached the edge, we saw cars, refrigerators, microwaves, washers and dryers, stereos, phones, and so on, for consumers. Those that won provided exceptional user experience or provided the most value for a low cost.

Now we see all these items computerized—sustaining innovation—and tons of new computerized products that miniature computers enabled. It's time to end the distinction between software companies and product companies. They are one and the same.

Your ability to know what your customer needs and your relationship with your customer are your competitive advantages. We will see many smaller companies nailing core value proposition for niche markets versus companies producing fewer products that serve many.

Startups spend *years* iterating on product and market segments trying to find the fit that propels them into product-market fit nirvana—a nirvana that is often short lived. Even after finding product-market fit, you must continue to learn, iterate, and discover new ways to disrupt again.

The new reality considers that to dominate like oligopolies of old, you must continuously improve known processes and continuously learn new ones; continuously reiterate new products or existing product functionality; or discover new market segments where you can provide value.

Much to the consternation of venture capitalists, we're witnessing the end of the dominance of big-win investing.

Tracing lean startup to its origins, one understands that it emerged from the realization that startups execute before learning. Why do we accept iterative learning processes when running scientific experiments, when conducting research, or even when building complex products, but not when determining whether we're building the right product, nor when we're attempting to market and sell the product?

To build a successful business, you must *learn* several things:

- What problem or passion to address.
- What solution to provide.
- For whom to provide it, segment by segment.
- How to market to the segment.
- How to sell to the segment.
- How to turn a customer into an advocate.
- How to scale a segment.
- How to innovate again.

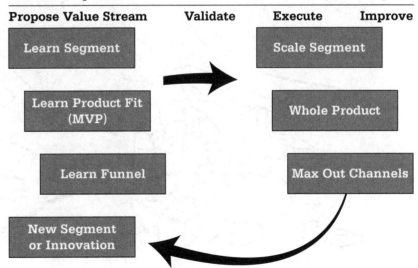

The idea is to evolve from lean startup to lean enterprise as you validate the answer to each question. In other words, you move from *learning* to *execution*.

The point is to embrace "I don't know" in your unrelenting pursuit of change. Whether you seek to change your own life, change your community, or change the world; whether you're seeking to support your family, or 10 employees, or thousands, you have to start small to be big. The lean startup is a language to describe how to create value as quickly as possible, to leverage deep knowledge of your customers, to discover your driving force, and to scale quickly once you've figured it out.

Case Study: Drinking Kool-Aid and Eating Dog Food

HubSpot

Marketing is broken. HubSpot was founded in 2006 by Brian Halligan and Dharmesh Shah to fundamentally change—to disrupt—how businesses market to customers. In our world of information overload—data; images; non-stop advertising; high-volume pitches; and the blurring of paid messaging, news and entertainment—we must adapt. The consumer creates new filters and incorporates new requirements, and businesses must somehow rise above the din.

"If you call me on my cell phone and I don't recognize the number, I don't answer it," says Mike Volpe, vice president of marketing at HubSpot. "So if you're a salesperson trying to get ahold of me and hoping to arm wrestle me into buying your product, it is really difficult today. It doesn't mean I don't buy things though. I'm buying all kinds of stuff for my business and for me personally."

The way that buyers buy things today is not the way people used to buy things. People hate to receive cold calls. They block out advertising. They look to friends on social media for product information. They search, they read blogs. They do a lot more research themselves.

It used to be that companies and their sales representatives could control information. That worked in a pre-Internet environment: before search engines, before social media. You had to talk to salespeople to get information and from the get-go, you were in the sales funnel, you were being sold to. That's simply how it worked: The sales reps had all the power.

"As marketers," Volpe explains, "we have not yet fully embraced the shift in power toward the customer. It requires a fundamental change in marketing, a fundamental change in sales."

This is the problem HubSpot focuses on. While apparent to some, most businesses don't even recognize the problem, and among those that do, no one knows the solution. It's a new world. While the phrase "lean startup" wasn't around yet in 2006, agile development and developing a customer feedback loop were attributes forward-thinking startups embraced.

"We were very much focused on getting product out the door and iterating. Not only iterating on product, but everything, marketing and sales. We were like: Try something, learn from it, iterate, improve it, and keep moving on from there."

Market segmentation has evolved, too. Traditionally, a B2B company would immediately divide its market by vertical industries, such as law firms, financial services, manufacturing, etc. Marketing, sales, and product development are oriented around these verticals and then further by firmographics, such as number of employees, revenues, and so on.

HubSpot initially took a fairly traditional approach. They looked at the Fortune 1000 market, but felt that was a path with multiple obstacles: long sales cycles, lots of competing technology, difficulty in reaching decision makers, high demands in terms of product functionality, and the likelihood they wouldn't even recognize they had the problem.

If we were to apply a segment matrix, it might look like this:

Segment	Sales Cycle	Competition	Reach	MVP	Level of Pain
Fortune 1000	L (unfavorable)	L	L	L	M

Not a good picture! So HubSpot looked at smaller businesses and within that, they thought about verticals, like law firms, car dealerships, doctors' offices, and accounting firms. What they found, however, was that segmenting based on such verticals didn't matter. The variables that differentiated market segments turned out to be based on a business's knowledge of pain and their revenue model.

Organizations that were already doing some amount of marketing, but felt is was ineffective and wanted to leverage the Internet, were good early adopters. Further, businesses that currently had a sales process and needed to generate leads were more favorable than transaction businesses like e-commerce sites or those generating revenue from advertising.

Vertical characteristics did come into play when marketing and sales tactics differed, as they did, for example, for nonprofits.

An updated segment table might look like this:

Segment	Sales Cycle	Competition	Reach	MVP	Level of Pain
Fortune 1000	L (unfavorable)	L	L	L	M
E-commerce	M	H (favorable)	H	H	M
Offline services	M	H	H	H	H
Advertising websites	M	M	H	H	L
Nonprofits	M	H	M	H	H

Being a startup whose products help innovate marketing funnels, HubSpot was forced to eat its own dog food. Build-measure-learn was the basis for learning how to market to their segments.

"It was execute a little bit, learn, execute, learn, execute, learn. It was definitely this type of feedback loop," Volpe says. They asked for beta sign-ups on their landing page, they started blogging. Then Dharmesh built "Website Grader," which is a free website evaluator. "We thought, 'Maybe people will be interested in using this and maybe after they grade their website then they will be more interested in trying to solve their marketing problems that the tool identifies.'"

So HubSpot started offering education: webinars, building up the blog, talking about how to improve inbound marketing. The fundamental insight is twofold: First, most organizations (yours, HubSpot's, HubSpot's customers) must innovate in areas other than the product. Second, funnel activities should be value-creating, where possible.

HubSpot's Website Grader (and other free tools) creates value itself, regardless of how it furthers customers' paths down HubSpot's sales funnel. The same can be said for HubSpot's webinars, blogs, and other content-creating activities. E-mail newsletters, for example, that merely sell or point to other resources, that don't provide value, are unlikely to move the needle of the business.

"It creates value on both sides of the equation, which has really been helpful. When I do a webinar or write a blog post or create an e-book or something that is purely educational, it absolutely is helpful to the other person," Volpe explains. "But it is also helpful to me, because now I have more people in the world that think about marketing in this new way. Even if they don't buy, they're talking to their friends and colleagues about that. They are trying to implement that. Maybe they move to a new company where they have a larger budget and it's a better fit and they end up purchasing."

Creating value in this way—throughout the value stream—creates passionate customers. HubSpot obsessively mines its data, segments customers, looks for patterns that enforce the notion of creating passionate, loyal customers who act as evangelists.

Like many forward-thinking organizations, HubSpot tracks its Net Promoter Score, which measures how likely customers are to refer its products to others. But they don't just track these scores; they double down on them. HubSpot doesn't just do case studies with them, or write them up for the website; they treat them special. They promote their content, send them swag.

"We gave them VIP tickets to our conference and they got to meet Cindy Lauper who had come to perform at the event."

In addition to NPS, they track non-product users who continuously interact with HubSpot through downloading content like e-books and attending webinars. They've demonstrated loyalty, though their currency is time.

"We put those people in a segment bucket. If they have gone through the download process and have been touched by the sales team more than two separate times—you know what? They love us, they love our content, but for whatever reason they are just not going to purchase, but we want them. We actually communicate with them more. We've found that those folks tend to be the ones most likely to share our content."

HubSpot takes data seriously. They hire quants, short for quantitative analysts, who use sophisticated mathematics and computer algorithms to analyze data. They're deep into the data looking for interesting patterns they can leverage to accelerate growth. They look at data in terms of:

- Pre-sales activity: website interaction data; how people interact with the funnel based on where they came from.

- Conversion activity: how the funnel steps differed; closing rates.
- Post-sales activity: how different segments use the application, what parts, and how often and to what benefit (e.g., lead generated).
- High-value customers: retention rates by segment, size of business, and parts of product used.

The data is used to determine how to prioritize marketing goals and tactics.

"I know that somebody in a five-person company who signs up for a webinar should average a few dollars of monthly revenue versus someone who is at a 100-person company and signed up for a demo, which averages $150/month or something like that. So I can tell one of my marketers: 'Hey you need to contribute $50,000 of pipeline and you can get there by a billion webinar registrations or you can get there with 1,000 demo requests.'"

And how do they reach the quota? Experiments, of course. HubSpot has created a structure around "how to experiment." Because the product is fairly mature, cross-functional teams do not normally have engineering members but can get them if needed, once they prove viability. The teams typically include marketing, support, sales, and sometimes web developers (as opposed to product developers). They have "experiment meetings" where teams pitch their ideas, get advice, and then report back regularly on progress. Experiments have included new channels, new segments, and lots of split-testing on landing pages, e-mails sales training, and so on.

"One great example is our agency reseller channel, which is now 30 percent of our revenue. That started out as an experiment when Pete Caputo thought it would work. Some of us, in our infinite wisdom, told him he was wasting his time. I came from a company that sold 100 percent through channel and resellers. We were saying, 'This is crazy, resellers are terrible.'

"Peter just kept doing it and we're like, 'Fine, just let us know what happens each month. We think it's a bad idea but you can do whatever you want.' Now he has a team of like 30 people and he's 30 percent of our revenue. He is director of this whole channel."

Selling into nonprofits started as an experiment. The e-commerce segment that originally didn't look promising is now getting traction, and that started as an experiment.

"We're doing one experiment right now where we're taking a specific type of lead that goes to our mid-size business team and instead giving them to three dedicated sales reps. We are trying to see if we can actually increase the conversion rate of those leads if those reps focus and we give them specific training on how to address them."

HubSpot is the ultimate lean startup. They focus on data that is relevant to moving the business forward: product satisfaction, passion, and the sales funnel. Their marketing activities not only further the cause of the business but provide value such that customers are more likely to be satisfied and passionate. They run purpose-built experiments to accelerate growth and provide the data to inform and prioritize tactics and product.

"I think a lot of what it really boils down to is in the old days marketing focused on helping your sales team," Volpe says. "Today what you really want to do is create marketing that helps your potential customers: creating marketing that they love, which then builds that love for your company."

Work to Do

For all those who want a step-by-step, bullet-proof blueprint plan for success, here it is. Treasure it. Hold it close. This is how to become a Visionary.

Job 1: Is There a Solvable Problem?

- Leave the comfort of your home and go find one person who is emotional about the pain or passion you are addressing.
- If you are a B2C play, find nine more to complete your LE Team of 10.
- If you are a B2B play, find two more to form your LE Advisory Board.
- If you are creating a multi-sided marketplace, serve both sides.
- Look for patterns in the people you compile.

Job 2: Is the Solution Tenable?

- Additionally, qualify your LE Team of 10 or LE Advisory Board.
- Find 10 (3) people who are excited about your high-level solution idea.
- If necessary, fill out your "team of 10" (Advisory Board) with new blood (starting from the beginning).
- What is the pattern?

Job 3: Solution Discussions

- Engage your LE Team of 10 or LE Advisory Board during product development.
- Are you on the right track?
- Is the customer on right platform?

- Perform usability testing with competitive products.
- Conduct a "high hurdle" experiment.
- If responses are lukewarm or uninterested:
  - Change the solution.
  - Change the segment (start over).

Job 4: Viability Testing

- What is most uncertain about your business model? Run purpose-built tests to resolve uncertainty:
  - Landing page
  - Concierge
  - Wizard of Oz
  - Prototypes
  - Wireframes, mockups, similar products
  - Test apps
- If you lose members of the Team of 10 or Advisory Board, refill.

Job 5: Minimum Viable Product

- Validate customer will do in product what they've said they'd do.
- Iterate.
- Develop discrete functionality that addresses the pain/passion.
- Iterate.
- Validate through customer use.
- Iterate.
- Perform usability testing.
- Iterate.
- If you lose members of the Team of 10 or Advisory Board, refill.

Job 6: Post-MVP

- As you learn, split off execution:
  - Learn "activated"; build toward "satisfied."
  - Learn "satisfied"; build toward "passionate."
  - Build toward "whole product."
- Developers should have the guts not to develop.
- If Team of 10 or Advisory Board members are not passionate, refill.
- What is the pattern?
- Turn your Team of 10 (3) into a team of 20 (6).
- Learn "passionate"; increase speed of customer acquisition.
- Create cross-functional teams charged with achieving specific objectives based on data that moves the needle of the business.

Job 7: Funnel Vision

- Use insights from your team of 20 (6) to:
  - Validate where customer segment "hangs out."
  - Validate that you can reach them.
  - Validate what messaging and positioning resonates.
  - Validate what makes customer trust you.
  - Validate what convinces customer to buy.

- Re-segment existing customers based on combination of:
  - pain
  - origin
  - value (revenue)
  - funnel
  - product usage patterns

Job 8: Minimum Viable Business

- Lifetime value > cost of acquisition
- Velocity: average revenue per user versus cost of acquisition
- Word-of-mouth: viral coefficient
- Acquisition channel viability
- Discovery of "shadow force"

Job 9: Long-Term Growth

- Execution + continuous improvement + continuous learning
- Continuous improvement of "shadow force"
- Resell, cross-sell, up-sell
- New products for existing customer segments
- Existing products for new customer segments
- Disruption: new products, new customer segments

Notes

Chapter 1:
Startup Revolution

1. Seth Godin, *Linchpin: Are You Indispensable?* Kindle Edition (Penguin Group, 2010), 8.
2. http://startupdigest.com.
3. http://lean-startup.meetup.com.
4. http://startupweekend.org.
5. http://gigaom.com/2011/12/01/its-time-for-startup-founders-to-think-bigger.
6. http://online.wsj.com/article/SB100014240531119034809045765122509115629460.html.
7. Brad Feld notes come from personal interview.
8. David ten Have greatly helped our understanding of emerging digital-fabrication trends.
9. Mark Frauenfelder thoughts come from personal interview.
10. Mike Maples thoughts come from personal interview.
11. http://articles.businessinsider.com/2012-03-21/tech/31218762_1_zynga-app-mobile-game#ixzz1yRwEPJ24.
12. Scott Patterson, *The Quants: How a New Breed of Math Whizzes Conquered Wall Street and Nearly Destroyed It* (Crown Business, 2010).
13. http://online.wsj.com/article/SB10001424052748704509704575019032416477138.html.
14. www.nbcsandiego.com/news/local/Feds-Set-to-Release-Power-Outage-Report-149584875.html.
15. Ryan Holiday, *Trust Me, I'm Lying: Confessions of a Media Manipulator* (Portfolio Hardcover, 2012), 150–151.
16. www.wired.com/wired/archive/14.06/crowds.html.
17. Bill Gross thoughts come from personal interview.
18. See this incredible New Yorker discussion of Philip Tetlock's book, *Expert Political Judgment: How Good Is It? How Can We Know?* (Princeton, 2006). www.newyorker.com/archive/2005/12/05/051205crbo_books1#ixzz2Em3VFcMC.
19. For an amusing and eye-opening read on the frailty of human rationality, please read Nassim Nicholas Taleb's, *The Black Swan: The Impact of the Highly Improbable*, (Random House, 2007).
20. Spirited conversations with Venkatesh Rao contributed to our thinking here. Please see: www.ribbonfarm.com.
21. Thanks to Paul Kedrosky for his contribution to this discussion and helping our understanding of what's actually going on in the world today.
22. Chris Guillebeau, *The $100 Startup: Reinvent the Way You Make a Living, Do What You Love, and Create a New Future* (Crown Business, 2012), 7.
23. Godin, op. cit., 9.
24. Donald E. Vandergriff, "Today's Training and Education (Development) Revolution: The Future is Now!" The Associate of the United States Army, 2010.
25. Dr. Stephanie Cooper is author Brant Cooper's sister.
26. Comments by Tim McCoy from personal interview.
27. Eric Ries, *The Lean Startup: How Today's Entrepreneurs Use Continuous Innovation to Create Radically Successful Businesses* (Crown Business, 2011), 8–9.
28. Jeffery Liker, *The Toyota Way: 14 Management Principles from the World's Greatest Manufacturer* (McGraw-Hill, 2003).
29. Steve Blank, *The Four Steps to the Epiphany* (Cafepress.com, 2005).

Chapter 2:
Vision, Values, and Culture

1. We strongly suggest reading the *Harvard Business Review* case study "The Vision Trap" (March 1992) by Gerard H. Langeler.
2. http://blogmaverick.com/2012/03/18/dont-follow-your-passion-follow-your-effort.
3. Tony Hsieh, *Delivering Happiness: A Path to Profits, Passion, and Purpose* (Business Plus, 2010).
4. Donal Daly and Paul O'Dea, *Select Selling* (Oak Tree Press, October 1, 2004), 19.
5. Interview with Stephanie Cooper.
6. Seth Godin, *Linchpin: Are You Indispensable?* Kindle Edition (Penguin Group, 2010), 26.
7. Liker, *Toyota Way.*
8. Ries, 189.
9. Liker, 253.
10. Ries, 232.
11. http://steveblank.com/2010/04/15/why-accountants-dont-runstartups.
12. VastuShastri Khushdeep Bansal, *Alchemy of Growth* (South Western College, 2000).
13. http://hbr.org/2007/07/to-succeed-in-the-long-term-focus-on-the-middle-term/ar/1.

Chapter 3:
All the Fish in the Sea

1. http://sethgodin.typepad.com/seths_blog/2009/11/choose-your-customers-choose-your-future.html.
2. Alexander Osterwalder, *Business Model Generation: A Handbook for Visionaries, Game Changers, and Challengers.* (Hoboken, NJ: John Wiley & Sons, 2010).
3. Marc Andreessen blog, blog.pmarca.com.
4. http://hbswk.hbs.edu/item/5170.html.
5. In "New Criteria for Market Segmentation," *Harvard Business Review* (March 1964), Daniel Yankelovich asserted, "Traditional demographic traits such as age, sex, education levels, and income no longer said enough to serve as a basis for marketing strategy. Nondemographic traits such as values, tastes, and preferences were more likely to influence consumers' purchases than their demographic traits were." http://hbr.org/2006/02/rediscovering-market-segmentation/ar/1.
6. Alan Cooper, *The Inmates Are Running the Asylum: Why High Tech Products Drive Us Crazy and How to Restore the Sanity*, 2nd ed., Kindle Locations 2250–2251 (Pearson Education, 2004).

Chapter 4:
Wading in the Value Stream

1. Ries, 49.
2. Godin, 26.
3. Cooper, *Inmates.*
4. See http://vimeo.com/26277733 (video).

Chapter 5:
Diving In

1. www.entrepreneur.com/article/222501.
2. By the way, in case you just thought of Henry Ford and his observation that "If I had asked people what they wanted, they would have said faster horses," that's not exactly what he said. But he did think along those lines. Read the whole thing here: http://blogs.hbr.org/cs/2011/08/henry_ford_never_said_the_fast.html.
3. We owe a great debt of gratitiude to Clayton Chrisensen and his must-read tome, *The Innovator's Dilemma* (Harvard Business Review Press, 1997).
4. Taleb, xviii.
5. Liker, 229.
6. www.fastcodesign.com/1669070/3-ways-to-predict-what-consumers-want-before-they-know-it.
7. www.zurb.com/article/588/hiding-in-the-bushes-with-steve-jobs and www.nytimes.com/2011/01/19/technology/companies/19innovate.html?_r=1.
8. Ariely's *Predictably Irrational* (Harper Perennial, 2010) is a fantastic book. If you haven't read it, we suggest you do so soon.

Chapter 6:
Viability Experiments

1. Ries, 113.
2. In 2004, Tim Ferriss popularized the Landing Page test in his best-seller *The 4-Hour Workweek* (Crown Publishers, 2009).
3. See http://wonder-tonic.com/geocitiesizer/content.php? theme= 2&music=12&url=leanentrepreneur.co.
4. Seriously, go try www.shoesite.com (domain name, not URL) right now.
5. Hsieh, 59.

Chapter 7:
Data's Double-Edged Sword

1. The matter of building data-informed sales and marketing funnels is important enough to merit a standalone chapter. To skip ahead please see Chapter 9: Real Visionaries Have Funnel Vision.
2. See www.youtube.com/watch?v=TgDxWNV4wWY.

Chapter 8:
The Valley of Death

1. If not congruent, you are ripe for a pivot.
2. See http://news.ycombinator.com/item?id=542768.
3. Our friend Sean Ammirati suggests, somewhat tongue-in-cheek, that some entrepreneurs can be helped by telling them to build MAPs (Minimally Awesome Products) instead of MVPs. This is the difference between calling a car "used" or "certified pre-owned."
4. www.forbes.com/sites/brianclark/2012/05/23/audience-lean-startup.
5. www.fastcompany.com/1837168/pop-goes-pivot.
6. For an amazing read on the subject, take a look at Ryan Holiday's *Trust Me, I'm Lying: Confessions of a Media Manipulator* (Portfolio, 2012).

Chapter 9:
Real Visionaries Have Funnel Vision

1. Whatever you do, do not fall for the "build it and they will come" type of thinking; even the best products need to be marketed and sold. In fact, the best products are often associated with very sophisticated marketing and sales processes.
2. Ries, 45.
3. Mark Leslie and Charles A. Holloway, "The Enterprise Sales Learning Curve: A Framework for Building Startups and Launching New Products." www.khoslaventures.com/wp-content/uploads/2012/02/Sales_Learning_Cycle.pdf.
4. Blank, 11.
5. Daly and O'Dea, *Select Selling*.
6. Chris Guillebeau, *The Art of Non-Conformity* (London: Turnaround, 2011). chrisguillebeau.com.
7. To risk belaboring the point, in some markets, your customers may not be capable of verbalizing or even recognizing the answers to these questions. Ergo, savvy entrepreneurs will need to frame these questions such that the answer reveals itself in customer behavior.
8. SteveBlank.com, http://steveblank.com/2009/04/02/supermac-war-story-5-strategy-versus-relentless-tactical-execution-%E2%80%94-the-potrero-benchmarks.
9. Internet usage by country available here: www.internetworldstats.com/top20.htm.
10. www.fourhourworkweek.com/blog/2012/07/18/ryan-holiday.

Acknowledgments

How does one write an acknowledgments section without it sounding like an Academy Awards acceptance speech? One probably can't. Yet this section is important to us, because without these individuals the book would not have been possible.

Unlike with the Academy Awards, when you might turn the channel once you know who's won an award, you should read this section. Why? Because they are people whom you should know or want to know. They are people who are doing things, people who are changing the world.

First off, we'd like to thank our editors at Wiley, Laura Walsh and Judy Howarth. One often hears horror stories about editors, and though they're always thanked in the end, the acknowledgment is often buried. This book is about disruption, and there's no better case study of an industry being turned on its head than book publishing. Laura gets this. She is forward thinking, open to new ideas, and infinitely patient. Note to Wiley: Promote Laura.

The most common question we get from frustrated intrapreneurs who see their efforts at real innovation inside their large organizations continuously thwarted is "How do we convince senior management to adopt lean startup principles?" We always have one answer: "Buy Eric Ries's book *The Lean Startup*. Ries's book is, hands down, the best way for big business to understand why they need to turn their continuously thwarting organization into a continuous learning one. Thank you, Eric, for leading the change and for supporting our efforts.

Similarly, when we encounter MBA students or professors seeking to actually teach entrepreneurship and not just market the teaching of entrepreneurship, we point them to Steve Blank. It's truly great that forward-thinking universities are using technology to make their courses available online, but the real disruption to education is coming from the few entrepreneurs who are changing what is being taught and how it's being taught. Blank's class at Stanford is the best example of that we've seen. Instead of a lab-to-market program that results in a business plan (ugh!), Blank's course results in real, live, functioning startups with validated business models and paying customers. Thank you, Steve, for leading the change and continuing to support our efforts.

We would like to single out one individual in particular. Hiten Shah embodies today's value-creation startup culture. He is a lean startup thought leader, kind hearted, magnanimous, and a great friend who has supported our efforts from the moment we first met. Thank you, Hiten.

We are grateful to Fake Grimlock for providing the artwork that makes this book special.

We are fortunate and privileged to be able to travel around the world and speak to entrepreneurs, investors, and other big thinkers. They've all influenced the way we view the world, what's happening globally, and, of course, this book. For taking time out of their busy schedules to speak with us, we would like to thank Paul Kedrosky, Bill Gross, Mike Maples Jr., Alan Cooper, Bill Burnett, Scott Summit, Nick Pinkston, Patrick O'Neil, Brian Clark, Mike Volpe, Brad Feld, Andy Butler, and David ten Have.

Similarly, thanks to Rob Fan, Bennett Blank, Hugh Molotsi, Marti Frederickson, Mark Frauenfelder, Nate Oostendorp, Tom Fishburne, Alex Douzet, Stephen Devereux, Tim McCoy, Yoav Lurie, Lucas Carlson, Chris Lindland, Nick Fellers, Chirag Patel, Richard Caro, Rob Emrich, Drake Pruitt, Steven Cox, Chris Waldron, Brent Freeman, Jeff Gothelf, Andres Glusman, David T. Lang, Dan Palacios, Danny Kim, Ryan James, Noah Kagan, Jeff Titterton, Patrick Llewellyn, Jason Sew Hoy, Lachlan Donald, Venkat Subramaniam, Bill Scott, Dave McClure, and Paul Singh for sharing their stories.

Special shout-outs to friends Jonas Koffler, Giff Constable, Trevor Owens, Eric Otterson, Eric Galen, Sean Murphy, Sean Ellis, Tristan Kromer, Jeremey Lavoi, Abbey Lavoi, Julian Bergquist, Kate Rutter, Janice Fraser, Jason Fraser, Venkatesh Rao, Al Bsharah, Bryan Hall, Aaron Eden, Parker Thompson, Nik Souris, Ryan Holiday, Michael Ellsberg, Stephen Sammut, Venkat Chandrasekar, Jin Lee, Salim Virani, Dan Martell, Ben Yoskovitz, Alistair Croll, Gary Whitehill, Sisha Ortuzar, Jeffrey Zurofsky, Johnny Chan, Rodney Rumford, Lindsay Dayton LaShell, Abby Fichtner, Alline Oliveria, Cindy Alvarez, Nate Berkopec, Casey Armstrong, Taylor Miles, Shervin and Vafa Talieh, Farsheed Atef, Keyvan Raoufi, Anthony Singhavong, Faiza Tajammul, Avesta and Cameron Rasouli, Joe Zulli, Pete Mauro, Molly Matthieson, Ryan Tanaka, Amir Banifatemi, Andres Buritica, Olin Hyde, Willy Huang, Maggie Finch, Lauren Gard, Tarek Pertew, Maciej Skierowski, Neil Patel, Philip Rosedale, Danny Beckett Jr., John Fries, Josh Payne, Chris Johnson, Alexander Osterwalder, Julien Smith, Steve Cheney, Derek Holt, Scott Case, Peter Hargittay, Debbie Landa, Clare Ryan, Brian Hall, Greg Isenberg, and Stephen Davies for providing some combination of content, review, big thinking, stories, inspiration, support, and friendship.

We would also like to acknowledge others whose thinking and writing are important influences: Seth Godin, Mark Suster, Marc Andresseen, Ben Horowitz, David Cohen, Brad Feld, David Skok, Tony Hsieh, Nassim Nicholas Taleb, Clayton Christensen, and Fred Wilson.

Thanks again to our early adopters who contributed to the book by diving in early, reviewing content, providing feedback, and otherwise supporting us through pre-orders.

Of course, the book is simply not possible without the support and patience of our family and friends.

Brant: I send love and thanks to daughters Riva and Eliza Cooper for being inspirational, smart and not least of which great human beings and excellent writers in their own regard! Thanks also to my parents, Ross and Cynthia, for all their support throughout the twists and turns of life. My brothers Craig and Todd and sister Stephanie, who also contributed to the book, are all big, independent, and inspirational thinkers. I'm not sure at all how my folks pulled that off, but I should probably thank them again for putting up with all that entailed. I'd also like to thank Daniella and Jackie Zucker for help with the family, Eve Zucker, and Karl Malone for their support.

Patrick: First and foremost, I could not have tackled this book without the loving support of my wife, Katalin Vlaskovits and our son, Shane. Kati and Shane truly know the burden of having a husband and a father not always present in the moment as *The Lean Entrepreneur* (unfairly) occupied my thoughts all too frequently. Thank you both for bearing with me, I love you.

It should go without saying, and perhaps too often does, but my parents Ludmilla and Joseph, my brother Jet and sister Vivienne have always been there for me. Thank you.

I am incredibly lucky to have an amazing extended family. My in-laws are a blessing: Istvan Csucsy, Gergo Csucsy, and of course, the indefatigable Krisztina Albert.

Alan Jones for his saint-like patience, unending generosity, good humor, and firm friendship since high school in Saratoga, thank you buddy.

It's important to know who the true entrepreneurs are in this world. Let us tell you: They are not the stewards of wealth creation. They are not those who claim that taxes kill entrepreneurship. They are not those whose motivation is purely money. They are not the gamblers posing as innovators, nor the smarmy marketing types trying to trick, guilt, or scare you into buying. They are not the self-promoters, real estate tycoons, the bankers, or the slash-and-burn business vultures.

The true entrepreneurs are those seeking to create value. Whether trying to support themselves or change the world, we thank you for facing down uncertainty, putting yourself out there on the line, risking it all to do what you believe *has* to be done. Above it all, you are optimistic, passionate doers, and we are fortunate to work *for* you.

About the Authors

Brant Cooper

Brant Cooper helps organizations big and small move the needle.

His startup career includes Tumbleweed, Timestamp, WildPackets, inCode, and many others. He has experienced IPO, acquisition, rapid growth, and miserable failure. Brant previously authored *The Entrepreneur's Guide to Customer Development,* the first purpose-written book to discuss lean startup and customer development concepts, earning a distribution of over 50,000 copies. Brant has worked with hundreds of entrepreneurs across the globe and is a sought-after speaker, having presented at leading companies such as Qualcomm, Intuit, Capital One, and Hewlett-Packard.

Brant is reachable @brantcooper. He lives with (and continuously learns from) his two daughters, Riva and Eliza, near Swami's in Encinitas, California.

Patrick Vlaskovits

Patrick Vlaskovits is an entrepreneur, author, and consultant, and more than anything wishes he were a polymath.

His writing has been featured on the *Harvard Business Review* blog, the *Wall Street Journal* blog, and The Browser.

Patrick routinely speaks at technology conferences nationally and internationally, including SXSW, GROW Conference, the Turing Festival, and the Lean Startup Conference. He co-founded two startups, currently advises multiple technology startups, and serves as a mentor for 500 Startups, a seed fund and startup accelerator. As a principal at Moves the Needle, he counts Fortune 100 companies in his client list.

The Lean Entrepreneur is his second book. The first, *The Entrepreneur's Guide to Customer Development*, is a required course text for MBA and undergrad at universities such as the University of Chicago Booth School and Berkeley. He has also guest-lectured at Stanford and UCLA.

For some unknown reason, Patrick holds a master's in economics from UC Santa Barbara. When he has spare time, he can be found on Orange County beaches with his family.

Tweet at him @Pv and read his blog at vlaskovits.com.

Winning organizations are fast, agile, and tenacious. They are focused on what *moves the needle*.

Led by principals, Brant Cooper and Patrick Vlaskovits, Moves the Needle Group offers lean innovation consulting, training, speaking, and workshops.

Learn to use customer interaction, rapid experimentation, and actionable data to accelerate growth.

(415) 347-1849 • insight@movestheneedle.com • movestheneedle.com • @movestheneedle

Index